THE
GHOST
HUNTER'S
SURVIVAL GUIDE

ABOUT THE AUTHOR

Michelle Belanger has repeatedly appeared on A&E's hit show *Paranormal State*, in addition to documentaries on HBO, the History Channel, and WE! She writes for paranormalinsider.com and regularly lectures at colleges across the United States. Visit her online at www.michelle belanger.com.

TO WRITE TO THE AUTHOR

If you wish to contact the author or would like more information about this book, please write to the author in care of Llewellyn Worldwide and we will forward your request. Both the author and publisher appreciate hearing from you and learning of your enjoyment of this book and how it has helped you. Llewellyn Worldwide cannot guarantee that every letter written to the author can be answered, but all will be forwarded. Please write to:

Michelle Belanger
c/o Llewellyn Worldwide
2143 Wooddale Drive, Dept. 978-0-7387-1870-5
Woodbury, MN 55125-2989, U.S.A.

Please enclose a self-addressed stamped envelope for reply,
or $1.00 to cover costs. If outside U.S.A., enclose
international postal reply coupon.

Many of Llewellyn's authors have websites with additional information and resources. For more information, please visit our website at
www.llewellyn.com

THE GHOST HUNTER'S HUNTER'S SURVIVAL GUIDE

PROTECTION TECHNIQUES FOR ENCOUNTERS WITH THE PARANORMAL

MICHELLE BELANGER

Llewellyn Publications
Woodbury, Minnesota

First Edition
First Printing, 2009

Cover design by Lisa Novak
Cover image © Bill Varie/Workbook Stock/Jupiterimages
Editing by Nicole Edman

Llewellyn is a registered trademark of Llewellyn Worldwide, Ltd.

LIBRARY OF CONGRESS CATALOGING-IN-PUBLICATION DATA
Belanger, Michelle A.
  The ghost hunter's survival guide : protection techniques for
encounters with the paranormal / by Michelle Belanger. —1st ed.
    p. cm.
  ISBN 978-0-7387-1870-5
  1. Ghosts—Research. 2. Self-defense—Psychic aspects. I. Title.
  BF1471.B46 2009
  133.1—dc22
                    2009017475

Llewellyn Publications
A Division of Llewellyn Worldwide, Ltd.
2143 Wooddale Drive, Dept. 978-0-7387-1870-5
Woodbury, MN 55125-2989, U.S.A.
www.llewellyn.com

Printed in the United States of America

This book is dedicated
to the cast and crew of *Paranormal State*
for fun times, chilling encounters, and the chance to help
ordinary people overcome extraordinary circumstances.
It's not your imagination!

CONTENTS

SIDEBARS

From ghosties and ghoulies and long-leggedy beasties
and things that go bump in the night—
Good Lord deliver us!

TRADITIONAL SCOTTISH PRAYER

Introduction

SHADOW CHASERS

Ghosts can't hurt you, you tell yourself. It's something you have to re-cite to the primal part of your brain every time you go out on an in-vestigation. Ghosts are just phenomena to be documented. At best, they're nothing but energy. There is no reason to be scared.

And yet, it's hard not to get the chills on this particular investigation. In the phone interview, the clients warned your team that the place was creepy, but creepy was an understatement. No matter how many lights you turn on in the living room, the place still seems claustrophobic, crowded with shadows. It's like the darkness is an entity in its own right, and it's huddling in all of the corners, watching you. For about the fiftieth time that night, you find yourself grateful that your paranormal crew doesn't insist on doing all of their investigations in the dark. You just don't think you could handle this place with the lights out!

The living room, with its cloying shadows, is bad enough. But the real center of the haunting, at least according to the homeowners, is the back bed-room. You can feel a presence waiting there, even before you approach the threshold. This room was where the previous owner lived and died, after the accident made it impossible for him to handle the stairs. He had been a fac-tory worker, and some mishap with heavy machinery crushed both of his legs. He hadn't responded well to his new disability, although according to all reports, he hadn't been the nicest of guys even before the accident. After he was hurt, he spent the remaining years of his life in the back bedroom, stewing over what had been taken away. He was a heavy smoker, and the walls of the room were still stained with nicotine. It was lung cancer that finally claimed him, and the young couple who bought the house after his passing insisted that his black personality had seeped into the walls of that bedroom just as surely as did the stench of his cigarette smoke.

The minute you approach that back bedroom, you can feel it—a tingling sensation like a weak electrical current applied to the base of your spine. Nothing registers on your trifield meter, but you know it's not your imagination. As clichéd as it seems, the sensation makes the hairs on the back of your neck stiffen, and you feel a cold knot of fear form in your stomach. But is it really fear that you're feeling, or is it genuine nausea? You've been to countless investigations. You know the dead can't hurt you (you keep whispering that under your breath like a prayer). There is nothing to fear—and yet you cannot shake those chills and that sour feeling in your gut.

The headache comes without warning. One moment, you're fine, and the next, it feels like someone is driving an ice pick into your brain. You haven't had a migraine since you were a kid, and there were no warning signs leading up to this pain. What on earth is going on here?

You can feel a malevolent presence all around you. The stench of stale cigarette smoke clogs your nostrils as you push farther into that back room, and the old man's hatred and frustration is an almost palpable weight pressing against your skin. You start feeling dizzy and a little weak in the knees. It's the adrenaline, right?

For perhaps the hundredth time, you remind yourself that ghosts cannot harm the living. But as the headache rages, you're starting to have doubts. If the spirit of this angry old man is somehow causing your headache, what can you do about it? If ghosts can actually reach out across the Veil to attack the living, how could you even begin to protect yourself?

How, indeed?

Ghost Hunters Aplenty

Ghost hunting has practically become a new national pastime. With the popularity of shows like A&E's *Paranormal State* and SciFi's *Ghost Hunters,* it seems that everybody wants to chase the unseen. New teams of paranormal investigators seem to crop up every week, and even college and high school students are getting in on the act, organizing ghost hunts at public locations or offering to document hauntings in private homes. Most of these groups are familiar with investigative procedures, and they're usually smart enough to take safety precautions when they go chasing shadows in the night. It's a matter of common sense to bring flashlights and extra batteries in order to make certain that no one is stuck in an unknown house without light to guide their steps. As a further precaution, most groups use the buddy system, making certain that no one ventures into unknown territory alone. But these are all physical considerations. How many ghost hunters know how to adequately protect themselves from paranormal threats?

Although spirit attacks are rare, the otherworldly can nevertheless have a palpable impact on a living person's health and well-being. How many people report unpleasant sensations purely as a result of being exposed to the energy of a negative haunting? How many people, living in a haunted residence, complain of headaches, dizziness, or even sensations of being touched by a phantom hand? In the most extreme cases, individuals can become obsessed or even possessed by entities, losing control of their own thoughts or actions for brief periods of time. Once again, such extreme incidents are exceedingly rare, but there is enough documentation to suggest that they do happen. If a spirit is malevolent, how can living people fight an enemy that is both invisible and intangible?

The living are not as helpless as our fear sometimes makes us feel. There are techniques that allow ordinary people to protect themselves under extraordinary circumstances. In some circles, these techniques are known as "psychic self-defense." These techniques are mental exercises that use a combination of focus, intent, and willpower to harness the natural human abilities that allow us to meet—and beat—spirits at their own game.

Psychic Self-Defense

In 1930, Dion Fortune published a book entitled *Psychic Self-Defense*. Fortune was the pen name of British psychoanalyst Violet Mary Firth, and she developed many of her techniques as the result of direct, personal experience with a variety of psychic attacks. The founder of the Fraternity of the Light and a veteran of the Hermetic Order of the Golden Dawn, Firth was a respected occultist in her day. Although she was not the first person to describe techniques of psychic self-defense, she was certainly one of the first to devote an entire book to the subject. The audience she was writing for was made up mainly of other occultists, but her techniques were of use to psychics of all stripes. This movement of people called themselves occultists not because they were involved in any kind of cult, but because they were dedicated seekers of secret and hidden knowledge—the real meaning of the word *occult*.

Firth was primarily writing about how to protect against psychic attacks from the living, and so few ghost hunters are likely to have heard of her, or her alter ego Dion Fortune. Also, there are some distinct differences in terminology, methodology, and ideology between traditional ghost hunters and those individuals who consider themselves students of the occult. These differences have led to a history of bias and misunderstanding between the two groups. Occult studies are a little too esoteric for most paranormal investigators, especially since most occultists tend to be focused on obtaining direct experiences of the unseen, while paranormal investigators are more focused on obtaining evidence of the unseen. However, the concept of psychic self-defense can (and should) be applied to the dead, and so Fortune's ideas and theories bear exploration within the context of paranormal investigation.

The movement that gave rise to writers like Dion Fortune influenced many great minds from the late nineteenth and early twentieth centuries. The Irish poet William Butler Yeats was a part of the Hermetic Order of the Golden Dawn, as was the wife of poet Oscar Wilde. Bram Stoker, manager of the Lyceum theater and celebrated author of *Dracula,* was also associated with the organization. From actresses to academics, from psychics to psychoanalysts, the occult movement appealed to a wide variety of individuals. It continues to influence people today, including a number of noteworthy writers and artists.

One of these is Alan Moore, a graphic novelist of some repute. If you've ever seen *Watchmen, V for Vendetta* or the more whimsical *League of Extraordinary Gentlemen,* you've been exposed to his work. In one of his less-known comics, *Promethea,* Moore tells a story that very neatly illustrates many of the concepts behind psychic self-defense. In the story, a man is riding on a train. The man holds a box in his lap, making his fellow passenger intensely curious about the contents of said box. In the course of several panels, the reader learns that this man is traveling to visit his brother, and he's bringing him a gift. The brother is an alcoholic and has progressed to the point where he hallucinates almost constantly. The poor man sees snakes all around him, and his brother has decided to help protect him from these snakes. Since the snakes are imaginary, his solution is to bring an imaginary mongoose. This invisible predator is what he holds in the box. That is both the punch line and the revelation of Moore's tale.

Consider that, in the field of the paranormal, we're confronted by beings that are not physical in any sense that we understand. Ghosts and spirits aren't typically perceptible to our five physical senses. Although theories on the nature of these beings diverge widely, most modern ghost hunters agree that spirits are not a part of the physical world. They may intersect with our realm of experience, but they are native to another aspect of being—call it a plane or a dimension, if you like—that only partially intersects our own. If we're to interact successfully with invisible beings that consistently elude most attempts to measure or quantify them, we need our own imaginary mongoose.

That is not to say that spirits themselves are imaginary. Moore's amusing little comic is actually a commentary on magick—magick as defined as humanity's inborn ability to influence reality through a concerted act of willpower. Moore believes that it is possible to affect reality, and many readers may have encountered the notion under a different (more mundane) name, such as "mind over matter." Whether you call it magick, psychic ability, or mind over matter, the fact is that we have more power over ourselves, our situations, and our environments than we often give ourselves credit for. The real lesson of the story is that it's best to fight fire with fire.

When you are trying to protect yourself from a nonphysical entity, bringing a sword or a gun will not do you much good. You need to meet that entity on its own turf and interact with it in the same fashion that it interacts with you. Ghosts very rarely physically strike the living. They have no body in a physical sense to do so. If a spirit really wants to physically lash out at someone, it has to muster a great deal of energy and produce poltergeist effects: knocking objects over or throwing them around the room. But how many times have you seen a spirit go this far? The effort is rarely worth the results, and so most spirits stick to tactics that can only be described as psychic in nature. The presence of the ghost is announced by a strange thickening of the air. The hairs on the back of your neck register this, but of course, none of your instruments do. You "hear" ghostly sounds and voices, only to play back the audio from five microphones placed at strategic points around the room and learn that they recorded nothing. Likewise, you "see" ghost lights, or a phantom form, or some dark shadowy thing out of the corner of your eye. And, once again, your technology is stymied. As far as the eye of the camera is concerned, there was nothing there.

If the technology insists that nothing is there, a number of ghost hunting groups will automatically discount the sensations reported by the human crew. But stop to consider how complex, how refined, the *human* machine really is. Do we understand every aspect of the body's functioning? Have we been able to produce a manmade construct that replicates everything human bodies are capable of doing? The skeptics in the community will be quick to point out that machines do not get confused or deluded; machines do not hallucinate. Human beings, although extremely complex, are also fallible and prone to regrettable errors, such as imagining things. In the skeptic's eyes, this immediately negates any of the nebulous impressions reported by so-called psychics, because these impressions are seen as unverifiable.

But are they, really? When five or six individuals report similar, if not identical, impressions independent of one another on a case, what is that if not empirical evidence? There are ways to verify a psychic's impressions. They often involve research and sometimes require the researchers to really dig deep, but a psychic who has learned how to interpret his or her perceptions can be surprisingly accurate. That's not to say that the human machine, as an instrument of perception, doesn't have its flaws. Psychic or otherwise, we have a lot of chaff that gets thrown up on our radar along with the few grains of wheat, and half of this comes from our own internal processes. Emotions, expectations, attempts to interpret a sensation that makes no logical sense—all of these factors can skew not the sensation itself, but an individual's *report* of that sensation. Add to that the fact that we can convince ourselves to see something that is not there, or that, since our brains are wired for pattern recognition, we will sometimes misinterpret real sensations, attributing to them a shape that they do not actually possess, and the process of interpreting perception becomes even more complex.

The human instrument is not perfect. Despite this, it still possesses a range of perception that manmade technology lacks. Call it psychic ability, call it instinct, call it one's "gut"—sometimes we sense things that cannot be explained from a purely physical point of view. Yet those sensations turn out to be accurate. Ghost hunters, skeptical or otherwise, would do well not to devalue this aspect of human perception, but rather, to weigh it, test it, and quantify it along with all of the other data gathered on a case.

Which brings us back to the problem of the imaginary mongoose. If you are hunting ghosts in the first place, you probably accept that they exist. They are not imaginary, but they are not physical either. In order to successfully interact with them—or, when necessary, combat them—it is necessary to respond to them in kind: energetically. Another thing that most people tend to overlook is the fact that we believe ghosts come from us. Human spirits are what's left, at least some of the time, after the human body dies. Some integral portion of who or what we are lingers, despite the lack of a physical body.

Do you think a spirit is produced only at the moment of death? Or is it with us all along? And if we, even when alive, are both body and spirit, doesn't that mean that we already have a leg up on the ghosts? We exist in the physical world, but some part of us—a part that we only dimly understand—also exists in the spiritual realm populated by ghosts. And in truth, these may not even be two different "realms," so much as they are like a double exposure on film. They are separate images, and yet they occupy the same space, each woven within and throughout the fabric of the other. If this is true, then we already have our imaginary mongoose. We just need to figure out how to let our mongoose out of its box, which—to take the metaphor to its most logical end—is our own flesh and blood perspective of the world.

Views on the Strange

Human response to the paranormal—especially when it comes to humans' ability to directly interact with or cause paranormal phenomena—falls broadly into three categories of belief. On one end, you have the people who perceive paranormal phenomena, and they call their ability to influence them "psychic." On the other end, you have the people who label the exact same abilities "magick." In the middle, you have the people who chalk all of it up to the fact that "God works in mysterious ways." They take a religious approach to paranormal phenomena and whether they see this phenomena in a positive or negative light depends on the specific religion.

This threefold spectrum is the believer's camp, of course. On the sidelines, you have the skeptics. They don't believe in any of it, yet from their vantage point, they can at least see that each of these three points of view describe the same thing with different words. When skeptics acknowledge that something is going on, typically they approach the human element of that interaction in terms of psychology. When people believe in something strongly enough, the skeptics say, they may experience it, but it's all just the placebo effect. The experience itself, from an extremely skeptical point of view, doesn't necessarily prove that anything paranormal is going on. It only seems that way.

All of these points of view—from magick to prayer, psychic phenomena to radical skepticism—are represented among the investigators of the paranormal field. Many paranormal investigation teams will contain a variety of individuals who subscribe to different points of view. Although they're sometimes divided by their beliefs about what paranormal phenomena may be, they are nevertheless united by a mutual desire to understand the truth and to obtain some proof of that truth to share with others. When a team is dedicated purely to discovering the truth about paranormal phenomena, it has the luxury of many different belief systems. Such groups seek out purportedly haunted places and devise methods to quantify, measure, or debunk the haunting. But when a team is called in by a family, the rules of engagement are often different. Typically, when a family believes that their house is haunted, they want a resolution to that haunting more than they want evidence that the haunting is truly paranormal. Certainly, some families welcome that evidence, because it helps prove that what they have been experiencing is real and not simply caused by madness or overactive imaginations. But time and again, when a family goes so far as to seek out a group of professional ghost hunters to investigate their home, what they want is peace of mind.

The four approaches—magical, psychic, religious, and skeptical—mentioned above are especially pertinent in investigations that seek to resolve, rather than to document, a haunting. Each of the approaches has a significant impact on how or if an investigator can resolve the haunting. Radical skeptics can seek to debunk all true paranormal activity, but in the end, they have to explain to the family that they were hoodwinked by their own senses and what they believed to be a ghost was some simple, mundane phenomena. Debunking a haunting is acceptable to some individuals who feel haunted, but it is often cold comfort—especially if the phenomena, debunked or not, continues after the investigators have gone. And if hardcore skeptics encounter something truly paranormal, their skeptical point of view may not equip them with the ability to respond. How does a skeptic drive a ghost from a home when the skeptic really doesn't believe in ghosts in the first place?

I'm not hating on the skeptics, although it may seem that way. I started from a skeptical stance myself although, at this point, it certainly may not seem that way. What I'm trying to do is point out a pitfall that some ghost hunting teams may stumble into, and that pitfall involves imposing their own point of view upon their clients. Investigators who fall into the believer's camp are not without their own problems. Consider the culture clash that must inevitably occur if an investigative team is made up of people who primarily espouse the notion that humans can impact the paranormal through magick. They are called in on an investigation, determine that there's a ghost, and then they break out, quite literally, bell, book, and candle to drive the spirit away. There's probably some incense or a smudge stick involved somewhere along the line as well. However, the family who called them in turns out to be Catholic. Not only does the family have no context for the investigative team's methodology, they may even find those methods offensive to their faith. The same problem arises when a very Catholic investigative team comes in to resolve a haunting for a family that is primarily agnostic. The Catholic ghost hunters perceive a very negative nonhuman entity and, as is appropriate to their point of view, they label it a demon and suggest that the family contact a priest. The family doesn't really believe in demons and they will either respond with incredulousness or abject terror, since demons are completely beyond their realm of intellectual experience. A psychic ghost hunter who goes into a Christian home may fare no better than the Wiccans in the first example, especially if the family is uncertain about the reality or accuracy of psychic powers. When a stranger walks into your home and claims to be conversing with dead Uncle Charlie, how do you fit that communication into a worldview that might not even allow for the possibility that Uncle Charlie is hanging out anywhere but heaven?

All of these are extreme examples, of course, and the folks from the believer's camp usually have a leg up on skeptics when it comes to families who feel haunted. Chances are, if the family has gone so far as to call in an outside team, they're not skeptics about the haunting themselves. Some experience, or a series of experiences, has prompted that family to believe not only that there are spirits in their home, but that those spirits have an undeniable ability to interact with and influence the living. If anything, hardcore skeptics going into such a situation are at a disadvantage because, even if the haunting does turn out to have a rational explanation, the family is oftentimes so worked up about it that a normal explanation won't satisfy them. And this is where we have to consider a very important factor in haunting investigation: the client's needs.

What do clients expect when they call in a team to investigate their haunting? Clients want a resolution. They want answers about what they have been experiencing, and they almost always want to know whether or not the things they have been experiencing are dangerous or harmful in any way. But more than answers, more than reassurances, more than anything else, they want the negative things they've experienced due to the haunting to stop. They don't feel confident in their own abilities to deal with the haunting and thus they have called in a team that they perceive to be professionals in these matters. And keep in mind that, to the average person, a professional in the field of ghost hunting often constitutes a person who simply has more experience dealing with ghosts than they do. And since there is no licensing, no oversight, and no way of regulating the field of paranormal investigation, the family that calls in a group is extending a level of trust that may or may not be justified. As the people who would be part of such an investigative team, you, dear readers, have a responsibility to live up to the clients' expectations in your professionalism, your knowledge of the subject matter, and your ability to solve the problem of the haunting. And that's where psychic self-defense and the techniques outlined in this book become invaluable tools for the aspiring ghost hunter.

A Ghost Hunting Survival Guide

This book is an attempt to take the concept of psychic self-defense and make it accessible to ghost hunters everywhere. Anyone who intentionally seeks out a reputedly haunted location and willingly exposes themselves to the presence of spirits should know at least the basics of psychic self-defense. Techniques like grounding, centering, and shielding, covered in the first few chapters of this book, are invaluable skills that can prevent unpleasant reactions to negative hauntings. Later on in the book, more involved techniques outline methods for clearing negative energy from homes and even removing unwanted spirits. These techniques can be especially useful to groups or individuals who seek to resolve hauntings for beleaguered families.

This book has two main parts. There is an ongoing story that unfolds from chapter to chapter. The story revolves around a haunting investigation I did with a friend several years ago. Each chapter of the story addresses a different issue that a team can encounter in a haunting. The story is meant to entertain and educate at the same time. After a portion of the story has been told, the chapter explores a variety of exercises and techniques that elaborate on the concepts encountered in the story. I chose to split up the book this way in order to make the subject matter more engaging. It is my hope that having the actual investigation as a point of reference will help put some of the exercises, and their ideal applications, into perspective for you. It may also help paranormal investigators relate some of their own cases to the situations outlined in the story, so in future they will have a better idea of how to deal with the specific problems presented.

In addition to the two main sections in each chapter, every chapter that contains exercises also ends with a section called "The Least You Should Know." This section is a chapter summary, and it recaps all of the important points made throughout the chapter. Often, this final chapter overview contains bullet points that can help guide you when trying to judge whether or not your application of the techniques has succeeded.

Throughout the book, I am writing with the assumption that readers are actively involved in paranormal investigation. I generally also assume that these investigations involve not just one individual but a team of people. From my experience, many of the people who are delving into paranormal investigation work in teams, and most of the material in this book is applicable to groups that specifically work to resolve hauntings for clients. That being said, the exercises in this book are not exclusively applicable to team situations. I strongly encourage anyone who finds themselves in a haunted situation to read through this book and practice its techniques. If you are the focus of a haunting yourself, you may find that this book can help you solve the haunting on your own without ever having to call in a team of strangers. If you are a member of an investigative team, you should practice the techniques outlined in this book on your own first. Become familiar with the techniques before attempting to use them in the course of an investigation so that you can be certain of their effectiveness.

Another good reason for learning the techniques independent of field investigations is so you can adequately explain these techniques to your clients. If you have been practicing the exercises in this book on your own, you will be better prepared to teach the techniques to your clients. Helping your clients learn how to defend themselves is the best method for resolving a haunting, because you empower them to deal with the spirits themselves, helping to transform them from victims to victors.

Skeptics versus Believers

Scattered throughout this book, you will encounter sidebars that elaborate on certain concepts and themes. Sometimes these sidebars also comment on exercises addressed in the text or offer alternate points of view. Roughly half of these sidebars are designed to speak from a religious perspective. These sections, entitled "Beyond Belief," exist because there is a sizable number of individuals in the paranormal community who approach their investigations from a religious perspective. The "Beyond Belief" sections speak to this religious perspective, offering alternate techniques or addressing concerns religious investigators may have about certain concepts covered in the text. The "Beyond Belief" sections may also seek to introduce readers to little-known techniques from exotic religious traditions, such as Tibetan Buddhism, putting these alternate practices into perspective for everyone.

Because there are a wide range of religions in the world and many different names for God, I repeatedly suggest throughout this text that faith-based practitioners appeal to their "higher power." Your higher power is whatever spirit, being, or divinity that you see as existing above or beyond you. Out of respect for the diversity of religions, I leave it up to each of you to give this a face, a shape, or a name.

Because the paranormal community is made up of both believers and skeptics, there are also sidebars entitled "Skeptic's Corner."

These sections function just like the "Beyond Belief" sidebars, only they come at things from a skeptic's point of view. Through these sidebars, I attempt to anticipate questions, concerns, or objections that skeptics may have regarding concepts and techniques addressed within the text. Oftentimes, the sidebars attempt to approach these concepts from a different perspective that speaks directly to a skeptical mindset but nevertheless allows a skeptical investigator to make use of the technique by approaching it from a direction that does not rely on faith or belief. Many of the "Skeptic's Corner" sections approach the exercises in this text from a psychological point of view, often pointing out how certain approaches may benefit clients even if those beliefs come down to nothing more than mind over matter.

It has not been easy, trying to balance the perspectives of both skeptics and believers within this text, especially considering the vast diversity of belief systems—both faith-based and science-based—that are represented among the members of the paranormal community. But I feel that it is crucial for aspiring ghost hunters to be familiar with some form of psychic self-defense techniques before going out into the field, regardless of their belief system or background. Knowledge of self-defense techniques becomes even more important if those aspiring ghost hunters seek to help others with hauntings, especially malevolent ones. The techniques outlined in this book are not the only right way to protect yourself from the spirit world, but they represent an approach to self-defense that has roots stretching back into traditions and cultures around the world. The exercises are written to be as general as possible, easy to implement, and accessible to both skeptics and believers alike. Even if you find that you want to change and add things to the methods that appear in this book, the material you hold in your hands right now will still provide a solid base from which to develop your own approaches to keep yourself and your clients safe from paranormal threats.

Making It Yours

The techniques in this book, although founded on very old ideas, are nevertheless based upon my own personal methods of doing things. I have done my best to make these methods accessible to as wide an audience as possible by boiling them down to their base constituents and presenting them in the most general terms possible. Even so, it is important to note that they remain my own techniques. As you progress through this book, you will learn that one of the key factors to harnessing the methods described in this book involves making those methods as personal as possible. All of the techniques here rely on a certain amount of visualization and symbolism, and it is important for these things to be relevant to you.

I suggest that all readers, regardless of their backgrounds, go through this book once and experiment with each one of the exercises. Try each of the exercises several times, just as they are written in the text, until you get the hang of them. It can be helpful to take notes about your experiences with these techniques, recording points that felt awkward or methods that seemed to work especially well for you. After you have familiarized yourself with the concepts and the basic actions underpinning each exercise, try innovating on the techniques. Change the wording or the symbols or change the technique completely. Adapt it to your particular belief system. In short, make it yours.

Because this book is also written for clients, keep the personalizing trick in mind when teaching some of the basic techniques to your clients. Remember to tell them that the initial technique they learn does not have to be repeated precisely word for word in order to be effective. In psychic self-defense, it's really the thought that counts, as long as you can bring yourself to genuinely believe in that thought. Clients, once they become familiar with a basic technique, should also be encouraged to innovate and tailor the technique to their own unique situation, perspective, and needs.

Finally, because the methods outlined here may present concepts that are new and may even seem a little strange, spend some time testing your results. If you are a part of a group of investigators, this can be easy. Practice the early techniques, like grounding, centering, shielding, and clearing energy, among yourselves. Ask for feedback to see how each technique affects the way people feel. If you are particularly skeptical about a given technique, set up a little experiment. Perform the exercise without telling others that you are doing so, then see whether or not they notice a change. Once you are regularly using the methods outlined in this book among clients, you should always solicit feedback on your performance. Pay close attention to the language others use when describing what they feel and see how closely that language compares to what you felt you accomplished.

Ghost hunters who typically employ technological gadgetry to gather evidence of hauntings may feel that a book devoted to energy work and psychic self-defense is too "woo-woo" to be scientific, but the biggest mistake anyone who delves into psychic perceptions can make is to forget to approach their experiences empirically. Psychic perceptions *can* be tested, and repeated feedback is one of the best ways to do this. Even if you yourself are uncertain about the success of a given technique, if five other people at a haunting independently notice a difference and use similar language to describe that difference, then it is fair to assume that you did something right. You might not be able to measure it on a trifield meter, but when it comes to haunting resolution, the most important thing is how the people exposed to the haunting feel. If you can make unwanted experiences stop, your work is successful, especially in the clients' eyes.

one

JULIE'S FIRST INVESTIGATION

The case seemed simple enough. Irving was a spirit medium who lived in a small house with his mother and grandmother. He was in his mid-thirties, and he had been sensitive all his life. Irving was one of those spirit mediums who seemed to shine like a beacon on the Otherside. Spirits flocked to him, frightening him more often than not. The spirits mainly wanted to communicate, but some of them seemed to hover around Irving, teasing and taunting him simply to see how he would react. Since Irving lacked any kind of formal training, he had no control over his gift. Try as he might, he could neither drive away the spirits nor block them out. Irving felt victimized by his gift, and the constant presence of spirits in his life was wearing him pretty thin.

Irving's mother had talked about his troubles with a friend of mine, and that friend had referred the family to me. From what I learned in the initial phone conversation, I was fairly certain that all I was going to have to do was perform a cleansing on the home to remove all the random spirits Irving had inadvertently attracted. Irving himself was worried that some of these spirits were dark entities or even demons, but as he described their behavior, they seemed to be more mischievous than malevolent. I didn't expect any of the spirits to give me any real trouble. Once the cleansing was finished, I planned to teach Irving some basic exercises to help him control his gift and block the spirits out. To help with this, I had also brought my friend Julie along.

Julie was a spirit medium herself. She had also been studying energy work with me for the better part of a year. Like Irving, she had started out feeling victimized by the spirits she attracted. She was raised in a religious household, and both of her parents were afraid that the voices she heard speaking to her were demonic in nature. Their fears passed to their daughter, who spent several years worrying that she was either crazy or besieged by the devil. Eventually, she got a handle on her gift, and I was hoping that she could share some of her learning experiences with poor Irving.

Irving lived about an hour away from me, not completely in the country, but definitely not in the city, either. The old farmhouse his family occupied was located a good distance away from the road, and we pulled up the long gravel driveway, tires crunching as we went.

The first thing that really stood out was how rundown the place seemed. The trim was flaking, the paint was faded and stained, and up on one corner of the roof, a gutter hung askew. All the windows seemed dark, and even the afternoon sunlight could not penetrate the layers of grime that streaked them from the inside. We saw no evidence of curtains, and several of the smaller windows near the back of the house were covered completely with insulating plastic. In at least one of these, I could see that the glass beneath was shattered and had never been repaired.

The same plastic sheeting, milky as a cataract, had been tacked up around the porch, closing the interior off from the elements. The stump of what at one time must have been a huge old tree jutted up in the front yard, surrounded by a crop of straggly weeds. Someone had left an old rusted axe half-sunk into the top of the stump, as if consciously trying to complete the stereotypical image of an old, spooky house in the country.

Julie's eyes were wide as the engine idled and I double-checked the address.

"People actually live here?" she wondered.

I was thinking pretty much the same thing myself, but I just nodded and verified that we had the correct address. I'd brought a briefcase stocked with some Tibetan tools and other things that I often used in house cleansings, and I got out and retrieved this from the trunk.

"Ready for your first experience in the field?" I asked, trying to sound light-hearted in defiance of the pall of neglect that emanated from the house.

"As long as there are no creepy old ladies mummified on rocking chairs somewhere in the attic, I'll be fine," Julie quipped.

And thus our adventure began.

I've been to a lot of reportedly haunted locations. Big houses, little houses, rundown apartment buildings—even a former abbey converted into college dorm rooms. While a beautiful, well-kept house can be just as haunted as some rat-trap rented out by a slum lord, there is no denying that the state of a residence can have a definite impact upon its energy. Just approaching the issue from a psychological perspective, a sad-looking, rundown home is going to have an effect on the subconscious minds of the residents. There are usually money issues that led to the home being rundown in the first place, and with money issues come stress, anxiety, frustration, and a feeling of being trapped. All of these negative emotions seem to soak into the very walls and floorboards of the home, creating residues of dark, heavy energy. Sometimes, a place with such a heavy build-up of negative residual energy doesn't even need a ghost to feel haunted—the "ghosts" of all those unpleasant emotions haunt the place quite sufficiently.

I didn't want to make the mistake of judging by appearances, but I began to suspect that at least a portion of Irving's troubles were going to come down to issues with residual energy. I didn't doubt that he was having problems with spirits as well, but many people who are sensitive to spirits are also very sensitive to emotional residues, and most places that looked like his home were thick with them. My suspicions were all but confirmed when we opened the flimsy screen door and walked into the front porch.

I'm not sure what bothered me more—the sheer profusion of boxes that were crammed into this makeshift room, or the haphazard way they had been stacked, floor to ceiling. Most of the boxes at the bottoms of the stacks were half collapsed under the weight of everything piled on top of them, so everything leaned at crazy angles, and there was only a tiny walkway for a person to get through from the outside screen door to the proper front door of the house. The plastic sheeting made it hot and muggy in the tightly enclosed space, and the air seemed barely breathable, choked as it was with dust, mold, and mildew. Flies buzzed frantically, trapped between layers of the plastic sheeting.

Julie looked like she was going to be sick.

I went up and knocked on the front door.

"Oh, my God. How can you touch anything in this filth?" Julie demanded in a hushed tone.

I shrugged. "I had a great-uncle who lived out on a farm about an hour farther east of here. This is nothing compared to his place. He had stacks of newspapers going back to the forties, and he kept this hammer tied to a string on his nightstand to hit the rats on the head when they tried climbing in bed with him."

Julie blinked. "You're kidding," she said.

"Wish I was," I said. With another shrug, I added, "Some people are just clutterbugs."

Julie considered this as we waited for someone to answer the door. If no one showed up to let us in, we wouldn't have to see what the rest of the house looked like.

"On a string?" she asked, shrinking away from the tattered, sagging boxes that penned us in from all sides.

"I guess so he wouldn't lose it," I replied. I was going to offer further commentary, specifically some details from an article I'd recently read equating this kind of hoarding behavior with an undifferentiated mental illness; there was also the possibility that it was tied to depression. But then Irving's grandmother answered the door.

It was impossible to tell how old the woman actually was, though "older than dirt" leapt immediately to mind. She had obviously spent a great deal of her life out of doors; her skin had that weathered, leathery quality that one might associate with antique photos of elderly Native Americans. She had a dusky complexion, and the way her nut-brown skin clung to the sparse flesh of her frame, I thought that she could have sprung from the stump of the tree that stood out in the front yard. I knew this was a ridiculous stretch perpetrated by my sometimes baroque imagination, but I could seriously have believed that, if a tree ever deigned to take on human form, it would emerge from the weathered bark in a shape not unlike this old woman. All she needed was to sport a few dry autumn leaves in her tangled hair, and the look would be complete.

"Hi," she said gruffly, in a voice reminiscent of those self-same dry, autumn leaves. "Come in."

Then, with no further commentary or greetings, she shuffled off.

From the look on Julie's face, I could tell she was regretting that line about mummified old women in rocking chairs.

"You gonna be okay?" I asked.

Julie just nodded, eyes never straying from the old woman's wizened form as it disappeared into the depths of the house.

I decided that anything was better than standing in that stifling, fly-infested front porch, so I took a deep breath and crossed the threshold. Julie followed a few steps behind me.

The inside of the house was little better than the front porch. As we threaded our way down a hall lined with stacks of newspapers and even more boxes, it became apparent that the front porch had just become a kind of spillway for the clutter that choked the house. Lights burned in every room, but the place still seemed dark. Some of this was due to the layers of dust and dirt that covered all of the lampshades, but there was something very oppressive in the atmosphere as well. I worked hard to separate my personal impressions of the home from my psychic impressions of its energy, but there's a point where the physical space affects the psychic space, and vice versa. I was already trying to determine how I was going to cleanse a place with so much clutter clogging the energy, when Julie stumbled against me.

"What's the matter?" I asked.

She was pale and holding her head.

"I know I'm a neat freak, and this place is kind of getting to me, but the farther we go, the worse I feel," she complained. "It's like everything in here is pressing down on me. I'm getting a headache, and I'm having trouble concentrating. It's just too much!"

She was talking about the energy. I was feeling it, too, but over the years, I'd learned tricks for blocking out emotional residues. I hadn't meant for Julie's first investigation to be a veritable trial by fire, but sometimes that's the way things work. I was going to have to teach her how to cope with an overwhelming energetic environment if she was going to be any use for cleansing the house.

"Let me find Irving real quick, and then I'll show you some tricks for handling this," I said.

Irving was in a room all the way at the end of the hall. It was a combination office and bedroom, and I got the feeling that Irving spent nearly all of his time in here. Notably, this was the one room in the house that was not piled high with clutter. Also, once we closed the door and effectively shut out the rest of the house, the atmosphere felt lighter. It wasn't perfect, but the difference was noticeable.

I did the necessary introductions, but then I excused us for a few moments.

"Julie's feeling a little overwhelmed right now, so I want to go outside and help her get back on her feet. I'll probably be teaching some of the same techniques to you, later on."

Irving was just happy that someone else felt all the negative energy in his home. He nodded and let us know that he'd be waiting in his room when we were done.

After steeling herself for a few moments to face the miasma of energy that roiled in that long, dark hallway, Julie indicated that she was ready to proceed. I led her back out to the front door. We rushed through the stifling little porch, and walked a good way down the gravel driveway.

"I feel so nauseated!" Julie cried. "And dizzy. It can't just be the clutter. There's something about the energy. No wonder Irving's going crazy!"

"It's just everything that's built up in there over the years," I explained. "The clutter's the physical aspect, but the energy is just as much of a mess. Because you're sensitive, it's hitting you really hard. Remember learning how to ground and center? We're going to do that now, out here where the energy is open and clear."

GROUNDING AND CENTERING

Grounding and centering should be your first basic response to any situation that has intense, chaotic, or overwhelming energy. It will serve you well in a variety of hauntings in addition to any situation where there are a lot of powerful emotional energies. Some psychics are so sensitive that even a trip to the mall can qualify as a situation with a lot of powerful emotional energy. We are all engaged in a constant exchange of energy with our environment, both taking it in and putting it out. Strong emotions increase the potency of this energy, and when people are emotionally agitated, they literally leave a wake of emotional energy behind them. Over time, these wakes of energy can build up to become emotional residues, something that one encounters in a lot of residual hauntings. Occasionally, an emotional event is so powerful and traumatic that it only needs to happen once in order to burn itself into the very fabric of the environment. Such events can lead to some of the most famous types of residual hauntings, like the ghostly battles at Gettysburg or the headless specter of Anne Boleyn.

Psychics who haven't learned how to tone down or shield their sensitivities encounter this wake of agitated energy and begin to feel overwhelmed. They will respond to the emotions carried on the wake of energy, sometimes mistaking the sudden wave of emotion as coming from within. A psychic who is specifically tuned into the emotions carried on other peoples' energy is known as an empath, and for them, emotional residues can be especially debilitating.

Highly sensitive psychics are not the only people affected by emotional energy, however. If a situation is intense enough, just about anybody will begin to feel the effects of these emotional residues. Think about how crazy a mall gets around the holidays, and then imagine all of those emotions experienced by all of the shoppers being emitted like fumes into the enclosed space. Most people's psychic "noses" aren't keen enough to clearly "smell" that energy, but in a figurative sense, they're still inhaling the fumes. In the case of emotional energy, that usually means you start to experience those emotions yourself, even if they aren't warranted for your current situation. It's a little like secondhand smoke, in that it can have an impact on you even if you are not actively participating.

Grounding is a simple technique that pays conscious attention to that secondhand energy and flushes it away. It functions on the principle that psychic energy works much like electricity. You are the wire that conducts the electricity, and a grounded wire can conduct the energy safely without burning out.

Centering is a technique that goes hand-in-hand with grounding. Oftentimes, it's such an essential part of the process that it hardly seems to be a separate step, although it is a very important one. In many of the grounding techniques that we will explore in a few moments, the exercises focus on pushing energy literally into the ground beneath your feet. For a lot of people, once they've done this for a little while, it tends to make them feel "bottom-heavy," at least energetically. Centering is a process that takes the focus of your energy and, instead of having it too high up in the clouds (light-headed) or too bogged down in the earth (sluggish), finds a balance in the center of your being.

Basic Grounding and Centering

Whenever you are feeling overwhelmed by the energy or impressions you are getting from a place, it's a good idea to ground and center. The first thing you should do is remove yourself from the environment that seems to be giving you problems. If you've gone to a haunted house to investigate and you begin to feel overwhelmed by negative or chaotic energy (or energy that is too intense), you should take a few minutes to step outside. Sometimes it's not always possible to completely remove yourself from the situation that is giving you trouble, but you should at least try to find a quiet corner where you can concentrate and be by yourself for a few moments. When your problem is just residual energy, you will feel better simply by removing yourself from the place where that residue is most intense. However, strong emotional residues and other types of intense energy have a tendency to throw us out of balance as well. You may feel spacey and have difficulty concentrating even after you've left. You may develop a headache, and, in extreme situations, you might even feel shaky and nauseated. To eliminate these symptoms, try going through the following exercise:

1. Stand with your feet slightly apart, so you have a balanced, solid stance.

2. Begin by taking three deep, cleansing breaths.

3. Close your eyes and focus inward. Imagine the energy as light. The bad energy is like static, or clingy dark globs. Picture this dark energy as it surrounds you, and begin to will that energy to flow down into the ground, through your legs.

4. Continue to focus on your breathing while you work with the unwanted energy. Each time you breathe in, picture yourself filling with warm, healing energy. When you exhale, use that expelling action to push the bad energy farther and farther down, until it gathers in your legs and seeps into the ground. You may find it helpful to make a pressing motion with your hands as you exhale, starting from a point just at the center of your chest and slowly pressing down toward your legs.

5. As the bad energy begins to flow out of your legs into the ground, picture some of your own energy extending into the ground like twin taproots growing from your feet. Imagine that the bad energy flows down these taproots, until it has seeped away, deep into the ground.

6. As you hold the image of taproots rooting you to the ground and lending you some of the stability of the earth, continue to focus on your breathing. Every time you exhale, expel

Let God Sort it Out

Most of the exercises in this book focus on your own ability to consciously interact with energy. I presume that we each have enough power in our own right to control what energies come into us and what energies we put out into the world. However, some people may feel more comfortable trusting in a power higher than themselves to make the final decision about where energy should go. If you aren't sure of your own abilities or if you simply feel better letting a higher power (e.g., God) handle the details of what you do, feel free to end every exercise with a simple prayer, asking your higher power to direct the energy in the best manner possible and for the greatest good.

the unwanted energy and emotions. Every time you inhale, breathe in light and allow that light to flow to every corner of your being.

7. When you feel balanced and stable and deeply connected to the earth beneath your feet, take a moment to reverse the flow of your energy. Instead of pushing everything toward the ground, reach instead for the heavens. You may find it easier to visualize if you actually reach your hands up above your head, although this is not strictly necessary.

8. Continue focusing on your breathing, but now extend yourself up and up until you feel connected with your higher power. When you connect, allow the perfect, healing light of that higher power to flow down into you.

9. With a sense that there is a part of you rooted to the earth and a part of you connected to the very heavens, begin to pull your energy back into yourself, focusing on a point just under your rib cage. As you marry heaven and earth internally, you may want to clasp your hands over that center. Focus on a clear, brilliant, and balanced sphere of energy burning in that space just beneath your rib cage.

10. Take a few moments to concentrate on the balanced feeling in your center. Finish the exercise just as you started it, with another three deep, cleansing breaths.

There are a number of concepts at work in the process of grounding and centering, and if you understand the concepts, you will be able to develop a style of grounding and centering that works best for you. The first main concept is that the earth is a stabilizing factor. You can approach this concept from a spiritual perspective, seeing the earth as a living force that sustains us, or you can simply look at it from a psychological perspective. We walk upon the earth, we build upon it. The ground beneath our feet is our stable foundation. Think about metaphors that we use for when we feel destabilized: "I need to go get my feet back under me," or, "I felt like I got my legs kicked right out from under me." The act of standing firmly on the ground is something we associate with being focused, stable, and balanced. Grounding and centering makes use of the mental connection we naturally make between our physical stability and our mental and emotional well-being.

Centering also draws upon potent metaphors that we associate with feeling both centered and balanced. "I've lost my center" expresses a sense of being unfocused and out of control. "Coming back to center" is about coming back to a place where you feel safest and most together. Someone who is "left of center" is out of kilter, usually in a bad way.

Maybe this sounds overly simplistic. Can grounding and centering be as easy as drawing upon metaphors that lie at the heart of certain figures of speech? Language has power, and every word we use speaks to us on an unconscious level, building profound meaning upon everything that each word symbolizes. These concepts about the power of language lie at the heart of techniques like daily affirmations, mantras, and neuro-linguistic programming (NLP, for short), all of which use words and phrases to reinforce unconscious patterns and habits.

Language is one of our most potent symbols, and one of the first things to be aware about working with psychic energy—your own or the energy in the world around you—is that we approach that energy through the language of symbol. To push energy into the ground, you visualize symbols that connect you to the earth. The most common exercise that many people use for grounding and centering involves imagining that they are a tree—what more stable and grounded image could one develop, really? The roots are sunk deep into the earth, the branches reach up to the heavens, and the trunk is that perfect, stable center that resides halfway between heaven and earth.

ALTERNATIVE APPROACHES TO GROUNDING

The main purpose of grounding is to get rid of unwanted, chaotic, or harmful energy. Going through the steps described above will not only help you to flush that energy out of your system, but will also help you feel more stable and balanced once you're finished. But the process of imagining all the ick going into the earth is really just a metaphor for flushing unwanted energy away. There are a number of different metaphors that can be used, and you may find each useful in different situations.

If you really have a hard time connecting with the concept of earth as a cleansing and stabilizing element, try using a different element as the basis of your visualization. Water, wind, or even fire can all be used in the same metaphoric way to help you direct the energy you need to clear from your system. Imagine a warm and gentle waterfall cascading over your head, trickling down your neck, sluicing down all of your body, carrying the unwanted energy away. At your feet, the water soaks into the ground, taking all the disruptive emotions and impressions with it. When you feel like the water has washed away everything you don't want, then you can reach up into the heavens to recharge yourself with positive energy, and bring everything back to center, just as in the main example.

With wind, you can imagine that both your body and energy are permeable to the wind, and cleansing gusts of wind blow through you, carrying anything unwanted away and scattering negativity like dust. With fire, you can imagine yourself standing in a purging flame. The fire burns away all impurities, leaving only a perfect light burning at your core.

The basic grounding exercise, which relies upon earth as your core symbol, is an exercise you can perform in the field. No matter where your paranormal investigations may take you, there will always be a floor to stand on and ground beneath your feet. Other elemental visualizations can be adapted to fit your circumstances on the road. For example, when I really need to clear myself of the energy I picked up from a particular case, I use a variation of the wind visualization while I'm driving home. With this exercise, you'll really see how physical activities and potent symbolism can help to reinforce the psychic work of visualization.

Blowing in the Wind

I feel most comfortable doing the exercise when I'm driving by myself, but you can definitely do it with other people around, presuming they're at least a little open-minded. As you drive, imagine that the wind of your passage is no longer blocked out by the physical exterior of the car. If the weather's nice, it can really help to roll down the windows as you visualize this, so you are literally surrounded by wind as you drive down the road. Imagine that wind is not just blowing around you, but also blowing *through* you. As with the simple version of the wind visualization mentioned earlier, picture the wind blowing away all of the bits and pieces of energy that you don't want attached to you. Let the wind blow away anything that is clinging to you, and let it break up and carry away anything lodged inside of you that is stagnant, negative, or just plain undesired. An argument can be made that this is not technically grounding, since you are not exactly sending energy into the ground in order to achieve balance, but the technique is nevertheless a potent one for clearing away energy, emotions, and impressions that are causing you trouble. Driving with the windows down, you literally feel immersed in the wind, which reinforces the visualization on a physical level. This enables those of us who might have trouble just imagining things and making them real in our heads to give our visualizations a little extra oomph.

Wash It Away

Sometimes, after I've been immersed in a very negative environment, I can still feel the energy of the place clinging to me even after I get home. Typically, I've already tried all my other approaches to grounding and clearing the energy to no avail. That's when I jump into the shower and use the act of washing my physical body as a launching point into cleansing everything else.

This exercise takes the water-based visualization and roots it in a physical activity. Coupling any visualization with physical actions that appeal strongly to the senses tends to give that visualization a great deal of added potency. Once again, it all comes down to harnessing symbols and metaphor to speak to the deeper part of our mind that controls a lot of our psychic activity. The more you are able to focus on your intent, the more powerful the results of your visualization will be.

For this very potent type of cleansing, you want to invest every action with intent, making it real in both a physical and a spiritual sense. When you disrobe, imagine that you are peeling away not only layers of clothing, but that you are also removing any layers of psychic dirt clinging to you as well. When you step into the shower and pull the curtain or close the door, imagine that you are sealing yourself off from the rest of the world, if only for a little while. You are now standing in your own private and perfect little space, free from the distractions of outside influences. As the water sluices down onto you, imagine that it is running through you as well as over you. Imagine that the water reaches into the very core of you, carrying away unwanted emotions and impressions just as it carries away dirt from the surface of your skin. As the water runs down the drain at your

Sacred Showers?

Can evil or negativity simply be washed away?
Holy water functions mainly upon this concept. Blessed by a priest, holy water is not only
a physical representation of that blessing, but it
is also a modern remnant of the practice of *ab-
lution*, or ritual cleansing. In very simple terms,
as the physical water has cleansing properties
for the body, once it is blessed, that water is
believed to help cleanse a person (or place)
on a spiritual level, too. This is why in many
negative hauntings, if the investigator is Catholic, he or she may seek to purge the home of
negativity through the use of holy water. Holy
water literally washes away the bad things, and
the same concept of ritual cleansing is at the
heart of the exercises here.

feet, imagine that everything you need to cast away, all the unwanted
influences that have clung to you throughout the day, are also being
carried away down the drain. This is where the concept of grounding
becomes expressed in this exercise: as you send everything you don't
want down the drain, you are performing essentially the same activity
as pushing all the unwanted energy down and away into the earth. Let
it be carried away to a place deeper than you, where it can be cleansed
and purified by cycles of the earth that are as old as time. Once you
feel that the water has cleared away everything that has burdened or
distracted you, focus your thoughts upward. Reach all the way to the

stars, all the way up to your higher power, until you can feel that pure, clear energy filling you, replacing anything you have lost. Then pull yourself down to your center, letting the rhythm and the sound of the water pounding around you help keep you focused in a kind of meditative state.

It is possible to perform this exercise with a bath instead of a shower. Simply adapt the visualization to suit the different circumstances. I strongly recommend that you do one thing that you probably wouldn't do in a bath under other circumstances: when you are finished with the cleansing, sit in the tub as the water drains out. As the water drains away from you, focus on imagining everything you have cast off draining away as well. Make a point of watching the water swirl down the drain, and remind yourself that all the unwanted energies and emotions are swirling down the drain.

A simpler variation of this, and one that you can make use of at virtually any home-based haunting, is to trade the shower for a sink and simply wash your hands. You can use soap and water and wash with the focused intent of also washing away the unwanted energy. Another option is to simply turn the faucet on and put your hands under the running water. Use the sensation of the water running over your hands as a focus, and extend that sensation to encompass your entire body. As the water runs over your hands, imagine that it is clearing away all of the unwanted energy and carrying it down the drain. The handy thing about this variation is that you can carry it out very discreetly. No one is going to raise an eyebrow if you go off to the bathroom and take a few moments for yourself. It has the added benefit of giving you space all to yourself that you can close off from the rest of the house, thereby assuming some control of your environment. The privacy afforded by a bathroom can be something you can take advantage of with any of the other grounding and centering exercises as well. When there are no better places to have a few moments to yourself in order to concentrate, this is a great place to withdraw and refocus.

The Least You Should Know

When you walk into a haunted location for the very first time, you can never be certain what to expect. Especially if you are doing field investigation or examining a haunting at a private residence at the request of the homeowners, you should be prepared for potentially intense situations. The energy in a haunted location may be strange, chaotic, overwhelming, or outright negative. If you know going into the investigation that you tend to be easily overwhelmed by such things, you should at least be aware of the basics of grounding and centering. It's even a good idea to go through the steps of the basic exercise *before* you enter the haunted location, just to give yourself a clean and stable foundation to work from. That way, you'll be in a better position to judge when (or if) the residual energies present at the haunting are beginning to affect you. Things to watch for should include:

- feeling unusually distracted or "spacey"
- experiencing strong emotions that seem to come from nowhere
- feeling light-headed or dizzy with no physical explanation
- oppressive feelings or a sense of pressure in your head
- headache or nausea with no physical explanation

If you begin to experience symptoms like these after entering a haunted location (and there are no physical causes), you're probably having a negative reaction to the energy. Once you identify that you're having a problem, you should try the basic grounding and centering exercise outlined in this chapter. In very extreme situations, this may not be enough to make you feel better, and you may want to leave the location entirely. As soon as you have a chance, go home and perform the cleansing exercise in the bath or shower. In future chapters, we'll learn how to effectively build up your tolerance for intense residual energies, so that, if you tend to be overly sensitive, you will be able to shield yourself when investigating hauntings.

Here are the four main points that you should take away from this chapter:

- Grounding involves restabilizing your energy.
- Flushing out the energy that originally destabilized you is a part of grounding.
- You may seek help from a higher power to guide you through the process.
- Centering, once you are done, involves finding a centered, peaceful point within.

two

DONNING YOUR ARMOR

I'm not sure I can go back in there," Julie said.

She stood, fidgeting in the yard, stealing uneasy glances at the old, weathered home. I had just walked her through a grounding and centering exercise, adding my waterfall technique for good measure. She looked worlds better than when we had first come outside, but I understood her trepidation. Although she was feeling better because of the exercises we had just performed, nothing inside the house had changed. Given that it had taken her all of about ten minutes inside the house to become overwhelmed, I didn't think she was completely ready to go back in any more than she did.

"This is a situation where your psychic sensitivity is working against you," I said. "You're picking up everything in that house all at once and you're basically suffering from sensory overload."

"I agree completely. That house is packed to the gills with all kinds of stagnant energy," Julie observed. She glanced back toward the house, frowning a bit as she adjusted her glasses on the bridge of her nose. "But you wanted me to come along and help with this. So what can I do so I don't fall over?"

"Shielding yourself from the energy would be one approach. You set up mental barriers to keep unwanted energy from getting to you. Think of it as donning your psychic armor."

"Armor?" Julie chuckled. "With that house, wouldn't something like a haz-mat suit be more appropriate?"

"However you want to look at it, you need psychic protection," I agreed. "Let's go through another visualization and then we can get on with our investigation."

SHIELDS UP, CAPTAIN!

In *Star Trek* and a myriad of other similar space operas, each starship sails through space surrounded by its own personal force field. The force field works like armor, keeping the ship safe from encroaching harm. Although the Starship *Enterprise* exists only in science fiction, the idea of a personal energy field is something we can borrow for psychic self-defense.

Shielding, in a psychic sense, is simply a technique that allows you to surround yourself with a barrier of protective energy (much like the fictional *Enterprise*). The technique builds upon the fact that we all have a bubble of personal space. We are generally unaware of this personal bubble—until someone we really do not like begins to intrude upon it. On one level, this bubble represents a psychological boundary. It is our personal comfort zone, and its boundaries can shift depending on our mood and our social situation. The psychological aspect of our personal space is important to our sense of safety, but, beyond the psychological level, this bubble of space also represents the limits of our personal energy.

The bubble of personal space that naturally surrounds us is connected with what psychics call the *aura*. The aura is a nimbus of personal energy that extends beyond the limits of our physical body. Depending on the individual, the aura can extend between one and three feet in every direction. The aura is like the halo of light that surrounds a candle—and we are the flame that burns in the center. The basic premise of the aura is that we are beings of both spirit and flesh, and we do not stop at the boundaries of our physical body. A bit of us leaks out around the edges, interacting with the world even when we are not physically touching or being touched by things.

Think of the aura as the psychic embodiment of your personal space. It represents your personal boundaries: emotional, physical, and spiritual. Have you ever felt invaded by someone just because that person got up in your space? Part of that intrusive feeling arose from the fact that, although no physical contact may have been initiated, the invasive individual was nevertheless standing in a part of *you*. Unwanted energies and even spirit entities can be similarly invasive, simply by interacting with the portion of personal energy that extends out around you. When someone intrudes on this boundary, we might say that they "got in my face," but what we really mean is that they got into a nonphysical part of us. With grounding, we learned how to shed unwanted energy that had a negative effect on us, and with centering, we learned to pull ourselves into our center so we didn't have so much of our own energy spilling out into the world around us. Shielding takes the concept of our personal bubble and harnesses it in order to create firm boundaries that not only keep us in but also keep unwanted energies out. Essentially, we are going to learn how to reinforce our psychic boundaries so invasive energies cannot get through.

The simplest method of shielding involves imagining a bubble of protective energy that surrounds you on all sides (on top and on the bottom, as well). Some people visualize this protective bubble as being made of brilliant white light. Others picture something more akin to an actual bubble of energy—something that is clear and see-through yet also tough and impenetrable. It does not technically have to be a bubble at all. Some people may erect their psychic shields by imagining themselves building a personal fortress, brick by brick. Others may prefer picturing walls of thick metal slamming down and closing off all the unwanted energies from the external environment. As with grounding and centering, the symbols you use are less important than your intent. You should use whatever symbols and whatever visualization has the

Again with the Imagining!

Imagination may be the key to using our whole mind. There are two sides to every argument, and there are two sides to every brain. The left side of the brain is the seat of language and reason; it is the dominant side of the brain if you are right-handed. The right side of the brain is more intuitive (rather than rational) and more invested in images than it is in language. Notably, when we go to sleep, much of our dreaming activity seems to take place in our right brains, with the left brain acting as a passive observer. According to Dr. Rhawn Joseph, there is a strong possibility that the memories of our dreams are also stored in the right brain, which explains why it can be so hard to remember dreams once we're fully functioning in our left brains after waking. Techniques like visualization and active imagination are not pure fantasy. They engage both sides of our brain, allowing us to use our whole mind when seeking to solve a problem.

most meaning for you, focusing all the while on your intent of protecting yourself.

How far should this protective bubble extend? A good rule of thumb is to extend your arm straight out in front of you. Imagine the bubble of protective energy extending about that far on every side. If you are trying to protect yourself from a living person's energy, it's a good idea to make sure that they stand at least this far away from you. You also want to discourage them from making physical contact—even if that contact seems casual. An energy worker can use physical contact as a very potent focus for connecting with your energy. Even if the person in question is not a trained energy worker, physical touch remains a potent method for connecting with and influencing a person's energy.

When should you shield? If you are in a situation where you need to ground and center more than once in order to maintain a healthy balance in your energy, then shielding is the next logical step. Grounding and centering help clear out unwanted energy and get you to a stable point, but they only clear out what was already there. If there is more negative or unwanted energy in a particular area and you know you are going to be exposed to it again, you'll want to ground, center, and then shield, to protect yourself from further problems. You will also want to shield if you know you are going into a situation with hostile entities or spirits that have had a history of negatively influencing the people around them. Make sure you have your protective barriers in place before you put yourself into such a situation to ensure that you do not fall prey to any of the spirits yourself.

When you find yourself in a situation where you need to consciously erect protective barriers, follow these basic steps:

1. Ground and center so you can start with a stable foundation.

2. Continue to focus on the energy at your center, just beneath your rib cage.

3. Imagine that this energy is a glowing ball of brilliant light. You may want to cup your hands around it, as if you are holding this sphere of light.

4. Picture this light expanding, farther and farther, until it completely encompasses you. You may want to spread your hands as you visualize the energy expanding, until it is so wide that you can barely touch it.

5. Picture the bubble of energy surrounding you on all sides. Focus on this image for a few moments.

6. Affirm the existence and purpose of this barrier by saying or thinking to yourself, "I am surrounded on all sides by the light. No darkness shall pass this boundary."

7. Go about your investigation—but periodically call up the image of this shield of energy and concentrate on it for a few moments, to reinforce the barrier.

CREATIVE VARIATIONS

There are many possible variations on this basic shielding technique. You can imagine your shields as a fortress that you build brick by brick, or you can call down spiritual fire that not only protects you but also burns anything that seeks to do you harm. As with grounding and centering, it's helpful to draw upon potent symbols that speak deeply to you when you are constructing your visualization. It also helps to tailor your particular visualization to your own preferences and needs. Some people will simply not feel comfortable imagining a nimbus of flame burning around them on all sides, but imagining a bubble of energy that functions as a one-way mirror, reflecting unwanted energy back to wherever it came from, will work instead. The main purpose of shielding is to construct a firm boundary that prevents you from being overwhelmed and invaded by unwanted energy. Your ultimate goal is protection, and given this, there is a wide range of images you can use to help construct a functional and powerful barrier.

Let's take a closer look at the concept of a mirror shield. This type of shield is a little more active than a simple bubble of protective energy and, while it can take more concentration to erect and maintain, in the end, it can be more effective. Once you've had some practice constructing a basic shield, try constructing a mirror shield instead. Go through the basic exercise outlined above, with one variation. As you focus on the ball of energy at your center, imagine that it is shimmering, silvery, and opaque on the outside. Picture this very clearly in your mind. You may want to cup your hands around this sphere of energy. As you look down at it, picture it reflecting back your own face. Expand this bubble of reflective energy just as you would a simple shield, until you can feel yourself surrounded on all sides by this

Armor of God

When shielding, you are constructing a barrier of spiritual energy to protect yourself from negative influences. If you feel that a situation warrants it, you can also reinforce this barrier through prayer, calling on your higher power to reinforce this protective shield. As you begin to visualize the glowing ball of light at your center, ask for God's protection. When you affirm the existence of the barrier, adjust the wording so it also becomes a prayer: *"Through the grace of God, I am surrounded on all sides by holy light. His power will protect me."*

protective barrier. As you focus on the boundary of the shield, keep in mind that a silvery, reflective surface covers the entire exterior of the shield. It is a perfect one-way mirror. You can send energy through the shield and you can see just fine from your side, but everything outside of you is reflected back on itself when it hits the shield. When you affirm the existence of the shield, say, "I am surrounded and protected by a perfect mirror. All harm directed at me will reflect back upon my attacker."

Why would you need to construct a mirror shield? Consider that you have been called to investigate a haunting with an ambivalent entity. The homeowners have had varied interactions with this spirit. Sometimes it seems harmless, as if it only seeks to communicate. At other times, the homeowners feel drained by the spirit. One of them believes that the entity has attacked them at night, although such attacks have not been a consistent occurrence. Is the entity evil? Does it intend harm when these attacks occur or is it simply attempting to interact with the living residents of the house and failing? There's a lot of uncertainty in a haunting like this. The entity may attack you, in which case you will want to defend yourself. But what if the entity is not malevolent and simply does not understand the impact its activities are having upon the living residents? You don't want to hurt the entity unless it tries to hurt you first—hence the importance of the mirror shield. A mirror shield is a little more proactively defensive than a simple bubble of energy, but it also allows for ambivalent situations. The shield simply reflects back whatever gets thrown at you. If an entity means no harm, the shield will do nothing to harm the entity in return. If something seeks to attack you, the shield will bounce that attack right back at its source. By reflecting any negative energy back at an attacker, a mirror shield not only keeps unwanted energy out—it can also help to dissuade negative entities from targeting you.

The fire shield, briefly described above, is another proactive shielding method that combines offense and defense. Let's consider that you are called to investigate a haunting where you know some very bad stuff has been going on. There is at least one entity present that is nasty and violent. Multiple people have reported feeling attacked by this entity, and at least one person involved in the haunting is worried that the entity was attempting to possess them. This is a highly volatile haunting, and you know going into it that you are marching into what amounts to a psychic battlefield. From the reports you have received, there is no doubt in your mind that any entity you may encounter in this haunting will seek to do you harm. So you want to erect a protective barrier that doesn't just keep it out—you want something that will dissuade it entirely from attempting to interact with you.

Fire, spikes, whirling blades—any of these images can be worked into your visualization of a basic shield to make that shield both offensive and defensive. Such a shield is not something you should seek

Calling All Angels

A religious variation on the act of shielding is to invoke the archangels to guard you. As you focus on the protective boundary surrounding you, cross yourself and say: *"Raphael before me. Gabriel behind me. Michael on my right side. Uriel on my left side. The Heavens above me. The Earth below me. I stand, protected and secure."* As you say their names, picture each of the archangels standing near you, armed with a fiery sword. They take up stances of protection around you, swords at the ready. With angels on your side, your shields will be superpowered!

to erect under ordinary circumstances. This is certainly not a casual shield to put up when walking through a mall, for example. A very proactive shield like this can also escalate a tamer haunting (or drive benign spirits away entirely), so you want to be careful how often you use something that attacks as much as it defends. Consider that you would not walk into a casual conversation with a weapon drawn unless you wanted to get a very negative reaction from the individuals participating in that conversation. When you erect an offensive shield, spirits will take notice. You only want to pull out the "big guns" when you know you are going to be under fire.

Once again, the method for constructing such a shield is deceptively simple. Go through the shielding exercise outlined earlier in this chapter. When you focus on the sphere of energy at your core, begin to picture that energy as a rolling ball of flame. Expand it outward until it encompasses you. As you do so, continue to focus on the roaring flames that wreath the exterior. When you have extended the shield so that it surrounds you completely, take a few moments to focus on the image of fire. See the flames licking around you on all sides—always focused outward, so that your personal bubble of space is still protected, calm, and cool. When you verbally affirm the presence and purpose of the shield, say, "I am encompassed and protected. Anything that seeks to breach this boundary will taste the flames."

FILTERING

Some psychics find shields to be inhibiting. When your experience of the world hinges upon taking in or at least perceiving the free-floating energy in your environment, shutting all of that energy out with a shield can be disorienting. It is natural for all of us—psychic or otherwise—to engage in a constant low-level exchange of energy with the world around us. We do it as regularly as breathing, and the process is just as essential to our well-being. Sometimes, the energy that surrounds us in a particular environment is detrimental enough to us that it warrants putting up solid shields that keep everything out. But for some people, cutting off everything is too much. All of the impressions that a psychic picks up from a person, object, or location are transmitted through energy. Emotional impressions, residues, even the communications of spirits . . . all of these things rely on our sensitivity to energy. This is why many psychics find that keeping shields up all the time makes them feel claustrophobic and even inhibited. So what are some options when you need to be protected, but still want to retain a certain level of sensitivity?

Filtering is a technique that takes shielding to its next logical conclusion. In a standard shielding exercise, the purpose of erecting the psychic barriers is to keep your energy in and everything else out. Shields are especially helpful when you are in a very negative environment where you feel threatened or overwhelmed by the energy surrounding you. But it's not always comfortable to go around completely surrounded by your own personal bubble, nor is it entirely advisable. This is where filtering comes in. Filtering allows you to set up a protective barrier, but it is a *selective* protective barrier. Rather than keeping everything out, no matter what, a filter allows you to protect yourself from the most extreme energies around you while still allowing you to breathe, psychically speaking.

The technique for setting up a filter is not much different from setting up a psychic shield. As with shielding, you want to concentrate on visualizing a barrier that surrounds you completely: front to back, top to bottom, and side to side. However, as you visualize this barrier, you don't want to focus on something that is absolutely impenetrable. Instead, you should imagine something that allows for some flow, some exchange. Good images to focus on include wrapping yourself in cloth or cotton—both of these substances can insulate you to a certain extent, but they also allow things to get through. Filters are less about keeping everything out and more about putting some distance between your energy and the energies in the outside world that might threaten to overwhelm you. Think of your filter literally like a psychic coffee filter: the water is allowed to flow through, while the grounds are kept out of your cup. You don't want coffee grounds in your cup, and you don't want all of the energy in the world around you just pouring willy-nilly into your energy. But, especially if you are psychic, you do want some energy to come through.

It may take a little experimentation for you to arrive at a level of filtering that allows you the balance of openness and protectedness that works best for you. When I am entering a situation where I want to filter some of the energy, but I don't really know what to expect out of the situation, I go in with a stronger filter in place than I probably need, and I gradually relax it as I go. The process of relaxing the filter feels to me almost exactly like clenching and unclenching a fist—only it's a fist inside my head that I cannot see. I relax the filter a little at a time, allowing more and more energy to pour through, until I reach a point where it feels like I am just on the edge of being overwhelmed. Then I back it up a step or two until I feel comfortable and secure again. If you want to experiment with filtering as opposed to shielding, try these simple steps:

1. Ground and center so you can start with a stable foundation.

2. Continue to focus on the energy at your center, just beneath your rib cage.

3. Gather the energy at your center as you would when shielding.

4. Imagine that this energy is light and airy—like cotton or spun sugar.

5. Wrap yourself in this fluffy, spongy energy, making sure that it surrounds you on all sides.

6. Focus on the porous nature of the energy surrounding you. Imagine that it makes a thick barrier that dampens the energy coming to you but does not entirely keep it away.

7. As you focus on the porous nature of this filter, think about what you definitely want to keep out and what you are willing to let in.

8. Silently or out loud, make a clear statement about the purpose of this filter: "May I remain open and sensitive to what I need to perceive, but may I be protected from anything that may do me harm."

9. Periodically stop to refocus your intentions on the filter and to reaffirm what you do and do not wish to allow through the filter.

Although you are using your imagination to guide your energy, the shields and filters that you create are not just make-believe. Your imagination is building upon symbols that are meaningful to you, and these symbols are speaking to a deeper part of your psyche. This deeper part of your mind has a better grip on your psychic abilities than you do, and by engaging it with symbols, you are essentially putting in a request for action—in a language that it understands. The very simple fact of going through the visualization and focusing on *being* protected is enough to empower your energy. All you have to do is focus on your intent and believe that this barrier will protect you. Remember: a wise man once said that all you need is faith the size of a mustard seed, and you can move mountains. Mind over matter is a powerful tool.

PHYSICALLY CUED SHIELDS

Once you visualize your shield, you should try to keep it up all the time—or at least as long as you feel that you're going to be exposed to unwanted or negative energy. But if you are concentrating on other things—like the details of an investigation—it can be hard to keep an awareness of maintaining your shield constantly in the back of your mind. Unless you put a little energy, intent, and awareness into your shield at least once in a while, it will fade. This is why, under especially negative circumstances, it is important to stop every once in a while to reaffirm those boundaries.

With practice, it is possible to make shielding so second nature that you barely have to stop at all to reinforce the boundary. Some people are really good at multitasking, and they have no problem focusing on one activity while also keeping the thought of something else in the back of their brain. But, if you aren't so good at multitasking, or if you find that your shields slip each time your attention wanders, what should you do?

Much of our work throughout this book involves speaking to a deeper part of your mind and allowing it to do most of the work for you. As we've seen, we speak to that part of ourselves through meaningful symbols, often delivered through imaginative visualization. But some people may find visualizations a little too ephemeral for them, or their subconscious simply responds to different cues. This is why it can be handy to train yourself to reinforce your shields through the use of physical cues.

Physical cues are simply one more symbol in the toolkit you're using to speak to your subconscious. Like the steps of a visualization, they are meaningful and they send a message to your subconscious mind. You should work to tie the physical cue into the visualization process, so you begin to automatically associate a gesture with a specific set of internal actions. A good physical cue for centering would be to periodically clasp both hands over your center, thus bringing your attention in a very physical way to that balanced point beneath your rib cage. This gesture could work for shielding as well, especially if you make it a habit to launch into a shielding exercise immediately after grounding and centering. By adding the gesture each time you do this, you establish a pattern of focusing on your center and then extending the shield. Eventually, the pattern will become so ingrained that each time you perform the physical gesture, you will instinctively go through the other steps as well.

When choosing physical cues, you probably want to pick something subtle and discreet that you can perform in a crowd without feeling self-conscious. If you have to shield in a social setting and your physical cue is too conspicuous, you may feel too embarrassed to use it; this does nothing useful in reinforcing patterns. My personal cue for shielding is to take the thumb and ring finger of my left hand and touch them together. This is a small, discreet gesture that I can do even if I keep my hand relaxed at my side. Touching my thumb and ring finger together completes a circle, perfect and whole. This circle then reminds me that my shields are similarly encircling me, perfect and whole. It's a very simple gesture that nevertheless speaks volumes as a symbol.

The specific gesture of touching the tip of the thumb to the tip of the ring finger is also a *mudra*. A mudra is a sacred hand gesture significant to the Hindu tradition—the same tradition that gave us yoga.

The fact that this gesture is also a mudra has additional meaning for me, which makes it a doubly potent symbol. If you are Catholic, consider making the Sign of the Cross your physical cue. Shaping a cross is one way to center—you touch your head, your chest, and then either shoulder. This has neatly acknowledged four quarters, placing you in the middle. It is essentially drawing a map of the cosmos, with your heart at the very center. As such, this can be a very potent gesture for centering, but it can be extended to encompass shielding as well. Because this gesture also has religious significance as a blessing, it further invokes your higher power in the guise of the Holy Trinity. By making this sign, you ask your higher power to help watch over you so your shield is not just energy. It becomes holy armor.

Other useful physical cues for shielding include:

- touching your heart (this brings you to center, and you can shield from there)
- touching your forehead
- folding your arms across your chest
- touching a necklace or pendant (such as a cross or other holy symbol)
- folding your hands together or lacing your fingers

Most of these are gestures that will initially help you focus on pulling your energy back into yourself so you can then establish the boundaries of a shield. Folding your arms across your chest is often an unconscious gesture that we make when we are in an uncomfortable social situation. We are literally protecting our vital organs with the gesture, and most people will do this when they feel nervous or threatened. Touching a pendant, charm, or religious medal relies on the personal significance of that piece of jewelry. Many of us wear a necklace that proclaims our faith, and often these items are blessed. Such jewelry serves as a constant reminder of our personal convictions. Touching that piece of jewelry is a way of reminding ourselves to

No Longer a Victim

Shielding is all about boundaries—not just boundaries of psychic energy, but psychological boundaries as well. If a person *feels* vulnerable, they often unconsciously put themselves into situations where that vulnerability can be taken advantage of. Every woman who has ever attended a self-defense class knows that the first step to protection is to walk with confidence and not look like a victim. Predators—human and otherwise—have an instinctive sense for weakness. By focusing on the steps of constructing a shield, you are telling your subconscious that you are not to be victimized. By tying this to a physical cue, you also link this intent directly to your body language. Your very belief in your safety helps to assure that safety on many different levels.

draw upon that faith for protection. It can even be helpful to have a specific piece of jewelry that you wear when you know that you may need the added protection of a shield. After using it in this capacity several times, each time you put on this particular piece of jewelry, it will be an unconscious cue that you are donning your psychic armor. Have this piece of jewelry blessed in whatever religious tradition you follow to give it added significance.

THE LEAST YOU SHOULD KNOW

Shielding is the act of surrounding yourself with protective energy in order to keep away unwanted influences. The process of shielding is typically guided through visualization, and one's visualization often hinges on one or more potent symbols that are personally meaningful. The symbols are mental cues that speak to a subconscious part of our mind that controls and understands the mechanics of energy work on a fundamental and instinctive level. Because each person's subconscious operates on a different symbol set—influenced by cultural background, religious upbringing, and personal views—it is important for each person to experiment with a variety of symbols in order to discover what works best for them.

The symbol, and even the visualization, is not the shield itself. These things are just tools for focusing your energy toward protecting yourself. Your symbols and visualizations can vary. The most important thing about the process of shielding is that you feel protected. You must have confidence in your own ability to protect yourself or, lacking that, you must have faith in a higher power's ability to protect you. If you are substituting prayer for energy work, it is still important that you focus within yourself and picture your prayers being answered. You may picture something like the healing light of divinity coming down to surround and protect you, or you can even envision your own personal envoy of angels warding off danger with flaming swords. Let yourself trust and be engaged by the process so that you feel protected and safe as long as the shields remain in place.

Shielding can become a habit that you perform instinctively with little conscious effort. You can link the internal process of shielding with a simple physical gesture that will help ingrain the process in your subconscious. In an ideal situation, after you have practiced shielding for a little while, you will be able to call up your protective barriers with almost no effort. Most of the work will be done by your subconscious, guided by symbols and physical cues.

When should you shield? Consider the same types of situations outlined in the chapter on grounding and centering. Whenever you feel overwhelmed by the energy in a given environment, you should ground and center to get your psychic feet back under you, and then you should shield, because grounding and centering do not make the energy in the environment go away. If you are in a circumstance where you know you may encounter an energetic predator—human, spirit, or otherwise—you should shield to prevent yourself from being victimized. If anything at a haunting starts to get out of hand, it's a good call to set up shields, even if only to remind yourself that you do have boundaries and you can be protected.

Of course, psychic shields can do nothing to protect you from direct, physical harm, so if you happen to run afoul of a poltergeist that's throwing items around the room, your best bet is to retreat and regroup until the physically dangerous activity has passed. But sometimes leaving is not an option, so we are going to explore ways of cleansing and even combating intense and negative hauntings in the coming chapters. When you find yourself called to be a psychic warrior, cleansing something negative or dangerous from a house, a strong protective shield is your first defense against any nonphysical attack a spirit might throw at you. It's always better to be safe than sorry.

three

CLEANING HOUSE

Do you think you're ready?" I asked Julie.

She was still standing in the yellowed grass, eyes closed as she concentrated on the visualization. Her hands were clasped over a point in the center of her chest, just beneath her rib cage. She was using the interlacing of her fingers as a subconscious cue for her shielding, just like I had shown her.

As she focused, her breathing was deep and regular, and the gentle rhythm was echoed by the rustling of the wind in the dry August grass. Finally, she opened her eyes. They were a striking shade of periwinkle, vivid even behind her glasses. I remembered that the other students at her college sometimes called her "Powder" because of those strange eyes and her nearly white-blonde hair. She fixed me with her pale gaze and finally nodded.

"All right," I answered. "Let's go."

I led the way back to Irving's unsettled home. The state of the front porch had not altered significantly in the ten minutes that we lingered in the yard. Nevertheless, Julie seemed far less affected by the oppressive energy that hung in the cluttered, enclosed space. She drifted, pale and serene, and she looked like some otherworldly being that was only on a brief sojourn in this realm. I reached up to open the torn and dented screen door.

"Is that better?" I asked, before leading her back into the depths of the house.

"Absolutely," she said. "And you were right about filtering instead of just shutting everything out. I'm still getting impressions from everything, but it's all muffled now. I can pick and choose what I pay attention to this way, and not be overwhelmed."

"You're going to describe that same thing to Irving when we teach him these techniques," I told her. "But first, we need to tackle the mess in this house. There's too much psychic clutter for anyone to properly concentrate. We need to clear it out if we're going to try to pinpoint the presence of any actual ghosts."

Julie nodded and continued to drift along a few steps behind me. I steeled my own protections and then re-entered the narrow, cluttered front hall.

I had to agree with Julie's earlier sentiments. It was hard to conceive of anyone living like this, my eccentric great-uncle aside. Boxes lined either side of the hall. Most were stacked at least chest-high, but in some places, the boxes were stacked nearly to the ceiling. The bottommost boxes sagged under the weight of those on top, their contents spilling out through dusty rips and tears. The contents were baffling: old yellowed papers, receipts from more than two decades previous, magazines, junk mail, jewelry. One box contained a few shattered Christmas decorations packed on top of a ragged collection of children's toys. There was a forlorn teddy bear with chewed ears and chipped eyes that could only have belonged to Irving, many years before. Half-crushing the teddy bear's face was an old teapot, so covered with grease and dust that it looked like it had sprouted a fur coat in sympathy with the bear. Every box was like this—trash and valuables packed helter-skelter together, antiques squashed beneath garage-sale junk, no discernible pattern to what belonged in which box, and all of it crumbling under an inch-thick layer of cobwebs and dust. We were going to have our work cut out for us!

There is a way of approaching the energy of homes and workplaces that has been imported from Asia. Known as *feng shui*, it is based upon principles of energy flow as they were understood by practitioners of the Taoist religion for many hundreds of years. In feng shui (pronounced *fung shway*), the placement of objects in a living space has a significant impact upon the way energy flows through that space. Energy is believed to flow in currents, preferring to move in straight lines (this is the reason for the sloped roofs on Chinese pagodas. The curve of the roof directs negative energy away). When a space is cluttered, energy collects among the clutter in much the same way as cobwebs and dust. Energy that becomes trapped like this stagnates and has a negative impact on the space as well as the health of the inhabitants.

As I threaded my way through the labyrinthine stacks of boxes that littered Irving's home, I couldn't help but think that this house would be a feng shui practitioner's nightmare. There were so many places for energy to collect and stagnate that it was hard to think of where to begin. An added problem was the sinking realization that it had taken years, if not decades, for the house to get like this. In an ideal situation, if Irving and his family wanted the energy in their home to improve, they would absolutely have to begin cleaning it out on a physical level. Given the state of things, I was just not sure that this would be done, no matter how strongly I made the suggestion to clean the place out.

We finally made our way down the hall and ducked into one of the rooms. This was a den or something, but it had pretty much been converted into a very large closet filled with—you guessed it—stacks and stacks of moldering boxes. There was a legitimate closet in one corner of this room, and it was open, one of its accordion doors hanging off the tracks and slightly askew. A lone lamp burned in the room, its glass shade fuzzy with a thick covering of dust. I didn't even realize, at first, that there was also a window in this room. The glass was covered with dust and some brown residue that could have been nicotine, although it didn't smell like there was a smoker in the house. The other side of the glass was sheathed in two or more layers of insulating plastic, and any sunlight that might have tried filtering into the room got lost along the way through the milky layers of that stuff. There was a mirror against one wall as well, but this was just as ineffective in its original purpose as the window. Covered in a layer of the same brown film as both the lampshade and the window, the mirror had trouble throwing back light, let alone any discernible reflections.

The dust seemed to drink the light, and the shadows were as deep here as they were everywhere else in the house. Nevertheless, the shadows in the closet seemed to have an even deeper quality to them and, when I wasn't looking directly at them, they seemed to shift and move.

"Julie," I asked, trying to sound casual. "What do you think of the closet over there?"

Her response was immediate.

"I don't like it," she said. "I've been staring at it this whole time. I swear, I keep seeing the shadows inside move."

She took a step back from the closet and discovered the mirror. She peered into its filthy depths with as much incredulity as I felt, then made a disgusted face.

"It might just be my imagination, but I think I keep seeing things skitter in and out of all the boxes," she said, hugging herself. "It's like the house is *crawling* with things. Not spiders or bugs or anything. Unless there are ghost-bugs." She looked around the dimly lit den and shuddered once more. "Michelle, where on earth do we start?"

The plaintive note in her voice echoed the way I was feeling. Even shielded against the oppressive energy that choked the house, it was hard not to feel overwhelmed by the sheer amount of work that cleansing this place would require.

"I think Irving's room," I finally said. "It's the cleanest place I've seen in here. Once we get his room cleared out, hopefully we'll have enough focus left between us to cleanse the rest of this nightmare."

Certain aspects of feng shui seem to hinge more on our subconscious responses to our physical surroundings than on a strict interaction with energy. It is believed, for example, that a home that has exposed beams in the roof can lead to an oppressive atmosphere in that home. Essentially, the beams give the residents the feeling that something is hanging over their heads. But is this just psychology? According to the principles of feng shui, our mental state and emotional responses to our surroundings have a distinct impact upon the energy of those surroundings. Psychology influences energy, which, in turn, influences psychology. In a home that is as dark and cluttered and oppressive as Irving's, this leads to a vicious feedback loop. If you feel very negatively about a space, you are less inclined to take care of it and once the space begins to look neglected, you are even less inclined to feel positive about that space. Living in surroundings that you hate, day in and day out, wears you down on several levels, and this psychological wear and tear can have a visible impact on your health and emotional state.

Negative energy also begins to attract negative entities. Some of these are like the spirit-bugs that Julie alluded to. They're the otherworldly equivalent of vermin, not exactly sentient, but driven to collect and feed in stagnant drifts of energy. I'd encountered them in hauntings before, and they were almost universally linked with cluttered, closed-off spaces. Usually, they inhabited closets and attics and basements, but because of his mother's hoarding compulsion, Irving's entire house had been transformed into one immense closet, with little portions of space eked out for the human inhabitants. It was no wonder the poor guy felt he was under constant attack. A psychic, with no training, no sense of shielding, forced to live in circumstances like this—he'd be hyperaware of each and every little thing that shifted or moved in the space, and that's not even considering his reaction to the oppressive atmosphere of the space itself. I was really beginning to feel bad for the guy.

We headed back to Irving's room, Julie picking her way carefully among the clutter so nothing bumped up against her and soiled her pantsuit. Delicately, I reached up and knocked on the bedroom door. It opened almost immediately. Irving, who wore a constantly haggard expression, ran his fingers through his disheveled, prematurely gray hair.

"You done looking around?" he asked.

He gestured us in and closed the door behind us.

"I think we really have our work cut out for us," I said, trying to be as politically correct as possible.

"Yeah. They don't like that you're here," Irving said. His eyes seemed wider than usual and they nervously darted around the room, lingering especially in the direction of the closet. I turned and followed Irving's gaze. That same blacker-than-the-rest-of-the-shadows darkness that we had seen in the den seemed to coil in the recesses of his closet here as well. I noticed also that Irving's closet was the only cluttered space in his room—full enough with clothes and boxes that he could not completely close the old accordion doors.

"They like the corners and the dark spaces, don't they, Irving?" I asked.

Wordlessly, he nodded, never taking his eyes from whatever he saw in the closet.

"On the phone you said you thought they were demons," I continued.

Again, he answered with a wordless, bug-eyed nod. I found myself staring at Irving's wasted frame, the shock of white in his otherwise dark hair, the lines scored around his mouth and eyes. I could hardly believe that I was looking at a man only a few years older than myself. He didn't just look haunted; he looked *consumed* by what was haunting him.

"They've got to be demons," Irving said in a hollow tone. "They come from the dark. They love the dark. That's why I keep a light burning in my room all the time."

Irving's room was indeed brighter than the rest of the house. Not only did he have several lights burning in the middle of the day, but he also had a huge window that covered nearly the entire back wall of his room. This was one of the only windows in the house that was not covered over with insulating plastic. It stood naked of any curtains or blinds, and light flooded in through neatly cleaned panes that were old enough to have that watery appearance that gravity inevitably bestows upon glass, given enough time.

His room was definitely brighter, and yet it still wasn't as bright as one would expect. The gray, watery quality to the light even in Irving's room spoke volumes about the unnatural pall of shadows that seemed to cling to the entire house. Could residual energy be so thick that it could physically obscure the light? I didn't think so, but I was willing to accept that it gave such an *impression* of darkness that our eyes didn't recognize the difference.

"I don't think they're demons," I said at length.

For the first time since I met him face to face, I saw Irving's expression light up.

"You don't?" he asked. "Really?"

"Those things we keep seeing in the closets," Julie chimed in. "They're dark and they're definitely not nice, but I wouldn't call them demons."

"Then it's not my music," Irving said with no small amount of satisfaction.

"Your music?" I asked, puzzled.

Irving retrieved a battered electric guitar from a stand behind his computer desk. Experimentally, he strummed the strings, which gave out a faint echo of the music that they could produce if plugged into a working amp.

"My mom thought it was my rock music," he continued. "She was afraid that I was inviting Satan into my life."

He said this so matter-of-factly that it was hard initially to raise the billion and one objections that leapt to my mind. Fortunately for me, Julie suffered no such hesitation.

"Are you serious?" she squawked. "Rock music? Rock music doesn't haunt your house! Do you really think your music's to blame? I mean, look at this place!"

Irving winced, but his next expression was more apologetic than offended. Again, he ran his fingers through his graying hair.

"Well, Mom keeps saying that she's going to clean it up some day. Some day just never seems to come," he sighed.

I took a deep breath myself, glancing from Irving to Julie and back again.

"Irving," I began, "I'm going to level with you. Your house is not haunted because you like rock music. It might not be haunted *only* because it's a mess, but the mess is not helping matters any. You're living in a toxic environment, psychically speaking."

Irving nodded. It didn't seem like I was telling him anything he didn't already suspect himself. Heartened, I went on.

Highway to Hell

In the 1970s and 1980s, a phenomena known as the "Satanic Panic" occurred. This social phenomena, largely inspired by books like *The Satan Seller* by Mike Warnke, led a number of people to believe that there was a widespread conspiracy of Satanists seeking to infiltrate society and subvert youth. One of the main methods used to convert young people to Satanism, according to proponents of the panic, was through the influence of heavy metal music. The loud, discordant sounds and often violent themes of heavy metal made it an easy target for this assertion. There were claims that subliminal messages were worked into the music or that, if certain records were played backward, they revealed Satanic prayers. There was no supporting evidence for any of these claims, but some heavy metal artists were inspired by the accusations to actually integrate references to Satanism in their work as a way of thumbing their noses at those who would criticize them. *Satanic Panic: the Creation of a Contemporary Legend* by sociologist Jeffrey Victor explores some of the social influences that lead to this special brand of hysteria and dispels a number of myths that persist because of it.

"I can clean up a lot of the energetic crud, but whatever I do here today, it won't stick unless you and your mother make some drastic changes."

Irving hugged his guitar as though he still missed the forgotten teddy bear that was currently half-buried under a teapot.

"I think I expected this," he admitted. "But you can clean it out at least a little bit before we clear out all of mom's stuff, right? And kick out those shadow-things that keep bothering me?"

Instinctively, I glanced to the closet again. The darker-than-darkness there seemed still for once. Maybe it was just waiting to hear what we said about it.

"I've got to clean out all the stagnant energy before I tackle anything else," I explained. "Once the energy in here has improved, I suspect that your spooky friends might just move along on their own. But if they don't, I'll have a few words with them," I promised, with what might have been a wicked grin.

"So what do I do now?" Irving asked.

"First, I need you out of here. Julie?" I asked. "Would you take Irving outside and show him the same grounding, centering, and shielding techniques I showed you?"

She nodded.

"Julie's a spirit medium just like you," I explained to Irving. "You might want to pick her brain about how to get a little more control over your abilities. You need to learn how to use your abilities, not let them use you."

Irving nodded.

"Are you sure you won't need my help clearing the house?" Julie inquired.

"I'm just going to start with this room. That will give you enough time to talk with Irving. After that, I'll be glad to have you help out. There's a lot of ground to cover before we're through."

Psychic Cleansing

Cleansing a living space functions on many of the same principles as grounding and clearing your energy. Your primary goal with cleansing is to flush out unwanted, harmful, or stagnant energy so that the space feels balanced and stable. The main difference, of course, is that you are seeking to affect the energy of a space outside of you, rather than grounding to affect your own energy. The difference can be subtle, but significant. For most of you reading this book now, it was probably not a difficult task to focus on and cleanse your own energy. It was simply a matter of turning your attention inward and letting your subconscious do the rest. But when it comes to influencing energy outside of yourself, it's easy to stumble a little. Some of this is a matter of having the confidence in your own abilities to believe that you *can* influence the energy in the world around you in a conscious and significant fashion. The other half is simply wrapping your brain around the fact that all it takes is a combination of visualization, focus, and willpower in order to achieve those conscious and significant changes.

You don't have to be psychic to notice that we can unconsciously affect the energy in the world around us. How many of us have encountered the following scenario?

Two people have been arguing in a room. The argument, though heated, has drawn to a close, and both people have vacated the room. Despite their absence, when you walk into the room, you can feel the tension of the argument still hanging on the air. There are no cues that you should be able to pick up with your five physical senses, and yet you are still aware that an argument just happened in this room. The atmosphere seems thick with something, and we've even got expressions that acknowledge this, like, "You could cut the tension with a knife." More intriguing are statements that we often make without even realizing what we're saying: "There's a bad vibe in that room," or "I don't like that room's energy," and even, "There's just something in the air."

All of these phrases unconsciously acknowledge the energetic component of our impressions simply through our language. We are forever going on about how we don't like a place simply because of the way it "feels," and yet we rarely stop to think about what we really mean when we make such a statement. What *do* we mean when we talk about the "feel" of a particular space? Are we talking about a quality that we can pick up with any of our conventional senses? Would we be able to bring in some piece of technological equipment to measure or quantify the "feel" of the space?

More than likely, the answer is no. The "feel" of a space has everything to do with the nonphysical quality that, for the purpose of this book, we are calling energy. And if we encounter it and unconsciously sense it on a daily basis, it's not a huge stretch to move our interactions with that intangible quality of our environments from an unconscious plane to a conscious one.

Cleansing the energy of a space first requires that you make this leap. You must accept that there is a nonphysical quality to a space that we will call energy. You must accept that, although this energy is not precisely physical in nature, it can nevertheless significantly influence our impressions and experience of that space. The next leap you need to make is accepting that you can not only sense this energy but you can also influence it through a conscious effort. Your tools for this conscious interaction with the invisible are the same tools that you have already explored with grounding, centering, and shielding. Visualization, symbolism, and focused intent are the building blocks that allow us to turn our minds to a conscious interaction with energy—both within ourselves and in the world around us.

However, before we delve into the basics of how to cleanse a space, let us first take a look at *why* we should cleanse the energy in our living spaces. Let me return to the example of the lingering argument that we considered earlier. We've all been in this situation, at least once or twice. Some of the people who share our living space have been arguing. Perhaps the arguments and the bad feelings have lingered on for a number of days. It's bad enough when they're actually shouting at one another, but it's actually worse when they just sit in silence, stewing over their differences. You can practically feel the negative emotions rolling off of them, filling up the room. Sometimes their negativity seems to completely eclipse all of the good emotions that linger in your space. Home doesn't feel like home any more. You can't stand to be around them or even in the same space where all that negativity keeps brewing. Pretty soon the whole atmosphere feels poisonous, and no one who shares that space is ever in a good mood.

This is a perfect example of how negative energy can build up in a residence or even a workplace. Energetic residues are like dust in that they're mainly generated by people. Physical dust is comprised mostly of cast-off human skin cells. Psychic dust, on the other hand, is comprised of cast-off vital energy. As suggested by the example of the argument, this energy is often heavily laden with emotion. When the emotions are negative ones—anger, fear, sorrow—we really notice how this residual energy affects our space.

Residual energy is a problem at a vast number of hauntings. In fact, a number of hauntings do not involve sentient spirits at all. Instead, the "haunting" is actually the residents' response to residual energy. This energy may have been imprinted upon the haunted location during a single traumatic event, or it might have simply built up over time through a series of negative occurrences. Often, a residual haunting will seem to replay the events that created it. Instead of being haunted by an earthbound spirit, the location is haunted instead with echoes of past trauma.

Although massive trauma can help to create a residual haunting overnight, it is not strictly necessary for residues to build up. We humans are constantly exchanging energy with our environments, both taking in energy to sustain ourselves and putting energy out, like a candle's flame sheds heat and light in its process of burning. Given enough time, energetic residues can build up in any place that people frequent. Some spaces are certainly more prone to collect residues than others.

Closed-off spaces and places choked with excessive clutter do not allow for a free and natural flow of energy, and thus residues are much more likely to collect and stagnate in such places. This highlights another salient quality of energy: as much as energy itself seems to be nonphysical, it nevertheless interacts in certain ways with our physical world. The Taoists of China had some good ideas when they were formulating the beliefs that gave rise to feng shui. In accordance with the principles underlying this ancient discipline, energy does seem to flow in currents, almost like water, and it does seem to build up particularly in spaces that are cluttered or ignored. The movement of people in and out of living spaces seems to stir up stagnant energy and the boundaries we construct even on a purely mental level can obstruct its flow. Those boundaries include the walls we erect to protect our living spaces from the mundane elements of the world, but those boundaries can also be conceptual things like shields—if they are shored up with enough belief and willpower.

There is a lot to be learned about how energy builds up and interacts with our environment, but as far as paranormal investigation is concerned, your primary concern about energy in living spaces is how and when it should be removed. Here is a summary of instances when you should seek to cleanse the energy in a space:

- there has been a consistent, negative haunting
- the atmosphere seems inexplicably heavy, oppressive, or dark
- there has been recent emotional trauma
- someone is sick or dying (or has recently died)
- the emotions of current or previous residents seem to linger in the home
- the space has been closed up or excessively cluttered

We are all constantly putting energy into our environments, just as we are constantly shedding the skin cells that make up dust. Given

Zen and the Art of Interior Design

Feng shui means "wind, water," and it is a technique that has its roots in Chinese Taoism. Although feng shui is derived from an Asian religion, it is not a religious practice itself. Instead, it is an approach to the world that takes its inspiration from Taoist philosophies. It is possible to study and practice feng shui without being a Taoist, and the principles of how energy flows between people, places, and things can shed some much-needed light on issues encountered in many hauntings. Essentially, feng shui is a structured approach to the invisible world that offers useful guidelines on how to manage and improve the energy in living spaces. If you are curious and want to learn more about this ancient Asian approach to energy, there are a number of good books available on the subject. I am particularly fond of Nancy SantoPietro's *Feng Shui: Harmony by Design,* and I also recommend Jayme Barrett's *Feng Shui Your Life.*

this, it's also a good idea to cleanse our work and living spaces every few weeks, just on general principle. You wouldn't let the dust build up in your home until it was thick enough to cover everything, so don't leave this psychic "dust" lying around either. When you investigate a haunting where residues play a significant role in the trouble experienced by residents, be sure to teach your clients the basics of keeping a tidy house in both body and spirit. Cleansing a home energetically can be worked into one's regular cleaning routine, so all it takes is a little extra effort to ensure that the troublesome residues don't build up to a point where they become a problem ever again.

DOWN AND DIRTY

We have looked at how residues build up as well as some theories behind why energy behaves the way it does in our homes and workplaces. We have explored the ways we are affected by energetic residues, not only in serious hauntings, but in simple day-to-day affairs. Now it is time to consider how to clear unwanted energy from a home. These are your goals when you perform a house cleansing:

1. Break up stagnant, blocked, or trapped energy.

2. Gather up unwanted and negative residues.

3. Clear all unwanted energy out of the home.

4. Promote a cleaner, healthier flow of energy.

There are a number of different ways one can achieve these goals. I'm going to start with a method that uses pure energy work, coupled with some physical cues to help focus your intentions. After that, we're going to explore a wide variety of methods that people of different religious and cultural backgrounds have used to cleanse the energy of homes and businesses.

To perform this first technique, you need a certain amount of confidence in your ability to work with energy. You should also have firm boundaries of your own, so you will not be easily overwhelmed by any of the negative and unwanted energy you are cleansing. For this reason, it's important to go through the steps of grounding, centering, and shielding before you attempt a cleansing. This gives you a clear, solid starting point where you are protected from any harmful energies you may encounter.

Confidence in working with energy comes from practice and experience. If you are the only person at a haunting who feels comfortable with the idea of cleansing the space, and you're still not entirely confident in your abilities, don't be afraid to make an attempt. In my experience, when a family or individual is experiencing problems because of a build-up of negative or stagnant energy in their home, it is better to make an unskilled attempt at clearing it than to do nothing at all.

That being said, it is still important that you try to get your practice in at home, where you have a lot more control over the energy, than to simply jump in headfirst and attempt your first cleansing at a haunted house. As you slowly master the technique, you will get a sense of what it feels like to clear out the unwanted energy, and once you start getting noticeable results, your confidence will grow. Another way to help boost your confidence in your ability to cleanse the energy of a space is to reach out to your higher power. Say a prayer at the beginning of the cleansing, asking the divine to work through you. If you work with spirit guides, you can ask for their help as well. An extra pair of hands always helps the work get done faster and more efficiently.

When you are cleansing energy from a home, you are essentially gathering up everything that is unwanted and casting it out of the house. For this reason, you should start in the back of the house and work toward the front door. If the house has multiple levels, proceed from the top down, methodically working your way down to the front door. Treat the basement, if the house has one, as a separate section entirely and only clean it out after you have cleansed the rest of the

99% Perspiration

It's natural to feel uncomfortable in a house that is excessively cluttered. Houses that have been closed up for long periods of time have stale air and there are often unpleasant odors lingering on that air as well. But is this bad energy or just bad housekeeping? Even if you don't buy into all of this talk about energy, cleaning the place up and airing it out is going to improve the overall feel of the house for the people who live there. It's simple psychology. If the state of a home is making the people who live there feel really negative about that home, that negativity will spill into everything. Their moods will decline. They will be more likely to experience nightmares in the house, and, in extreme situations, the stress levels will be palpable. Helping people to feel more positive about their space, reassuring them that it can be healthy and safe, and showing them how to maintain these improvements will all help to change the atmosphere of a home for the better—whether or not you believe in any psychic aspect of that improvement.

house. Also, if the house has pets, secure these outside or in the basement for the duration of your work, so they do not get underfoot. Toward the end of the cleansing, you are going to have the front door wide open, and you want the pets secure so Spot doesn't follow the cast-off energy out into the yard.

You may find it helpful to open all of the windows in the house as well (or as many windows as you can manage to open). This not only encourages airflow, but it also helps to open up the energy of the house. Just as an opened window can help alleviate the stale air in a dusty room that has been closed up for too long, so too can the open window help to alleviate some of the stagnant energy in a similarly closed-off room.

If it is cold outside, or raining, you can forego opening all of the windows in the house. Instead, as you go room by room, open a window or two in the room you are cleansing. Even if you open the window just a crack, letting in that fresh air from the outside will help your cleansing efforts tremendously.

Once you have a general game plan for how you are going to proceed through the house, select a room in which to begin. For each room, start by standing in the center of that room. Take a moment to center yourself and focus on that ball of energy burning at the core of you. It will be helpful to cup your hands just above your center, or, alternately, you can hold them out in front of you, palm-to-palm, about an inch apart. When shielding, you worked to take that ball of energy and expand it until it surrounded you. Now, all you need to do is to focus on that energy and transfer some of it down to your hands. You can imagine energy pouring out of the center of your chest, filling your cupped hands with light, or you can picture the energy pulsing and glowing at your heart, then flowing down your arms to gather in your hands. However you want to visualize it, your goal is to move energy from your core to your hands. As you concentrate on this flow of energy, it is normal for your hands to grow tingly and warm. Once you begin to feel the flow of energy moving to your hands, cup it in your hands and rub or press it gently in that space between your palms. Visualize the energy as light or fire, and picture this brilliant power radiating off of both of your hands. If you are having serious difficulty calling up the energy, ask your higher power to work through you, filling you with divine power.

When you feel that you have successfully called energy into your hands, you are ready to begin. Cleanse from top to bottom and back to front of the room, using the door or entryway as your marker for what constitutes the front of the room. The door is where people—and thus their energy—come into the room, and the door is where you ultimately will be guiding the energy back out of the room. With open layouts or rooms with multiple doors, select the entrance that sees the most frequent use and treat this as the "front" of the room. With one hand, reach up as high as you can toward the ceiling and make sweeping motions down the walls. You don't have to touch the walls directly, and I've found that it's actually better if you don't. Instead, concentrate on the space just an inch or two away from the surface of everything in the room. Let your fingers hover above the walls and the other objects, and just wipe through the energy that clings to everything in the room. Open closets and sweep them out as well, leaving their doors to stand open once you are done. Do not pull the energy of the room *into* you. Instead, simply concentrate on wiping the energy down and away, just as you would cobwebs and dust. You do not have to wipe down every inch of every wall; general sweeping motions will suffice.

Gather the cast-off energy together in a growing ball and cradle this collected energy with your other arm. As you go around the room, sweeping and clearing, the pile of cast-off energy that you are carrying will grow until it starts to feel like an actual weight in your arms. Continue top to bottom and back to front throughout the room, wiping down every surface that catches your attention. Pay attention to how you feel about certain portions of the room. If a particular object or corner seems especially heavy or dark, take a few moments to concentrate your efforts on this item or area. Keep sweeping and clearing the energy until you feel satisfied that it is clean.

When you are done with the room, push the collected stagnant energy out the door. Alternately, if there is a window in the room, you can sweep the main portion of this collected gunk out of the window. As you do so, picture the mass of stagnant, unwanted energy being picked up and scattered by the wind. It is still important to sweep the little bits that are left out of the room using the main door. Not only does this help to clear the unwanted energy, but it also builds upon the natural flow of energy in the home. Energy is moved mainly by people, and thus it comes in and out of a room by the main door. Focusing on this natural flow and encouraging energy trapped inside the room to flow out the door through your own focused movements will ultimately improve the flow throughout the home.

Once you have finished with the first room, move to the next room, continuing to work from top to bottom and back to front. Sweep at the energy with your hand, guiding the stagnant energetic clutter out of corners, closets, and out from under beds. Do a complete circuit of the upstairs (if there is one), pushing the energy of each room into the hall when you are finished. Once you have gone through every room in a particular area, you should then sweep through the hallway, continuing top to bottom and back to front. Move down the hallway (and possibly down the stairs), all the while working your way toward the front door.

Once you have made an effort to clean each individual room from top to the ground floor, take everything you have gathered, pushing it in front of you, up to the front door. Open the door and push all of this energetic detritus out of the house. If the porch or patio is screened in or otherwise enclosed, you should treat this as another room and clear it out as part of your final step of sweeping the energy from the home. Once you are outside, release the energy to nature so it can be fully cleansed and returned to the earth. Let the earth soak it up, imagine the wind dispersing it, or picture a future rain washing the last remnants of it away.

If possible, you have left the front door open (as well as all other interior doors) through this entire process. Once you have released the main portion of cast-off energy you collected in the home, you should go back inside and do one final, quick sweep-through. Leave the front door open and walk all the way to the top and back of the house. Sweep quickly through each room in turn, making certain that there are no lingering residues that you missed. Move down the stairs, down the halls, and back out the front door. Concentrate on the flow of energy throughout the various rooms and hallways of the home and, as you move from room to room, consciously pull energy in your wake. It may help to imagine that all the energy in the house is like water and you are intentionally forming currents in that water through your swift and focused movements. Ultimately, you are encouraging those currents to pull everything out and down to the front door. Once you reach the front door in this final sweep-through, stand at the open door and imagine the currents of energy making a final pass throughout the house, picking up all the little dark and stagnant bits and carrying them away into the yard. When you are satisfied that the house is clear, close the door. Then go through the house and close any other windows or doors you left open during your work.

If the house has a basement, now is the time to pay attention to that. With the basement, you should move from back to front but bottom to top, starting at the floor in the area farthest from the basement stairs and working your way back up to those stairs. Once you've cleared the basement, open the basement door and sweep everything you have gathered out the front door of the house.

To sum up, here are the steps of a basic cleansing:

1. Ground, center, and shield so you can start in a good place with your own energy.

2. Call energy into your hands so you can better interact with the energy of the space.

3. Move through the house from top to bottom and back to front.

4. Sweep through each room, starting farthest away from the main entrance, then sweeping energy out of the room through that entrance.

5. Cleanse individual rooms, then work on common and connecting areas like hallways or stairs. Give special attention to areas that seem especially dark, heavy, or stagnant.

6. Finish at the front door to the house and sweep everything outside, focusing on improving energy flow.

Spic and Span

In the swampy wilds of Louisiana, there is a folk tradition called hoodoo. Hoodoo blends a variety of beliefs, drawing upon the folk rem-
edies of the French, Spanish, Native American, and African peoples
who settled and intermingled in the region around New Orleans.
This colorful Creole tradition has a fascinating and very hands-on
method for clearing bad energy and unwanted spirits out of a house:
the van-van floor wash.

"Van-van" is simply a phonetic rendering of the Creole pronun-
ciation of *vervain,* the main essential oil traditionally included in the
blend. In English, this herb is also referred to as verbena and one variety, lemon verbena, has a crisp, lemony scent that lends itself well to
a clean-smelling floorwash. In the traditional floorwash, van-van oil
was diluted in water. The water sometimes also contained salt, vin-
egar, ammonia, or lye. The oil was believed to help draw in good luck
and positive energy while chasing out bad energy, ill-intentions, and
anything else that could be harmful to the business, the home, or the
people who spent time there. When using a floorwash to clear bad
energies out of a house, the practitioner would move top to bottom
and back to front throughout the house, saving the front step of the
door for last. Special attention was paid to the threshold of the front
door and the space just outside of it, because the door was the por-
tal through which energies—both good and bad—entered the house.
When the cleansing was done, the scrub water was thrown out—typically emptied out in the yard.

For our purposes, the most interesting thing about hoodoo floor-
washes is the fact that they combine the energetic cleansing of a home
with a hands-on, down-and-dirty cleaning. In this sometimes exotic
tradition, the very process of physically cleaning the home or business is thought to help clean things out on the Otherside as well. This
is a theme we will return to again and again. Consider how a physical, concrete action can help to focus your visualization and intentions when shielding. Hoodoo floorwashing is simply an extension of

That Voodoo You Do

Voodoo, and its Hispanic cousin Santería, are two of the most misunderstood traditions in the Western world. Voodoo, contrary to all the spooky portrayals it's gotten in Hollywood, is a legitimate religion. Imported from Africa, it mixed with a number of other systems along the way, including Catholicism. This is why the gods and goddesses of voodoo, known as loas, have African names but are also represented by Catholic saints. Santería, a version of voodoo popular among Spanish-speaking people, also uses Catholic saints to represent the ancestor spirits. The most intimidating aspect of both voodoo and Santería is that these religions sometimes practice animal sacrifice and use exotic rituals to communicate with their deities. However, keep in mind that animal sacrifice played a role in early Judaism, and the Catholic Mass seemed so esoteric to some that the term "hocus pocus" was originally derived from a garbled version of the priest's words at the height of the ceremony of the Eucharist: *Hoc est corpus,* Latin for, "This is my body." Religion is in the eye of the beholder.

this concept of physical cues. It takes the everyday act of scrubbing a floor and marries it to the intent of clearing away more than physical dirt. This is a concrete action that helps anchor and focus your energetic intent. For people who have a hard time focusing on things they can't otherwise touch or see, this marriage of action and purpose is invaluable.

For ghost hunters who find the purely energetic house-cleaning technique a little too ethereal, I recommend taking a few tips from the Creole folk of Louisiana. You don't have to use van-van oil to wash the bad energy out of your home; any simple cleaning agent will do. The real power comes from the work itself focusing on the process of cleaning not only as something that cleanses the physical dirt from the home, but as something that cleanses the home on every level. Since many modern homes have carpets rather than wooden floors, you might not specifically be able to scrub the floors as part of your cleansing. However, consider some of your other options: dusting, running the vacuum, wiping down the walls. These all seem like such perfectly mundane activities, and yet because they are so normal and familiar, they speak to us on a very profound level. There is no reason that a house cleansing cannot go hand in hand with a good old-fashioned house cleaning.

Going through the entire house and lightly wiping down each of the walls is an activity that can allow you to combine the act of cleaning with something like a van-van floorwash. Get a sponge and a bucket of water and add a little salt and a few drops of your favorite essential oil. Lavender oil or rosemary oil both have clean, pleasing, and invigorating scents, so they would make ideal choices for this van-van alternative. If you feel it's appropriate, add a little holy water to the mixture instead and use this to spiritually clean the house as you also wipe away literal dirt and dust.

Holy water, as we've seen in earlier chapters, is based on the idea of ritual cleansing. For a Catholic, one alternative to preparing a floorwash (or wallwash, as the case may be) is to simply go through the house with a vessel of holy water. Move from top to bottom and from

back to front, and instead of scrubbing down the walls, sprinkle drop-
lets of holy water around the room. As you do so, focus on the cleansing properties of the water, and say a little prayer asking the divine to
help the water wash away all the unwanted and negative energy in the
home.

In some traditional hoodoo cleansings, once an individual room has
been cleaned, a candle is lit in that room and a prayer is said over the
candle. Researcher Catherine Yronwode, in her online work, *Hoodoo in
Theory and Practice*, suggests a prayer of thanksgiving, such as Psalm 23.
Surprised that something as exotic as hoodoo uses a bible passage? Even
though it draws upon a lot of notions that can best be described as folk
magick, hoodoo has a strong Christian element as well, and it makes
wide use of biblical passages, especially the Psalms.

Sacred Smoke

There is a long-standing belief that certain plants have cleansing properties. For the Creole folk of Louisiana, vervain was one of the cleansing herbs of choice. In the Middle Ages, the herb known as fumitory
was one of several plants, woods, and resins that were burned to drive
evil from a home. The practice of fumigation was believed to carry
away bad air and cleanse the general atmosphere, improving the health
of the home on both a mundane and a spiritual level. In the Middle
Ages, fumitory was known as *fumus terrae,* or "smoke of the earth," for it
was believed to have been created by vapors rising from the earth. The
herb was connected with the practice of exorcism, as it was believed to
have the power to drive away evil spirits.

In modern times, one might encounter a practice very similar to
fumigation. It's called smudging, and it uses smoke from a bundle of
sacred herbs to cleanse and purify a person, place, or thing. Smudging
is a practice borrowed from the Native Americans and now widely
used by a variety of New Age practitioners. The traditional herbs for
smudging are sage, cedar, and sweetgrass. In the original practice,

clippings of the herbs were smoldered in a clay pot or tied together in a dried bundle. A person or object was then essentially bathed in the smoke to cleanse negative energies. The smoke was rubbed into the hands and gathered into the body, or it was wafted along the insides of a new home. Sometimes wing feathers from sacred birds were used to guide the smoke and sometimes it was simply directed with the hand. Because smoke in general has such an airy quality, it was seen as a substance that could cross the barriers between the physical and the spiritual planes. Half-spirit itself, it had the power to interact with the nonphysical aspect of our world.

Like most of the techniques explored above, smudging is another method of cleansing that combines a physical element with energetic intent. If you choose to adopt smudging into your own practice, keep in mind that the cleansing is not solely the action of the smoke itself. Simply lighting a smudge stick in a haunted house and letting it burn will not drive all of the bad energy out. Proper smudging requires some conscious intent on the part of the smudger. The smoke from a smudge stick is another tool to help you focus your own abilities to reach out and interact with the world of spiritual energy. If the symbolism of bathing a person or place in sacred smoke to help cleanse them appeals to you, then smudging is a tool you should be able to use to good effect.

You can purchase smudge sticks at a variety of locations online or at most New Age stores. Modern smudge sticks are made up predominantly of white sage, although some may also contain cedar or the rarer herb sweetgrass. Many stores will sell smudge sticks alongside abalone shells, suggesting that you use the abalone shell as a receptacle for the smudge stick. However, an abalone shell will scorch if you set a smoldering smudge stick into it, and if you set the shell down anywhere, it may burn anything else beneath it. A much better idea is to go back to smudging's true Native American roots and pick up a clay pot to use as your receptacle. Make sure the pot is deep enough to contain a layer of sand at least an inch thick. That way, if you set the smudge stick down, the heat from the smoldering end will be contained.

To use a smudge stick, light one end until several portions of the stick catch fire. Allow it to burn for a short period of time, then blow it out (and be careful not to scatter embers from the smudge stick on any flammable objects when you do so!). The stick will smolder for a long period of time, releasing pungent curls of smoke. When you smudge, smudge yourself first. You can do this as part of your grounding and centering exercise. Shield yourself once you have purged your energy with both the smoke and the visualization, and you are ready to begin.

Use the same pattern of movement through the house for smudging as you have for all other cleansing techniques. Start at the top and back of the house and move down and forward, toward the front door. Smudge each individual room, starting at the farthest corner and moving toward the main entryway or door. As you watch the smoke curl up around the corners and the walls, picture that smoke spreading from the physical world to the realm of energy. As the smoke naturally rises up and up, picture it moving through heavy and stagnant energy, loosening that energy and carrying it away. Smudging is not just blowing smoke in the face of residues and negative energy. The process of smudging is often described as a "smoke bath," and you want to concentrate on this idea. As you waft the smoke through the house, concentrate on problems areas. Allow your intuition to be your guide, and if some corner or object in the house seems especially heavy or dark, take time to linger over it with the smoke. As the smoke envelopes this problem area, imagine the smoke scrubbing the dark spots away, until everything comes clean.

When you have finished with the entire house, step out of the front door. Smudge the threshold, starting at the bottom on the left side and following the lines of the door up and around. As you smudge this main entrance into the house, imagine a barrier of smoke coalescing on the door. Focus your intentions so that this smoky barrier will behave much like a shield, allowing only good energy to pass into the house and trapping anything harmful, negative, or chaotic outside the door.

If, during the course of your investigation, you decide that the problems being experienced by the residents are mainly coming from outside of the house, you should consider repeating this process for every door and window that leads to the outside. After you've cleansed each room, take a moment to trace the lines of the windows and envision the smoke weaving a barrier against unwanted and harmful energies. Affirm your intent, either as a statement or a prayer: "May no harm pass into this house. May all good things gain entrance." Be certain to do this not only for windows, but for any doors that lead outside, even if those doors are no longer in use.

Tolling of the Bells

Throughout medieval Europe and beyond, deep-voiced bells in massive cathedrals would call the faithful to prayer at matin, nones, and vespers. By tolling the time, bells also helped guide and unite the community members in their daily tasks. During the celebration of the mass, smaller bells chimed during the process of transubstantiation—the Christian rite by which the communion bread and wine become the body and blood of Christ—calling the parishioners' attention to the mystery unfolding before their eyes. The tolling of bells marked transitions in peoples' daily and spiritual affairs, and their sound, heard by all, could help draw the community together. But did you know that in the Middle Ages bells served another function as well? Throughout Europe, there was a persistent tradition that the chiming of bells—especially church bells—had the power to drive away evil spirits.

Europeans weren't the only ones who believed that the reverberating music of bells could cross the barriers between our world and the realm of spirits. In the snowy heights of old Tibet, several varieties of bells appear among traditional ritual tools. One type of ritual bell, called a *drilbu*, is used in conjunction with a small scepter, known as a *dorje*. The dorje is a stylized lightning bolt, and it represents the masculine principle. The bell, often crafted of a blend of five metals and decorated with symbols sacred to the Buddhist faith, represents the feminine principle. The scepter is clasped in the right hand and held against the heart to remind the practitioner of active compassion. The bell is held in the left hand as a sign of wisdom. The sound of the drilbu is believed to penetrate every level of reality when it is rung.

Another Tibetan ritual tool, the *tingsha*, is used in the Tsog ceremony. This is a ceremonial meal that dedicates and sanctifies the act of eating. Tingsha resemble large finger cymbals. They come in pairs, and they are typically joined together with a length of leather or cord. During the Tsog ceremony, the tingsha are struck together to summon different types of spiritual entities to the feast. The sound of the tingsha is believed to open the doors between realities. They shatter the boundaries between the physical and spiritual worlds, and when a good pair of tingsha are struck together, they help to raise peoples' awareness of their own spirit-selves so they can interact more completely on that other level.

In traditional Tibetan practice, the opening power attributed to the tingsha's clear, piercing sound is typically used to invite interactions with spirits. In my own practice, however, I have found that the resonant chime of these small cymbals is also highly effective in house cleansings. As the pure, clear sound reverberates through a room, the very vibrations seem to spill from one world to the next, knocking loose the blocked and stagnant energy of accumulated residues. The sound of the tingsha also seems to bring the many different levels of reality into sharper focus, making it much easier for a physical being to reach across the boundaries of flesh and interact with the world of spirit. While Tibetans might use these bells to invite spirits to join in their ceremonies, I retain my Western belief that the sound of bells is much more likely to drive spirits away, and perhaps because of these beliefs, I have found the tingsha very useful in clearing not just energy but also entities from a home.

I suggest using the tingsha in much the same way that you would use a smudge stick. Move in the same, familiar pattern throughout the home, starting at the top and working your way down, from the top to the bottom and from the back to the front. When you work on each individual room, instead of wafting the smoke of a smudge stick at the problem areas to clear them, use the tingsha. Strike the bells together and move them around so the walls, corners, and objects of the room are bathed in sound. Focus on the ringing reverberations of the tingsha and imagine those sound waves washing over everything in their path, shaking loose unwanted energy and carrying it farther and farther out of the space. As with smudging, go through the room, paying close attention to areas that seem heavier or darker than others, slowly working your way to the door or main entrance to that room. When you have cleared every individual room in the house, you should finish at the main door of the residence. Open the door and strike the bells as you stand on the threshold. Use the reverberating bells in your hand to guide the remaining unwanted energy out of the house and into the open yard, where it can be picked up and truly cleansed by the natural elements.

Tingsha, when struck together firmly and with intent, are loud. They have a high, clear, piercing, and slightly dissonant ring. Even with the noise, however, I have found that many clients prefer tingsha over smudge sticks. The smoke from a smudge stick is pungent, and not everyone finds it pleasant. Some homeowners prefer to keep a smoke-free home, excluding all types of smoke, not only tobacco. Some residents have allergies, and these allergies make smudging the home problematic. In each of these cases, the tingsha are a workable option, providing a strong, visceral, physical action you can use as a focus for your cleansing without inconveniencing the people for whom the cleansing is being performed.

Many New Age shops as well as online stores sell tingsha. Any store that carries Tibetan Buddhist objects will also carry tingsha. But what if you simply cannot find a pair of these useful little bells? In my experience, the effect of the tingsha is a result of their sound. If you can find another bell that has a similarly high-pitched, resonant ring that reverberates for a lengthy period of time after the bell has been struck, you can probably use it in place of a traditional tingsha. I think the construction of traditional tingsha gives them the best possible sound for their intended purpose, but that does not mean another bell could not possibly match their effectiveness. Experiment with the sounds of other bells, and pay attention to how the space around you feels when you strike the bell. If you can feel a noticeable change in the energy of the room when you strike the bell, particularly a sense of things clearing or becoming more open, you should be able to use that bell for house cleansings.

THE LEAST YOU SHOULD KNOW

Cleansing a house is the energetic equivalent of sweeping out the cobwebs and dust. The energy that builds up in a house is produced mainly by the people living there, although spirits can also contribute to residues of energy. Many hauntings do not involve sentient spirits at all but are instead caused by residual energy, most commonly energy that is heavy with emotion. Whenever a traumatic event occurs in a home, it contributes to the negative residue of energy that builds up naturally over time, coloring the residence with the unpleasant emotions of the trauma. Negative residues are not created merely by incidents of trauma, however. They can also build up over time as a result of long-term stress, sorrow, or conflict in the home. When someone living in a home suffers from a protracted illness and mainly endures this suffering while living in the home, this has an effect on the home's energy. Similarly, when someone dies in the home, that death leaves an imprint.

The built-up emotions trapped in energetic residues often have an impact on the emotional state and even the physical health of the people living in the house. Like attracts like when it comes to energetic residues. If the primary emotions that have built up in a house over time are positive ones, the overall effect will be to improve the mood of the people living there. If the overall emotions are negative, then the people exposed to those residues will begin to mirror those emotions, often experiencing anger or anxiety without realizing their source. Some individuals who are exceptionally sensitive to such emotional residues may even find themselves repeating a cycle of emotions or events that was imprinted upon the home during a past traumatic event. In these rare instances, one or more residents of the house may find themselves unconsciously acting out roles that lead them to repeat the emotional trauma that echoes in the home.

Certain Asian systems, most notably the Taoist religion, have established methods for dealing with the energy that naturally builds up in a home. The technique of feng shui, which is based on Taoist beliefs about the behavior of energy, seeks to modify the flow of energy in a home in order to minimize the creation of residues and improve the overall energetic health of the home. A number of other cultural groups, including Native Americans and the Creoles of Louisiana, have also developed methods for clearing the energy in a home. All of these methods, regardless of their cultural background, focus on clearing stagnant, negative, and unwanted energies and improving the overall flow of energy in the home.

A house cleansing focuses primarily on the energy of the home, although it can often have the added benefit of driving away unwanted spirits. Some spirits are attracted to the energy that gets trapped and built up in certain homes, and a simple way of dealing with the spirits is to clean up this stagnant energy. Physically cleaning the house can help clear some of the trapped energy in the home, particularly if the individual doing the cleaning is intently focused on also *cleansing* the home. The idea that physical cleaning can be coupled with energetic cleansing is a useful one, as it provides a concrete set of physical actions that an individual can engage in as a focus for the energetic work of cleansing. As we have seen with shielding, pairing energy work and visualization with concrete physical cues can help the energy work feel more tangible to those who have a hard time connecting intellectually with a visualization.

When cleansing a home, the main point is to scrub away the energetic residues through an act of focused willpower. The individual performing the cleansing can clear the house purely through energy work and force of will, or the act of cleansing can be paired with a symbolic physical action, such as smudging, bell ringing, or physical washing. Pairing the cleansing with actions and/or visualizations that focus on scrubbing, sweeping, cleaning, and otherwise clearing out the unwanted energy in the home is the most effective approach. When cleansing a house, the ultimate goal is to clear the energy and improve the overall flow of energy throughout the house. For this reason, one should always work from top to bottom and back to front when clearing energy out of a house, ending the process at the front door to encourage any leftover detritus to leave via this entrance. A house has been successfully cleansed when you have

- broken up stagnant energy,
- cleared away unwanted energy, and
- opened the way for healthier, positive energy.

four

PICKING UP HITCHHIKERS

I had just finished breaking up all of the psychic gunk I sensed in Irving's room. Once I had started, the process went more smoothly than expected. There were only two real problem areas: the closet and the corner behind the main door. Every time I swept my hands past these areas, I felt something heavy and cold. So I made a point to focus in these places, clearing away the residues until I felt better about the whole space. When I was finished, I gathered everything and swept it out that huge back window. Once I had a chance to tackle the rest of the house, I'd hit this room again, doing a quick sweep-through and pulling the last dribs and drabs of negative energy down the hall and out the front door. This final sweep would help clear out the last remnants of negative energy and help encourage a healthier energetic flow throughout the house. As long as the energy was open and flowing, it was less likely to stagnate and promote residues.

I was surveying my work, trying to determine if there was more I could do, when I heard a polite knock on the door.

"Michelle?"

It was Julie. She opened the door a crack and peeked in. I could only see about half of her face as she peered in from the hallway, but she looked worried. I thought at first that she was just nervous about interrupting me. Then she must have gotten a sense of the room, because her expression suddenly transformed.

"Wow!" she exclaimed. "You've been busy."

She opened the door all the way and took a step in.

"It actually looks *brighter* in here," she said, taking it all in.

I grinned, pleased to know that the change I felt in the space wasn't just wishful thinking. No matter how long I've been working with energy and spirits and cleansings, I always appreciate confirmation of my work.

"Well," I admitted, "I kind of cheated. I started with these."

I retrieved a pair of tingsha from where I'd left them on Irving's bed. The twin metal cymbals were slaved together with a piece of leather cord. I pinched this cord between the fingers of both hands, careful not to let the bells clang together.

Julie stepped farther into the room. Behind her, we could hear Irving's grandmother making some ungodly noises in the bathroom down the hall. Julie grimaced and quickly closed the door behind her, shutting out the disturbing sound.

"I've seen those in your library before," she said. "What are they?"

"Tingsha," I replied. "They're a Tibetan tool. Their sound is supposed to shatter barriers and make it easier to interact with the realm of spirit."

"Do they work?" she asked.

I handed them off to her, and she examined them more closely, peering at the subtle Tibetan characters scribed on the underside of each cymbal. The bells were otherwise unadorned, but they were elegant in their simplicity.

"They look like cymbals," Julie observed. "Do I bang them together or what?"

"You grab the thong above each bell and strike their edges together," I instructed.

With a very determined expression, Julie took her hands and mimicked the way I had been holding the bells when I passed them over to her. Squeezing her eyes shut as if uncertain exactly what to expect, she clanged them together. When the sides of the tingsha collided, they reverberated with a pure, clean tone that seemed to vibrate every particle of air in the room. Julie's periwinkle eyes flew open, suddenly wide as saucers. For a moment, I was afraid that she was going to drop the little bells.

"Wow," she managed. And again, "Wow."

I couldn't help but grin. "It goes right up your arms, doesn't it?" I asked. "And then it kind of hits you right about here." I touched the spot just beneath my rib cage, where I had taught her to focus when centering.

"What do you mean, *kind of*?" Julie demanded. "I felt that down to my toes! I'm still buzzing."

Gingerly now, she handed the tingsha back to me, holding them as far apart from one another as the thong allowed so there was no possible way they could accidentally chime together. I took them and just as carefully set them back down onto Irving's bed.

"I've found that striking those together right before I start cleansing a room makes everything go much easier," I explained. "I'm not sure it's a use the Tibetans intended, but I swear, when you clang those things together, they just blast apart blockages and residues."

Julie nodded. With one manicured finger, she absently pushed her glasses up her nose. She seemed to be pondering the many uses of the tingsha when her expression suddenly changed. "Irving!" she exclaimed, smacking herself in the forehead. "I almost forgot. I came here to ask you about Irving."

"Where is he, anyway?" I asked.

"Out front, practicing grounding and shielding," she answered. "But there's something really weird going on with him."

"Weird?" I inquired carefully. "Weird how?"

Considering the circumstances, I didn't know what to expect.

Julie's brow furrowed and she struggled to find the right words. "Well," she said haltingly. "When I was explaining how to ground and center, he started asking me these questions about what kinds of things spirits can do to people. The way he was talking, at first I was afraid he was going to start telling me that he had some sort of alien implant in his head," she laughed. "But the more he talked about it, the more it started to make sense. So I looked at his aura, and I saw them."

I blinked. I was glad that it made sense to her, because I was lost. I hesitated before responding, trying to figure out exactly what she was talking about. In the silence, Irving's grandmother started howling again at the evils of her stomach from the bathroom. With the door closed, the sound was muffled, but that didn't make it any less disturbing. Julie and I exchanged glances before going on.

"Okay. I'm stumped," I admitted. "I have no idea what you're talking about with Irving."

Julie furrowed her brow, apparently looking for the right words. Gesturing agitatedly with her hands, she said, "He's got these . . . things . . . coming off of him." She shuddered.

"Things?" I asked.

"Energy things," she persisted. "Like wires or tendrils or something. I think they're from the spirits that keep bothering him in this house."

Oh, I thought. Not good.

"You said he's out in the yard?" I asked.

She nodded.

"Bring him back in here, would you?" I asked. "Let me take a look."

Julie hurried out to get Irving. As she made her way down the hall to the front door, Irving's grandmother finally finished wrangling with whatever gastric demons had afflicted her bowels and emerged from the bathroom. Then she shuffled off down the hallway, eventually disappearing into one of the front rooms. As she went, I couldn't help thinking how much she looked like something out of a creepy horror movie. I felt terrible for thinking that, but that did not mitigate the creep factor one bit. Finally, I heard the front door open as Julie headed back with Irving.

When they got back to the room, I ushered them in through the door, then shut it tight behind them.

Turning to Irving, I said, "Julie mentioned that you might have some attachments. I wish you'd have said something sooner."

Irving stared at his shoes, looking sheepish. "I didn't want to sound any crazier than I already sound, thinking there's demons in my closet," he admitted.

"Well, you're no crazier than the rest of us, because we've seen them, too," I assured him. "So why don't you tell me what else you think is going on. It sounds like it could be serious."

The minute I said that, Irving looked scared. It was that kind of scared that you get when you're at the doctor's office, and you really don't want to hear the diagnosis. But after standing in tense silence for a couple of moments, Irving finally dredged up enough courage to start talking.

"Well," he said. "I know I told you that I can feel them watching me at night." He glanced furtively in the direction of the closet, just in case I wasn't clear on who "they" were, at this point. "But they don't just watch me," he continued. "They did at first, but then they started getting closer every night, coming right up to the edge of the bed. I could feel them standing there, leaning over me. And," he said, choking a little with the intensity of his emotion, "and sometimes . . . sometimes they were touching me. Taking things from me."

Irving was ashen-faced with remembered terror. Shaking, he eased himself down on the edge of his bed. I quickly scooped up the tingsha and set them elsewhere, lest his weight on the bed caused them to shift and clang together. Even muffled as they lay on the comforter, I expected that their sound would make my tightly wound client jump straight out of his skin.

As he continued his harrowing tale, it became obvious that Irving not only believed that the shadows had taken things from him—he also felt as if they had put things into him as well. I could see what Julie had meant about the alien implant thing. From the way Irving explained it, it sounded like he thought they had put pieces of themselves inside of him.

"I don't want to be possessed," he insisted. "They're trying to get inside of me, aren't they? But you said that they weren't demons. Why would they want to get inside of me if they're not demons?"

"Whoa. Slow down, Irving," I said, placing my hands on his shoulders and trying to catch his darting eyes. "I still don't think that they're demons. I don't believe that they're trying to possess you either." Then I gave him the bad news. "But it does sound like maybe they left things attached to you."

Poor Irving looked like he was going to cry.

"But why?" he wailed.

Julie looked like she was getting just as distressed an Irving. Strong emotions have a way of spilling over like that among those who are sensitive to them. I sat down on the bed next to Irving and laid a comforting hand on his shoulder.

"There's no need to panic," I told him. "This is a lot more common than you realize and it's not something we can't deal with."

"But why are they attached to me?" he demanded again.

"Well," I explained, "it's usually to take your energy. You and me, we eat food to fuel our physical bodies. We also take in energy, but we usually don't notice that part. We get some with the food we eat and we get some every time we take a breath—it's so natural, most people never even think about it."

Irving nodded to indicate that he understood. I also noticed that he was visibly calming as he listened. Heartened, I went on.

"We need food and energy, but spirits are all energy. They can't eat food any more, and they don't breathe, so they have to take energy a lot more directly. Most of the time, they prefer to take that energy from people. And sensitive people like you are a lot more open energetically, so you're easier to prey upon. You also do a lot more with your energy, so you're basically tastier, too."

"I'm tasty?" Irving asked, nonplussed.

I couldn't help chuckling at the expression he wore.

"Think of it like this," I said. "Psychic people sense energy. That means that you're also more likely to work with your energy, since that's what you use to sense things. The more you work with your energy, the cleaner and stronger it becomes. It's a better quality of energy than the stuff that comes off of someone who's never consciously done anything with their energy at all. Hence, you're tastier to hungry spirits."

Irving squirmed on the bed beside me.

"I think I understand," he said, but he didn't look convinced.

"I'll try to explain it better in a little while," I promised. "But for now, why don't you have a seat on your computer chair? I want to take a look at these attachments myself."

UNDER THE INFLUENCE

Although they have little power to interact with us on a purely physical level, spirits can nevertheless influence us by interacting with our energy. This can affect the way we feel emotionally and, if a spirit is draining our energy, it can also affect our health.

Consider what spirits are. If you accept that they exist, you probably also accept that they are not physical beings. In the case of human spirits, they are whatever is left when you take away the physical aspect of a living person. What is left of a person when the physical body is gone? The soul is the obvious answer, but how does this nonphysical portion of a person continue to linger and interact with the physical world? What qualities of a person might transcend their physical flesh?

There is emotion, willpower, memory, and that subtle, vital force which, for the purposes of this book, we have labeled energy. Of these things, energy is the key. Almost everything a spirit does comes down to energy. This is why so many ghost hunters drag things like trifield meters or thermographic cameras out into the field. Nearly all of the gadgets employed by paranormal investigators seek to measure some manner of energy. When a piece of investigative equipment is not directly concerned with measuring some type of energy, it is still very often connected with an indirect measurement of energy.

Consider an EVP. Electronic voice phenomena is predicated on the belief that spirit voices can sometimes be captured on audio equipment. Tape recorders, digital recorders, and even personal computers armed with a recording program have all been brought to bear in the quest to obtain EVPs. But most people who work to capture EVPs do not expect to hear these ghostly voices with their physical ears. The most common type of EVP session involves someone with a digital voice recorder, speaking to the spirit, then allowing for a long pause, during which it is presumed the spirit is responding. After the session, the investigator plays back the recording, listening to those empty pauses for any indication of a spectral voice. Some investigators believe that the spirit voices are inaudible the first time simply because they exist outside the range of human hearing. But if that were the case, then why would the voices be audible in the human range only *after* the EVP is played back? Wouldn't a voice, recorded when speaking beyond the human range of hearing, still occupy that same inaudible range when played back on the recording device?

A more likely explanation than such a radical shift in frequencies is the notion that the spirit is somehow interacting with the recording device itself. If the spirit is not manipulating the recording device in a physical manner, that only leaves some manner of interaction involving energy. The fact that so many paranormal occurrences are accompanied by a sudden and inexplicable battery drain or electronic equipment failure further suggests that whatever spirits are doing, they are doing it with some form of energy. This might not be energy that exists on a spectrum that we can consistently measure, but it certainly has the ability to interact with other known forms of energy, such as electricity.

With this line of thinking, it seems easy to see how spirits might be able to interact with things like light bulbs, computers, or recording devices. Most investigators, at one point or another in their career, have witnessed some sort of electronic phenomena associated with a spirit manifestation. Maybe a light bulb turned itself on. Maybe the same light bulb then suddenly blew out. Perhaps an appliance turned on by itself or refused to turn itself off, even after it was unplugged. When these things happen at a haunting, they can be terrifying, because they offer us that rare, fleeting proof that the world of spirits can and does interact with our more reliably solid physical world. The ways in which a spirit can interact with a living person's energy may be subtler than these examples, but it is no less frightening for its subtlety.

How do spirits influence our energy? One way is to simply influence the energy in our environment. Living humans are not the only beings capable of producing emotional residues. Typically, we produce residues wholly unconsciously. They are, in many ways, merely a byproduct of powerful emotional experiences. A sentient spirit can consciously produce emotional energy, building an intentional residue that lingers in a space. When we encounter that energy, we tend to respond to that emotion unconsciously. More often than not, we simply start to resonate with the emotion, answering the external emotion that we are psychically sensing with an internal experience of the emotion as well. This happens with residues naturally—they are self-perpetuating. When a powerful emotion lingers in a space, everyone who encounters that emotion tends to experience a little of that emotion themselves. By reacting to the residue in kind, we pump more of the same emotional energy right back into it, thus making the residue even stronger.

Although these residues might be products of the living, there is always the chance that they were intentionally seeded in an area by a spirit. Why would a spirit do such a thing? Some spirits fill the places they haunt with very negative, unpleasant emotions in an effort to

encourage the living residents to leave. Others emit these intentional
residues specifically to inspire the same emotions in anyone who encounters them. This can be a primitive method of communication:
the emotion in question is important to the spirit or to some aspect
of the haunting and, lacking any better method of communication,
the spirit pumps out all of this raw emotion with the intent of having
that emotion spill over to the living. This is an uncertain method of
transmitting a message at best, and there is no guarantee that the living residents of a haunted location will pick up on the emotion and

respond accordingly. Furthermore, the vast majority of such intentionally emitted residues do not have such a benign purpose. Many spirits that produce these residues willfully do so in an attempt to manipulate the emotions of the living.

Intentionally filling a space with residual emotions so that the living will encounter those emotions and react is a fairly roundabout method of attack. There are far more direct and pernicious methods that a spirit can employ to affect the energy of living human beings. One of these methods involves building attachments. Rather than passively emitting energy into a particular location, a spirit can forge a direct connection with a living being in order to actively manipulate that person's energy. Before we launch into a discussion of the mechanics of such spiritual attachments, however, let us consider *why* a spirit would go to the effort of establishing such a connection in the first place.

As discussed in previous chapters, living beings are both body and spirit. Our flesh interacts with the world that we typically think of as "real"—the solid, physical world that is tangible to our five senses. Our spirit, like all spirits, is energy, and it is capable of interacting with the world on a different level. This is the numinous level of energy, sometimes called the subtle reality, where spirits dwell and energy ebbs, flows, and occasionally builds up into residues. We are aware of our flesh and sometimes we are aware of our energy. The five physical senses tend to be much more intense and immediate than the senses that perceive the world of energy, and so many of our perceptions of that half of our existence come through subconsciously. We often acknowledge them only as intuition or instinct, but they are, nevertheless, present and a very real part of us.

As living beings, we need food to fuel our physical flesh, and, although we are frequently ignorant of the process, we also need subtler nourishment to sustain our spirit halves as well. For instance, think of someone who says they need a vacation or time off to "recharge their batteries." We take in energy from our environments in nearly everything we do. Every breath we take pulls in some vital energy along with the life-giving oxygen we process with our lungs. Every piece of food that we eat has at least a small portion of vital energy that is digested by our spirit-bodies as surely as our physical bodies digest the food. When we touch one another, interact, and converse, we share energy and—if the Chinese concept of *chi* holds true—even our footsteps as they fall on the earth help to connect us to the life-giving energy of the planet we call home.

A spirit is just energy. The physical body has long since passed, and the energetic component of the person lingers. Some spirits were never human to begin with, and they may never have had physical bodies. They exist only on that subtle side of reality, and their reasons and motives are much harder to discern than those of formerly human spirits. Like living beings, spirits need nourishment to sustain themselves. Unlike physical beings, they cannot rely upon food or breath or a connection to the earth to provide this vital, sustaining energy. As beings that only exist in spirit, they are cut off from a full half of the experiences we ourselves can use to draw in energy. And yet, since spirits are pure energy, they need this vitality to sustain everything they do. Every action a spirit takes, every attempt they make to reach across to communicate with us or interact with our world—each of these things requires an expenditure of energy.

Lacking the ability to gain portions of vital energy by eating or breathing, what source is left? *People.* As unsettling as it may sound, we are the most extensive and efficient source of vital energy out there. Spirits seek us out because we are living fonts of the energy they so desire. Even benign and helpful spirits feed on us, at least a little bit—often seeking to engage us emotionally in order to strengthen the connection that allows for the transference of vital energy. The energy we living human beings emit into our environment is heavily influenced by emotion. When we experience powerful emotions, we tend to give off greater amounts of energy—almost always spiked with the flavor of that strong emotion. This process contributes to residues like those that had been allowed to build up and stagnate in Irving's home over the course of decades. Often, it takes extreme situations for an emotional residue to be powerful enough to linger longer than a few days, but every time we experience a powerful emotion, we imprint at least a small portion of that emotion upon our environment, in the form of vital energy.

It's not frightening to think about benevolent spirits that may be drawn to us when we're experiencing love or contentment or joy. But what about spirits whose taste for energy runs along a darker spectrum? Spirits that feed upon anger or hatred or fear are what most investigators classify as negative entities, and such entities generally care little about what their predations may do to the living. Further, as we have seen in previous paragraphs, it is not impossible for a negative entity to manipulate people specifically to elicit a desired emotional response. Not only that, but some negative entities may latch on to a victim, sucking directly from their energy much like a remora or lamprey feeds directly from a larger fish.

In most cases, the predations of a vampirizing spirit manifest as attachments—tiny little threads of energy that adhere to the surface of a person's aura and trail off to the spirit itself. Think of attachments as little straws that a spirit (or spirits) have sunk into our energy so they can sip directly from our vitality.

In hauntings, it is rare to run across a spirit that has become so parasitic that it has actually forged these attachments with a living person. But, as rare as it might be, it still happens. It seems to happen most often to people who have very weak personal boundaries. People who are emotionally damaged are prime candidates, as are victims of extreme addiction and abuse. Some types of mental illness can also wear a person down to the point where they are vulnerable to a parasitic entity. Chronic depression or simply living immersed in a lot of negativity can wear down a person's defenses, making them vulnerable to this manner of attack. People who are very psychic may also be targeted, although they are generally only vulnerable in cases where they have repressed their abilities or failed to gain control over them. From this list, the emotionally damaged remain the most significant targets, largely because their emotions tend also to be volatile. They usually experience extremes of emotions, and they often respond to specific triggers that inspire fits of emotion. As we have seen, people in heightened emotional states produce massive amounts of energy, and this is just what a vampirizing spirit wants. Most cases of parasitic attachments involve a combination of all of these factors: emotional vulnerability, weak personal boundaries, chronic depression, a history of abuse, and latent psychic abilities. One of these factors alone may open up someone to such an attachment, but when all of these factors combine, you have a recipe for disaster.

There are signs of such parasitic attachments, and they often help to perpetuate the conditions that made the victim vulnerable in the first place. These include:

- lassitude, lethargy, and depression
- emotional damage, volatility, and vulnerability
- chronic illness, especially general systemic complaints
- lack of motivation; unwillingness to leave the negative space
- inexplicable aches and pains, especially at the point(s) of attachment
- insomnia, pallor, premature aging, or a sense of always being cold

It should be noted that many of these symptoms are also symptoms of chronic depression. Here is a major catch-22: chronic depression can make a person vulnerable to parasitic entities, but many of the physical signs of depression are identical with or without an attachment. Before assuming a paranormal cause, you should explore and rule out every traditional medical and psychological explanation for the condition. As Freud famously said, sometimes a cigar is just a cigar, and sometimes a depressed and emotionally fragile person is that way without any "help" from paranormal circumstances. If you are running an investigation and encounter someone you suspect of having a parasitic attachment, learn as much as you can about that person's real-world circumstances before even bringing up the possibility of a parasitic attachment. That being said, it certainly cannot hurt to do energy work on someone who is suffering from chronic depression, as any physical or psychological ailment inevitably has an impact on a person's energy. Teaching them how to shield or at least going over the importance of developing healthier boundaries is going to help them in the long run, attachment or no attachment. But you should avoid suggesting a paranormal explanation if you think there is any possibility that the person in question will then use this as an excuse to avoid seeking help for a perfectly treatable organic condition.

You should consider the possibility of a parasitic attachment if and only if:

- all medical reasons for the symptoms have been ruled out by qualified professionals
- symptoms persist despite medical or psychiatric treatment
- onset of symptoms is connected with exposure to the haunting (i.e., the person was fine until the family moved into the haunted house, or the person was fine until he or she started to experience the haunting themselves)

It also helps to have a trained energy worker or trusted psychic examine the person in question. If you are being exceptionally cautious, do not tell the examiner what you suspect about the condition. Wait to see whether or not this outside source picks up on the attachment and allow their independent perceptions to provide some measure of verification.

Attachments or Depression?

Many of the symptoms associated with parasitic attachments look suspiciously like symptoms that are associated
with chronic depression. When running a paranormal
investigation, it is very important that investigators rule
out real-world causes for the complaints of the clients.
This includes exploring the possibility that the experiences being reported are the result of mental illness. If
only one client is experiencing the range of symptoms,
a qualified professional should examine the person to
be certain there is not a psychological or organic cause.
When multiple people in a residence are complaining of
very similar symptoms, this is still not a guarantee that
the situation is paranormal. Psychological issues may still
be at work, and this angle should always be explored.
Paranormal investigators should make helping their clients their first priority, and encouraging an individual in
a delusion or preventing them from the proper treatment
of a real disorder is no help at all.

As with Irving, the victim of a parasitic attachment might report an
awareness that the spirit is preying upon them. This awareness most
commonly manifests as a sense that the spirit is attacking the person, touching them, taking something out of them, or even putting
something in. The victim may also suffer from night terrors fixated
on the entity. Victims often report a sense that the parasitic entity
looms over them in their sleep, invades their dreams, or directly attacks them as they lay in bed. As with depression, night terrors can
occur with or without a parasitic attachment. Examine the content of
the reported experiences carefully and with an open mind. Consistent details focused on the same entity or entities, coupled with the
signs previously outlined, very likely indicate actual spirit attacks. Be

aware, however, that there are vivid hypnagogic hallucinations that people can experience falling into and rising out of sleep, and some of these are nigh indistinguishable from actual spirit attacks. The realm of dreams is a strange and shifting territory where spirits are concerned, and we will explore it more fully in the next chapter.

Removing Attachments

If you are removing attachments from another person, you should first ground, center, and shield. This helps you focus your energy, but it also helps to protect you against any of the entities that forged the attachments in the first place. Have the person with the parasitic attachment sit in a chair (a straight-backed chair like a kitchen or dining room chair is ideal). Have them sit on the edge of the seat with their back several inches away from the back of the chair. This will allow you 360-degree access to the front, back, and sides of their body. If such a chair is not available, or if some medical condition on the part of the subject precludes sitting in this manner in a chair, make do with what you have. You can have the person lie down on a bed (in which case you should work on their back first, then have them roll over so you can go over their front), or you could even have them stand while you work so you can maneuver around them and examine all angles of their body. Once again, the positioning is dependent on your circumstances and environment, as well as the physical capabilities of you and your subject. Be aware that some people get a little dizzy or weak in the knees when receiving energy work, so you want to take care that, if this happens, your subject will not stumble and get hurt.

Removing attachments from another person is a very intuitive and energetically intensive undertaking. Many of you reading this book right now already have some background in energy work or psychic awareness, and you will probably pick up this technique with little difficulty. For others, this whole notion of energy work might seem strange, and if you feel that you are not cut out for this kind of thing, you should endeavor to find someone on your investigative team who does have a knack for it. Even if you feel that you have a handle on energy work, you should not undertake this particular procedure lightly. Before attempting something like this in the field, you should practice sensing other peoples' energy and be entirely confident in the accuracy of your perceptions. You may find that it is extremely helpful to have two people working in tandem to remove attachments. When you work with another person whose impressions you trust, you have someone to verify your own perceptions of the subject's energy. You can each also double-check the other person's work, ensuring that all of the attachments have completely been removed.

If you find yourself in a situation where parasitic attachments must be addressed but no one present feels entirely confident about their ability to handle the problem, as a last resort, you can call upon a higher power to help guide you through the process. For those of you who are deeply religious, it is always helpful to integrate your faith into your practice, opening your work with a prayer that you find personally empowering and asking your higher power to help guide your hands for the greater good. Just don't get into the habit of using God or other aspects of the Divine as a Swiss Army knife. Faith is powerful, but your work will be even more powerful when you combine faith with practice and expertise.

Here are the steps to a basic procedure to remove attachments:

1. Ground, center, and shield.

2. Focus your energy and call it into your hands.

3. Direct your attention to the person's aura (typically between three and twelve inches beyond their physical body).

4. Pass your hands along the exterior of the person's aura, starting from the top of their head and working down to their feet.

The Blade of the Dakinis

In Tibetan Buddhism, when a soul detaches from a body and starts to move into the afterlife, it is believed that the soul undertakes an extensive journey before getting to its final destination. Along this journey, the soul may encounter a number of other spirits, including gods and goddesses that present themselves in both peaceful and wrathful aspects. In addition to these deities, one of the spirit-beings a soul may encounter when undergoing this journey is a Dakini. Dakinis are something like the Tibetan Buddhist version of angels, although they are definitely the type of angel that needs to introduce itself first with the statement, "Be not afraid!" Dakinis are wild-looking women whose purpose is to inspire the soul to release its attachments to its previous life. They often wield a special blade, sometimes known just as a "chopper" and sometimes also called a *katrika*. This blade is used to cut away spiritual attachments, and the concept of the Dakini's blade can be harnessed in visualizations involving attachments. Consider acquiring a small, dull-bladed knife or even a real *katrika* to help focus your intentions when slicing away attachments from a subject's aura.

5. Make note of places where you feel a snag, dark patch, or cold spot in their energy.

6. Go back to the top of their head and make firm, sweeping motions downward with your hands.

7. At the trouble spots, picture yourself either plucking away the attachments or severing them with the side of your hand.

8. When you have swept away everything that does not belong, place your hands over the person's head and call down warm, healing energy to envelop them.

You may find it easier to sense the trouble spots if you close your eyes and allow yourself to be guided entirely by your intuition. Most attachments will feel like threads or tendrils that extend from the outside of a person's aura. Some attachments go a little deeper and seem to trail off of the edges of the person's physical body. Most parasitic attachments that have been formed for the purpose of siphoning portions of a person's energy are relatively thin and they can connect anywhere. You may find them on the person's back, trailing off of their arms, or even on their legs. Most attachments tend to focus on the torso or head, but be certain to do a complete sweep of the person in question, checking them from head to foot just to be certain that you catch everything.

With particularly stubborn attachments, you may want to visualize a sanctified blade of energy in your hand. Imagine that this blade allows you to cut cleanly through the foreign tendrils. When the blade cuts through an attachment, the energy of that connection withers, until all vestiges of that invasive energy drop away from the aura of your subject. Another powerful visualization for removing attachments is to imagine your energy as fire. Picture potent, healing flames wreathing both of your hands. As you pass your hands along the other person's energy, this fire burns away all foreign intrusions at the same time that it warms and heals the energy of your subject.

As with all energy work, visualization helps you to speak to that deeper part of yourself that really understands what is going on. The more powerfully the symbols of the visualization speak to you, the more potent your energy work will become. And your visualizations should not be limited to the suggestions I provide. I have a medium friend who is also a seamstress, and she imagines a pair of scissors in her hands. She calls these up from her higher power and then simply snips all the unwanted attachments away. When she is done with the scissors, she gives them back to the Divine until she needs them again. Develop visualizations that are relevant to you, and experiment with different images and symbols until you find what works best to empower and direct your energy.

If you are cleansing someone's aura of intrusions and attachments, you can also draw upon some of the cleansing techniques covered in the last chapter. If you found that you worked well with a smudge stick, consider smudging the person with the attachment. As you bathe the person in sacred smoke, focus on clearing away attachments in addition to stagnant energy and unwanted residues. If you have better luck with cleansing a space through the use of a bell, apply the same basic technique to your subject in order to remove the attachments. Strike the bell in front of them, behind them, to their right, to their left, and finally over their head and down by their feet. Each time you do this, allow the vibrations of the bell to linger on the air for a little while and imagine this sound shattering all of the unwanted energy and attachments as if they were made of glass. When you are finished with the bell, make sweeping motions with your hands down the person's aura to clear away any psychic debris left over from this sound-empowered shattering.

No Wrong Way

There are a number of energy workers out there who will tell you that, when it comes to cleansing energy, there is no wrong way to do it. But this is not entirely true. To suggest that there is no wrong way implies that there is no real technique at all: that it is all just feel-good mental gymnastics. There *is* a technique, but it relies very heavily upon your ability to focus on your purpose. With energy work, your intent has a powerful influence upon your result because that intent is what helps to focus your ability to manipulate energy in the first place. I realize that to a hardcore skeptic, these past few sentences probably still make it sound like energy work is nothing more than feel-good mental gymnastics. However, consider breathing for a moment. Take a breath. Take another one. Think about how that makes you feel. Now stop for a moment and think about the mechanics of breathing. Think about why you breathe and how life-giving oxygen is pulled into your body through the action of your lungs. Now take a breath and breathe like you mean it. Breathe with the full knowledge that this is something you need to do to keep yourself alive.

How do you feel? Isn't it different to breathe with intent?

There is a right way and a wrong way to do energy work. The wrong way is to do something by rote or simply out of habit. With no focused intent, action becomes empty motion, devoid of meaning. The right way to do something is with focus, purpose, and intent. From energy work to working out, this will improve your results.

Frequently, when you remove parasitic attachments from someone, you will get a general impression of the spirit that made them. Sometimes, this spirit hovers close to the procedure and may even attempt to re-establish connections as you sever them. When this is the case, shielding the person you are working on just as you shielded yourself will help to prevent the immediate formation of new attachments. Of course, if the spirit responsible for vampirizing the individual is very persistent in maintaining its connection, you will absolutely have to remove that spirit from the house as quickly as possible. But what if you follow these parasitic attachments to their source and you discover not a spirit but another living person?

Psychic vampirism is a condition wherein a living person has to regularly and actively take in vital human energy in order to maintain their own mental, physical, and psychic well-being. A psychic vampire possesses an instinctive psychic sense of this vital energy, as well as abilities to connect to it, harness it, and direct it for their own purposes. Most psychic vampires also suffer from a chronic health condition that has most likely been with them from birth. As a child, they learned to prey upon the energy of those around them in order to use that energy to heal their own ailment. It is possible for a psychic vampire to become aware of what they are doing; with awareness comes a choice. A self-aware psychic vampire can learn how to control their natural capacity to take the energy of others and, with practice, they can even learn how to harness their in-born abilities to perceive and manipulate energy to become powerful psychics and healers. Nevertheless, some still choose to be predators, willfully vampirizing the energy of those around them. Others simply never become aware of their actions, and these unconscious psychic vampires can be even more devastating. Without a conscious awareness of their predations, they siphon energy off of family and loved ones and anyone else they come into contact with, never completely understanding why they seem driven to force these people

God Will Provide

What do psychic vampires lack that God cannot provide? This question has been asked by Christians and Pagans alike, both of whom believe that divinity is benevolent and nurturing and seeks to support us with abundant life, light, and love. But, in a world where thousands of people die of starvation every year, this question is a little naïve. Beyond physical starvation, consider the number of health conditions that exist that prevent a person from gaining the nutrition they need, even when they have enough food to eat. Divinity may seek to provide, but we live in an imperfect world, and things still manage to go wrong despite all the best intentions. How difficult is it to consider that, in addition to ailments that affect our physical bodies, there are also ailments that affect us psychically? We are living in a sea of vital energy, it's true. But all the water in the world cannot slake the thirst of someone who cannot swallow.

into highly charged emotional confrontations in order to get an even more intense rush of energy off of them.

As we have discussed, every living person needs to take in vital energy and, typically, they acquire portions of this energy every time they eat, breathe, or interact with other human beings. What distinguishes a psychic vampire is not the fact that they take in energy, since everyone does that. A person earns the psychic vampire label if the amount of energy they need to take in is significantly greater than the amount of energy provided through natural means. Chronic illness can often bring this about, but some people are psychic vampires even without a chronic health condition. Their condition may purely be psychic in origin: either they burn energy quicker than their systems can keep up with or, for some reason, they do not get the same sustenance from natural sources. Many different factors can play into the actual cause of a person's psychic vampirism, but the end result is still the same: they are driven to make up the difference by taking energy from those around them.

If you find yourself investigating a case of parasitic attachment, do not rule out the possibility that the parasite is a living person. Examine the relationship dynamics between the victim and everyone that he or she lives with. In the course of every investigation, you should get reports from all of the residents of the haunted location, encouraging them to recount their own experiences and impressions of the alleged haunting. Ideally, you should get these reports separately so that the individuals involved do not compare or alter their stories based on what another person has said. When parasitic attachments are part of the problem, these interviews should also include observations about the individuals in residence.

Unconscious psychic vampires tend to be either very needy people or very dominant people. The needy ones have learned to get their energy through attention, even if it's negative attention. They often create situations where people have to pay attention to them, or they fixate on their personal troubles, constantly reaching out for validation, caregiving, and support. The dominant ones are confrontational, and they have learned to get their energy by inspiring powerful emotional conflicts with and between others. Both types of unconscious psychic vampires often get right up into peoples' space, trying to make physical contact in order to reinforce the psychic connections they use to siphon energy.

Self-aware and predatory psychic vampires are much more difficult to identify, but most psychics will be able to sense them. There is generally a dark flavor to a predatory psychic vampire's energy, or the sense that they are negative space: a psychic black hole. Intentional psychic predators will also be highly resistant to any inquiries regarding their involvement in the victim's situation. If there's an intentional psychic predator in the equation, that person may likely be absent for the duration of the investigation, but other individuals involved will probably report how that person voiced very negative things about the investigation. There's a lot of negativity connected with intentional psychic predators, and if they are living in a home with their victim, it's a good bet that the relationship they have with that person is abusive in other ways, as well. Keep an eye out for these dynamics and you'll almost certainly find the person responsible for the vampirism.

Fortunately, removing the attachment works exactly the same way for living vampires as it does for vampirizing entities. However, since you can't very well use ghost-busting techniques to kick a human psychic vampire out of somebody's life, you will want to teach the victim shielding techniques and strongly encourage them to bring their association with the harmful person to an end. This may include suggesting that the victim seek professional counseling—not on the pretense of talking about their vampire, but because most unconscious psychic vampires get into abusive or codependent relationships with their victims, and intentional predators create their own style of abuse. Encourage the person suffering the attacks to seek out a caring professional who is willing to help that person learn how to maintain healthy boundaries in a relationship and how to say no when a relationship grows dangerously codependent.

Dangerous Liaisons

The vast majority of spirit attachments are forged simply to siphon off portions of a person's energy. However, every once in a while, you will encounter a different type of attachment with a more malevolent purpose: control. Some negative entities are not content merely supping on the energy of a weak or damaged person. Sometimes that entity wants to establish a foothold in the person with the ultimate goal of being able to influence their behavior. In truly extreme cases, the entity can worm its way so completely into a person that it can occasionally speak through them or direct some of their actions as its own. This type of attachment is most commonly associated with demonic possession, but it is not limited strictly to the entities we understand as demons. A variety of sufficiently powerful, sentient spirits exist that can establish this type of connection. Most are simply not interested in doing so.

It's important to recognize the distinction between a parasitic attachment that has begun to influence a person's health and mood and this more pernicious sort of attachment intended to gain control over a living being. A spirit that has forged any attachment with a living person has some amount of influence over that person, mainly through the connection to that person's energy. Most of this influence manifests in altered emotions and, at worst, a decline in their mental and physical health. Truly destructive attachments begin to obsess the victim so much that it seems as if some of their thoughts and actions are not their own. At these times, a gifted psychic may even perceive a shift in the victim's energy where, at least for a moment, they seem to change into someone else entirely.

Before we begin to fully explore this type of attachment, I feel that it is important to stress how rare it actually is. Over the past ten years, there has been a tremendous rise in the number of paranormal investigators out there, and there has been a similar rise in the number of people interested in demonology and demonic possession. As a result, there have been plenty of folks eager to save the world from demons, and their zeal has, on more than one occasion, led them to mistake something prosaic for a true possession. I am including the information here because I know it is a topic that people in the paranormal community are interested in—but I hope that, in reading it, you approach any case of suspected possession or even attempted possession with extreme caution. Do not allow fear to make you jump to conclusions. As with every case you investigate, study all angles, gather as much background information as you can, and try not to believe *or* dismiss anything prematurely based on your own expectations.

That being said, if you feel that someone is laboring under the more pernicious sort of spirit attachment, there are three main places you should look for attachments. Parasitic attachments may occur just about anywhere, and they tend to be superficial, clinging to the outside of a person's aura or the surface of their bodies. In my experience, attachments that are forged to influence or control a living being are sunk much deeper and placed with more intent. These attachments are much thicker than parasitic attachments, and this represents the extra effort and energy expenditure that goes into forging such connections. Connections of this nature do not occur overnight. They almost always build up slowly over time, and the pernicious spirit has had connections to the victim for quite some time before those connections grew into something that could be used for control. Rather than simply trailing off from the person's aura, these attachments are sunk deep into the person's very core. For those who can perceive energy, the attachments will look as if they have literally taken root inside of the person. The three places to look for these pernicious attachments are as follows:

- the middle of the back, at the center of the body a few inches beneath the shoulder blades
- the base of the neck, typically right over the vertebrae just between the shoulders
- the base of the skull, sunk into that little hollow that opens onto the spine

The Devil Made Me Do It?

Is so-called possession just an excuse for not taking personal responsibility for one's actions? How often do the so-called "weak personalities" so often presented as the prime candidates for possession also exhibit signs that they are prime candidates for more prosaic—but nonetheless devastating—mental illnesses? And where does one draw the line? A diagnosis of possession is something that should not be handed out lightly, and every other possible explanation for an individual's behavior should be thoroughly explored. Only when no other option seems to fit should the idea of possession or obsession by a malevolent entity even be considered. In cases of suspected possession, it also helps to have someone with some background in psychology on the team (even if you have to call this person in just for this particular case) so that possible psychological disorders can be completely ruled out.

Note that all of these points of connection are focused on the spine. The spine is the main causeway of the central nervous system, and it relays all of the messages that control the body to and from the brain. By connecting to significant points along this central highway of the nervous system, the obsessing entity is seeking to essentially "jack-in" to the victim, plugging its energy into the "machine" of the victim's body. A connection at just one point allows a greater transference of energy and intent between the entity and the victim. Each additional point allows a greater measure of influence and control.

The good news is, if you can still perceive the lines of attachment, they can still be severed and the obsessing entity can be sent packing. The process of severing these pernicious attachments is essentially the same as the process for severing any energetic attachment. When obsessing entities are involved, however, there can be a struggle for control over the victim. Obsessing entities have devoted a lot of time and energy into establishing attachments profound enough that they can gain even limited control over a living person's body. They typically do not relinquish this control easily.

If you undertake to sever these attachments, you should also be prepared for the obsessing entity to retaliate. With minor attachments, shielding the victim will almost certainly keep out the entity responsible for the attachments. But pernicious attachments are more complicated. They essentially provide the obsessing entity a direct pipeline to the victim's energy, which often allows them to circumvent shields and lash out through the victim even as you are working to sever the attachment. To make matters even more difficult, most people who have been victimized so completely by attachments have actually grown accustomed to the presence of the obsessing entity. Even as you sever the attachments, the victim may unconsciously reach back out to the energy of the entity, simply because that entity has become so familiar as to seem to be a part of them. Like a battered wife who goes right back to her abusive husband, the victim may seek to reconnect to the entity simply out of habit.

A lot of paranormal investigators do not feel confident in their ability to tackle cases of destructive attachment, and it is certainly something to be approached with great caution. The types of entities that seek to establish this level of control over a living person, against that person's will, are almost universally malevolent. Some investigators assert that *only* demonic entities seek to establish such control, but I disagree. I don't think it's as simple as angels versus demons, good versus evil. There are more types or species of entities out there than one can possibly classify in a lifetime, and many of them defy easy categorization. Anything of sufficient intelligence and power can feasibly take advantage of these points of connection in people. Benign entities can establish the same level of control—they simply seek to do so with the full knowledge and cooperation of their subjects.

Willful Possession

Some systems, such as voodoo, actually allow for willful possession. In voodoo, for example, one way that the loas (gods) are summoned involves inviting them into a willing individual. This person may use a variety of methods to induce the possession, such as dancing continuously until the body and mind both become so exhausted that the normal boundaries that prevent a spirit from entering a living person's body are weakened or broken down. These willful possessions are always short-term and the person who is possessed is looked upon as vehicle for the spirit. Individuals who channel spirits, although they do not typically give themselves over to full possession, are nevertheless relinquishing a portion of their control over their own body so that a spirit can speak through them. Mediums from the late nineteenth and early twentieth centuries also opened themselves up to a type of limited possession, where a spirit control would step into their body and speak through their mouths.

But, whether we agree that all possessing entities are demons or not, we can almost certainly agree upon one thing: only people who feel wholly confident in their ability to handle such a malevolent entity should ever undertake to do so.

Before we delve into some methods for removing pernicious attachments, I want to make a few things absolutely clear. Although, in my experience, there is a progression of connection that develops over time, this progression may not hold true in absolutely every case. Most obsessing entities start with a malevolent attachment at the center of the back. Once this is sufficiently established, they then up the ante by forging the connection at the base of the neck, ending finally with the connection at the base of the skull. But spirits can establish connections at any of these points without having forged attachments at any of the others. The difference in the method of connection can depend upon the spirit itself or it may be influenced by that spirit's overall agenda. Either way, be aware that you might find a harmful attachment at the base of the skull alone, and, even if you do not find attachments at the other two major connecting points, you should still approach the situation as a pernicious attachment if all of the other signs are present.

Finally, I want to stress that these points of connection are not universally bad in and of themselves. In fact, everyone has certain points along their energy bodies where it is easier to connect and exchange energy. People with strong personal boundaries never have to worry about outside entities randomly coming up and taking advantage of these points as if they were open ports on a computer. Weak personal boundaries, however, do leave people vulnerable to outside entities that can sense and take advantage of these connecting points.

The Devil You Know

If you feel that you have run across a victim of pernicious attachment in the course of one of your investigations and you feel confident in your ability to handle it, the first thing you want to do is to talk with the victim about their situation. Do not give in to fear for what might be happening and discourage fear in the victim. Fear only makes people more vulnerable, so keep a level head as you have this conversation. Find out if the subject of the attachment realizes what has happened. Are they aware of the entity and its influence over their life? How do they feel about this influence? As mentioned briefly before, the victim of a pernicious attachment frequently develops a mindset similar to that of victims of long-term abuse. They may not recognize that the entity's influence over them is negative or they may acknowledge that it is sometimes negative, but then seek to defend the attachment. Others will feel trapped and yet will give in to the entity again and again, believing themselves to be too weak to resist the entity's influence.

Before you even begin to struggle with the attachments themselves, you need to try to change this mindset.

1. Reinforce the individual's value as a human being.

2. Encourage the individual to be confident in his or her ability to resist the obsessing entity.

3. Discourage the "victim mentality."

4. Stress how faith, belief, and "mind over matter" can empower the individual to fight off the entity.

5. Seek the support of family and friends to reinforce the individual's strength, value, and empowerment.

6. Address any issues of addiction, depression, or other problems that led to the initial vulnerability, directing the individual to seek proper help.

Faith can play a significant role in an individual's ability to fight off an attachment like this, but it may not take the form of hugging a cross or reciting sacred prayers. When dealing with a pernicious attachment, you do not have to fall back upon the Hollywood stereotype established by *The Exorcist*. Realistically, you can scream "the power of Christ compels you" until you are blue in the face, but if neither you nor the victim have any real faith in that power, the phrase is nothing more than empty words. Faith is not the trappings of religion. Faith is a quiet certainty that there is both a higher purpose to life and a higher power that oversees that purpose. Faith is knowing that we do not have to go it alone during our darkest hours and, even when we feel utterly victimized and weak, there is still something brighter, purer, and more potent than anything we can imagine that cares enough to reach out and offer a shoulder for us to lean upon. The object of faith takes many forms and many names, but the universal truth is faith itself. And this is something that can help to save the victim of a pernicious attachment. Learn what they believe in and, if they believe in nothing, at least encourage them to believe in themselves. Finally, adapt your language to their beliefs, even if your personal faith takes a different form than the victim's. Wrestling with a harmful attachment is trouble enough without the complications of a theological debate.

Once you've shored up the victim's belief in themselves, as well as their belief in the fact that they can be released from this invasive entity, your next step is to set up a safe and energetically clean space where you can address the attachments. Consider that, in cutting these attachments that have been sunk completely into the victim's energy body, you are performing a type of surgery. A responsible surgeon does not even remove so much as a mole without having sterile equipment and a sterile environment to use it in. Your approach here should be no different. Pick a room where you will not be disturbed. Turn off distracting appliances like the television or the computer. Switch the ringer off on all phones. Ensure that the room is safe, secure, and comfortable on a physical level, and then be sure to cleanse it energetically as well. Sweep everything out of the room. Do this even if you have very recently done a cleansing on the space, just to be sure. When you have cleared everything out, touch each wall, reach up to the ceiling, and reach down to the floor. Each time you touch one of these physical barriers, imagine that the walls, floor, and ceiling surrounding the room are more than physical structures. Picture power streaming from your fingertips and flowing through the walls. The entire room glows with energy, and this energy forms a barrier, a personal shield extended to encompass the entire room. In chapter six, we will delve more completely into the concept of warding a space, but for now, the simplest way to approach the technique is to think of it as an extension of your personal shield. As always, you can do all of this by force of will alone, or you can use any of the cleansing techniques outlined in chapter three. You can also frame the actions as a prayer, inviting your higher power to work through you in order to cleanse the space and erect barriers against any possible intrusion.

Once you are satisfied with your work space, invite the victim and any assistants to come in. Have everyone ground and center before they come in, sweeping away any residual energy that might be clinging to them as if they were surgeons scrubbing before a surgery. Have someone cleanse the subject as well. Obviously, this is not going to clear away the pernicious attachments themselves, but you want to cleanse that person's energy as completely as possible, despite the attachments. Once again, think about prepping a patient for surgery. Use any of the cleansing techniques outlined in chapter three. It's usually a good idea to remain consistent in your techniques, so if you cleansed and prepped the room using energy work only, use these same techniques and visualizations to cleanse the people subsequently entering that room. If you smudged the room to help cleanse it, smudge the participants before they come into the room. If you used holy water to help cleanse the space, anoint the participants with holy water before they enter, offering up a small prayer of protection for each of them and focusing especially on the subject.

To remove pernicious attachments, you should:

1. Ground, center, and shield.

2. Have the victim sit so you can easily reach the energy of his or her back.

3. Focus on your own energy and call energy into your hands. Alternately, you can gather energy by invoking your higher power and asking that higher power to strengthen you and work through you.

4. Vividly imagine energy flowing from your heart into your hands. Envision this energy as brilliant, purging flames.

5. Find the attachments. Start with the lowest one and work your way up.

6. Vividly imagine yourself cutting through the attachment. This may take some effort, and you should focus on being certain that the attachment is completely severed and cauterized by the flames surrounding your hands.

7. Remove each of the main attachments, then sweep the entire aura clear.

8. Walk the victim through grounding, centering, and shielding, and encourage them to develop stronger personal boundaries.

You want to engage in potent and vivid visualizations when removing attachments. You have to be focused and firm, with no doubt about your own ability to resolve the situation. If you lack faith in yourself, seek strength in your higher power. It is important to teach the victim how to shield immediately after the obsessing entity has been detached. You must encourage the person to have faith in their ability to repel future attacks from this entity. The victim should also be discouraged from fearing or otherwise fixating on the entity. By paying any kind of attention to the obsessing entity, even once it has been detached, the victim is still giving that spirit energy and this encourages it to continue to try to re-establish its connections. Instead of dwelling on past events connected to the entity, victims should be encouraged to move on with their lives, heal, and become whole.

THE LEAST YOU SHOULD KNOW

Parasitic attachments typically manifest as thin threads or tendrils extending from the victim's aura. They may also manifest as threads extending from the very surface of the victim's physical body. Attachments are most commonly forged by entities in order to suck up portions of a person's vital energy. Spirits, as they are comprised completely of energy, require energy to sustain themselves as well as to fuel any manifestations. Typically, the most effective source of energy that spirits can tap into is living people.

Strong emotions increase the quality and quantity of energy that a person naturally emits into their environment. Some spirits will intentionally manipulate people or the environment in order to encourage strong emotional reactions. If you have ever encountered a mischievous spirit that seems to delight in causing chaos with no purpose other than attention-getting, you have likely encountered a spirit that was using the attention people focused on it to gain energy. It is perfectly natural for living beings to emit energy into their environments, much like the flame of a candle naturally sheds heat and light. When the energy is no longer directly attached to a person, it becomes ambient energy, free-floating energy that may become trapped in certain places to become a residue. Spirits that intentionally inspire strong emotional reactions in people are most likely feeding only on the ambient energy and thus have not formed direct attachments with any individuals involved in the haunting. But some spirits are not content with free-floating energy alone, and they go straight to the source to take directly from a living person.

Spirits that forge attachments are seeking more than mere energy. These spirits seek control. Pernicious attachments can lead to obsession and even possession, and they should be identified and handled with the utmost care. These attachments tend to run much deeper than parasitic attachments, often focusing on specific points. These points are located at the base of the skull, the base of the neck, and the middle of the back. A harmful attachment almost always involves at least one of these points, and some involve all three. Pernicious attachments, although deeper and tougher to remove than parasitic attachments, are nevertheless removed using virtually the same techniques. Victims of harmful attachment must be encouraged to develop strong personal boundaries and to change the negative circumstances in their lives that helped to make them vulnerable to the attachment in the first place.

Spirits are not the only things that forge attachments in order to take other people's energy. Some living people form these attachments as well. We commonly label such living individuals *psychic vampires*. They are not vampires in the traditional cloak-and-coffin sense of the word, but they are called vampires because they feed off of the vitality of others. Psychic vampires are not exclusively evil or predatory individuals. Some psychic vampires are aware of what they are, and they meet their needs ethically, only taking from willing and knowledgeable energy donors. Many other psychic vampires are unaware of what they are. Such unconscious psychic vampires function purely off of instinct and thus can make no ethical decision about the manner in which they feed.

Unconscious psychic vampires prey upon those immediately around them, including family members, spouses, and friends. They are often driven to inspire strong emotional reactions from these people in order to achieve the greatest share of energy. When an unconscious psychic vampire focuses on one person, taking energy from that person repeatedly over a period of time, an attachment naturally builds up between the victim and the vampire. This attachment is indistinguishable from similar parasitic attachments established by vampirizing entities. In addition to unconscious psychic vampires, there are some self-aware psychic vampires who intentionally prey upon others; these may be more difficult to identify.

Removing parasitic attachments that have been formed simply to siphon a person's energy is a relatively simple affair. The first step is to accurately identify the parasitic attachment, distinguishing it from ordinary physical and/or psychological disorders. The attachments themselves are almost always superficial, although a sufficient number of them can be devastating to a person's health and well-being. Although no one has ever died from having their vital energy depleted, either from a parasitic spirit or from a living psychic vampire, sufficient predations can certainly affect someone's quality of life. The attachments should be removed by sweeping down the victim's energy. Cut the attachments or pluck them away, then focus on healing and protection. When a person has been victimized by parasitic attachments, it often leaves their energy vulnerable to further attack, and so it is also imperative that they be taught effective shielding. Helping a former victim to learn how to establish firm personal boundaries will help to stave off the predations of both parasitic spirits as well as psychic vampires. Because emotional disorders, chronic depression, abuse, and addiction can all contribute to an individual's vulnerability to such attacks, the victim should be strongly encouraged to address these issues with a qualified professional.

five

THE INVADER OF DREAMS

Irving blinked from his position on the computer chair. Julie had scooted out to grab a cigarette while I worked on removing the attachments. I could tell the atmosphere of the house was still getting to her, so I didn't object. Although terribly unhealthy, smoking is a ritual that helps some people achieve calm and focus. It doesn't hurt that, in the very act of smoking, one typically takes regular, deep breaths. Of course, a smoker could probably gain most of the same calming effects by omitting the cigarette entirely and simply taking the deep breaths, but we all have our little vices. While Julie was out communing with her favorite brand of carcinogen, I tracked down and removed all of the parasitic attachments that I felt trailing away from Irving's energy. There were about half a dozen, all told.

Stretching, Irving said, "I could feel that." He leaned forward in the computer chair, clutching his head in his hands. His voice was muffled, but not so muffled that I missed the slight tremor in his words. "I could feel it when you got the things they put in me. But now I'm kind of dizzy. Is that normal?"

I put a hand on his narrow shoulder, seeking to comfort him. "Yes, it's normal to feel a little dizzy. I wouldn't recommend standing right away. Most people feel a little woozy right after intense energy work, and you're more sensitive than most. Your hypersensitivity is one of the reasons these things were attracted to you in the first place."

"And that's why they put things into me?" he asked.

"Well, they were really just attachments," I explained. "Like little threads of their energy running into you. There were a few of them, but I'm pretty confident that I got them all."

"And they were eating me?" Irving pursued, running his fingers through his already disordered hair. It was a nervous habit that I had observed him doing about half a dozen times already. I was beginning to appreciate why the poor man's hair resembled a haystack half of the time.

"They were feeding off of your energy," I confirmed. "My guess is that they were attracted to the atmosphere of this place first, especially given how much stagnant, blocked energy has been allowed to build up over time. And when they discovered that you were so easy to interact with, they decided to stay. They've been feeding off of your fear."

Irving was silent for a little while. He hugged himself as he sat in the computer chair, and I was struck again by how thin and wasted he looked. His shoulders were visible knobs under the dark fabric of his T-shirt. Quietly, he said, "They attack me in my sleep, you know. That's when they put those things into me. Can you fix it so they don't come when I'm sleeping?" he asked plaintively. "I'm tired of seeing shadows in my dreams."

"Julie taught you how to shield, didn't she?" I asked. "If you keep doing those exercises and work on developing stronger boundaries, they won't be able to prey on you as easily as they've been doing."

Irving did not look convinced. "I can't shield in my sleep," he said.

"Well, you are most vulnerable when you're sleeping," I acknowledged. "But there's a lot I still need to do here to clear things out. I haven't even started on the rest of the house."

"Please?" Irving begged. "I wake up at night and I can feel them hovering around me. Sometimes, it's like they're pressing me down into the bed. And they've even appeared in my dreams. Is that possible? Can a ghost haunt your dreams?"

"Dreams are complicated things, Irving," I told him. "It's possible that you're just having night terrors, since you're so stressed out all the time. But yes, spirits can invade your dreams."

"Show me how to protect myself," he asked.

"Fine," I relented. "I'd be showing you all of this eventually anyway. It's not like the rest of the house is going anywhere."

"So what do I need to know first?" Irving asked.

"First, let's talk about the nature of dreams. Dreams can be funny things, especially when spirits are involved."

DREAM A LITTLE DREAM

In much of the ancient world, it was believed that the gods communicated with mortals through the medium of dreams. In ancient Sumer, kings would sleep in special chambers atop lofty ziggurats, seeking dream-borne wisdom from the gods. The ancient Greeks believed that not only did the gods sometimes visit mortals in their sleep, but also the spirits of the dead walked the shifting byways of the dream-space. The technique of dream incubation—intentional dreaming with the purpose of communicating with beings beyond the mortal realm—became a popular method for seeking answers about illness and disease, for gaining insight into important financial decisions, and even for seeking advice on marriage prospects. A whole cult of dreamwork grew up, and people would travel for miles to sleep in special temples or at the tombs of fallen heroes. The tomb of Achilles was especially popular, and seekers would bed down directly on top of the tomb in the hopes that the dead hero would visit with words of wisdom in their sleep. In the tale of Jason and the Argonauts, the Golden Fleece so fervently pursued by the Greeks was a sacred sheep-skin used for dream incubation. Such sacred sheepskins were the bedding of choice in many of the temples devoted to dreams.

Although many of the ancient Greek dreaming practices may seem strange and esoteric today, the realm of dreams remains deeply connected to paranormal phenomena. Perhaps the most common modern psychic experience is the death-announcing dream, where a friend or loved one appears to a sleeper in order to bid them farewell. The sleeper awakens from the dream only to later learn that the loved one in question passed away at or near the exact time of the dream. Death-announcing dreams have been reported the world over, and because the sleeper often rouses from the dream to check the time before going back to sleep, they remain some of the most verifiable psychic experiences.

Why is the dreamspace such a fertile ground for the paranormal? A lot of it has to do with how our minds work. The realm of dreams is the realm of the subconscious. This vast and shifting territory in our psyche lies just beneath the conscious portion we mentally inhabit throughout the day. The subconscious is the seat of our intuition, and it communicates in image, symbol, and metaphor. When we use visualization and guided imagery to perform psychic feats and energy work, we are communicating directly with the subconscious, speaking to it in the language it best understands.

The subconscious is the repository of instinct, repressed memories, and all of those mental processes that take place beyond the corner of our mind's eye. When we go to sleep and dream, our conscious mind, which narrows our focus so we can deal with the minutia of day-to-day life, descends into this deep and fertile sea. We relinquish our linear method of thinking and become submersed in myth and metaphor—often inscrutable, but nevertheless meaningful.

Our minds do not simply turn off when we dream. Instead, our consciousness changes states, shifting its focus inward. We process memories in our dreams, and some scientists believe that dreams are primarily a side effect of this memory consolidation (that's the technical term for the process of moving remembered material from short-term to long-term memory). However, memories are not the only focal points of

Psychic Content in Dreams

Given the surreal and disjointed nature of typical dreams, it is easy to discount our nightly visions as nothing more than meaningless fancies conjured by an exhausted mind. However, there is ample evidence that there is more to dreams than meets the eye. Chemist Friedrich Kekule famously discovered the structure of the benzene molecule in a dream, and Elias Howe, inventor of the sewing machine, had the vision of how to structure the needles come to him in a dream. In addition to problem-solving dreams where a sudden inspiration is transmitted through dream imagery, early psychologists noted another widespread phenomena in dreams: dream telepathy. Psychoanalysts working in the early half of the twentieth century noticed what they termed "psychic leakage" between analyst and client, with very private information about the analyst often manifesting inexplicably in patients' dreams. Although some analysts insisted that these details must have been unconsciously transmitted through body language or other ordinary cues during the course of a session, psychic leakage was one of the phenomena that led Dr. Sigmund Freud to assert that proof of the paranormal would most likely be obtained first through a study of human dreams.

our dreams. Emotional dilemmas, anxieties, and even logic puzzles that frustrated us during the day can manifest in our dreams—often leading us to intuitive solutions that would otherwise have eluded our waking minds. In addition to these types of dreams, people the world over have also reported psychic dreams: visions of the future, telepathic communication between friends and family members, and the previously mentioned death-announcing dreams. Psychic experiences are so prevalent in people's dreams that Sigmund Freud, often recognized as the father of modern psychology, eventually acknowledged that the most likely proof for paranormal experience would be achieved through a careful study of dreams.

So what does all of this have to do with protection and hauntings? Remember how the Greeks believed that gods and spirits were able to appear and communicate with the living in the realm of dreams? It turns out that you don't need to sleep on a sacred sheepskin or on top of the tomb of a fallen hero in order to invite spirits into your dreams. Something about the dreamspace—or the very nature of our dreaming minds—allows us to connect the world of spirits. It also makes it easier for spirits to reach out and connect with us while we sleep.

Lay Me Down

Once asleep, our dreaming minds can sometimes move beyond the boundaries of our physical flesh, reaching out to the minds and spirits of others—both living and dead. With dream telepathy and death-announcing dreams, this can be useful. But the gates of the dreamworld swing both ways: just as we can learn to use dreams to reach beyond our ordinary space, so too can spirits use the shifting boundaries of the dreamspace to invade our dreams. While not every nightmare is a clear sign of a spirit attack, it is certainly possible for a malevolent entity to use this vulnerable state to prey upon us in our sleep.

One of the main methods a spirit can use to attack us as we sleep is to invade our dreams, inserting itself into the dreamspace and engaging us in this hazy inner realm of myth and symbol. When a spirit directly invades our dreams, it utilizes a method very similar to dreamwalking. Dreamwalking is a technique wherein living people can reach out to one another and communicate through dreams. Halfway between lucid dreaming and out-of-body experience, dreamwalking takes advantage of the hazy boundaries of the dreamspace, where the dreams of one person can sometimes spill into the dreams of another. When someone you know employs this technique (either consciously or unconsciously), they appear in a shared dream, often to pass along a message. In extreme situations, this may be a message that they are in danger, as in a death-announcing dream. The prevalence of death-announcing dreams suggests that dreamwalking is an ability that we all possess, and it is something we can tap into instinctively given a serious enough need. This dream communication is not limited to bad news, however. People can reach out to one another in dreams when they are lonely and seek to communicate, when there is an unresolved emotional issue that the subconscious seeks to address, or even when they have a strong mutual attraction that cannot be acted upon in the waking world, either due to time, distance, or circumstance.

When one person dreamwalks to another, one of them typically acts as a sender and the other acts as a receiver. When the active party is dreamwalking on instinct and the act is not a conscious effort on their part, they may remember the experience as nothing more than a dream, because the real significance of the content simply does not stand out to them. It is far more likely for the receptive party to remember the experience, because the dreamwalk will stand out as being significantly different from their ordinary dreams. This is because the contents of the dreamwalk are foreign to the receiver's dreamspace. Anything that is unfamiliar to your habitual nightly experience will stand out in memory once you awaken. In studies done at the Maimonides Dream Institute in the 1960s and 1970s, Drs. Stanley Krippner and Montague Ullman discovered that the same was also true for instances of dream telepathy. When foreign content is inserted into our dreams by an outside agency, we are far more likely to remember those dreams. This is important in hauntings, because it means that dreams that have been invaded by an entity are also very likely to stand out as unique, unusual, and memorable events.

When a spirit manifests directly in our dreams, whether to communicate with us, intimidate us, or attempt to do us harm, the spirit is using much the same technique as a living dreamwalker. This means that this type of spirit contact follows many of the same rules as dreamwalking.

As the de facto receptive party, we find that the spirit contact we receive in dreams almost always stands out as something qualitatively different from our ordinary dreams. When a spirit seeks to contact us through the medium of dreams, those dreams will stand out for a number of reasons. Those reasons include several of the following:

- You recall the dream with greater clarity than usual.
- The dream was lucid (i.e., you were aware that you were dreaming).
- The dream was qualitatively different from your customary dreams in content, feel, and imagery.
- The dream featured a being, person, or presence that seemed foreign or invasive to the dream.
- You were having an ordinary dream that changed noticeably once this individual or presence manifested.
- Your interactions with this individual or presence were more coherent than in ordinary dreams.
- Upon waking, physical symptoms experienced in the dream lingered for a significant amount of time.

The presence of just one of these qualities is not necessarily an indication that your dreams have been invaded. However, if you experience three or more of these qualities in a single dream, you should pay special attention to that dream and any subsequent dreams you may have that are similar to it. A qualitative difference in a dream could be one of several things, but it usually involves the feel of the dream, its symbolism, landscape, and overall coherency. Our dreams, though strange and unpredictable at times, nevertheless have a familiar quality that you might not realize until you start thinking about all of the dreams you typically remember. If you notice something in a dream that really sets it apart from what you are accustomed to, this is a strong indication that some force other than your own subconscious is involved in orchestrating the dream. This dream could be a premonition, it could be an instance of dream telepathy, or it could indicate spirit contact.

Physical injuries or symptoms experienced in dreams that linger past waking are another strong indication that something unusual is going on. These injuries or symptoms need to last more than ten or fifteen minutes after waking, as it is not uncommon for some dream sensations to linger very vividly when we are still in the hypnopompic state (the state of consciousness that occurs as we emerge from sleep). Document the phenomena, taking clear, color photos whenever possible. Try to take these images as soon as you notice the marks and, if you have the option, take multiple images throughout the day to document how the marks change or fade over time. You should also make every effort to determine whether or not the symptoms have an ordinary, physical cause. If you regularly wake from a certain type of dream feeling tired and achy all over, go to a doctor and get a clean bill of health before you start plumbing the depths of the dream for the cause of your ailment. If you wake up from a dream where you are being slashed or battered by an evil force only to find that you have visible cuts and bruises in the same places where you were attacked in the dream, do not rule out the possibility of a physical cause. Do you have a cat? Do you sleep with someone who may have had a nightmare themselves, and lashed out unconsciously in their sleep? Check the angle, shape, and size of the marks. Could you have scratched or struck yourself in your sleep? It has been well documented that when a sleeper is exposed to external sensations, those external sensations are often interpreted in that person's dreams.

The best example of this—and one that nearly all of my readers have likely experienced at one point or another—is the dream manifestation of an alarm. Your alarm clock is going off, but you are still asleep and dreaming. Suddenly, in the context of the dream, there is a noise. It clamors and will not stop. In the dream, it may manifest as a foghorn, a particularly loud jet whizzing by overhead, or even a person screaming nonstop. But, as the incessant sound continues to drag you out of sleep and the dream shatters to pieces around you, you eventually realize that the horrible noise is nothing more than your alarm clock, going off in time to wake you up for work. Physical sensations can be interpreted in dreams in much the same way. Anyone who has injured themselves has probably experienced the pain of that injury bleeding over into their dreams, sometimes manifesting in unexpected ways.

We are not insensible to our surroundings when we sleep. We simply stop being conscious of those surroundings. If our sensations and perceptions of the world around us cross a certain threshold (such as an alarm clock's annoying buzz), they filter in through our dreams. Rule out all of the waking world's possibilities before committing yourself to the suspicion that something like physical scratches carried over from your dream. Given what we know about dreams and sensory input, it is equally possible that you dreamed about being attacked because, in the waking world, you sustained an injury at the time of the dream. In the case of symptoms like headaches, dizziness, nausea, or shooting pains, assess your physical condition and make absolutely certain that you aren't just coming down with a migraine or the flu. When you're just beginning to get sick, your subconscious mind is often the first to know, and, as we have seen before, this wiser, more intuitive part of our mind typically communicates its messages to us in dreams.

If you have determined that there is not a waking-world explanation for the symptoms or injuries, and you are satisfied that there was something distinctly unusual going on with the dream in question, then there is something else you have to determine: Was the dream a one-time experience, or is it a recurring phenomena? The best way to know for certain is to start keeping a record of your dreams. Keep a pen and notebook near your bed. If a dream wakes you up, take a few moments to write down as many details as you can remember. These details will be clearest if you write them down as soon as you wake up from the dream, even if you wake up in the middle of the night and

Conscious Dreaming

Shamanism is a spiritual practice that can be found in a wide variety of primitive cultures, from the tribal peoples living along the Amazon River basin to the aboriginal people of Siberia and Australia. In shamanism, specially trained individuals serve the community by communicating with the spirit world. These shamans achieve their communication through ecstatic trance, sometimes reached through drumming or dance and sometimes reached through the ingestion of hallucinogens. The dancing, drumming, or entheogens are all used to help the shaman break down internal barriers so that he or she may journey into the spirit realm. This journey can have a dreamlike quality and, notably, the shamanic spirit-world is referred to as the Dreamtime among the aborigines of Australia. Shamans typically journey like this in order to learn how to cure a certain disease or to lead spirits to their proper resting place. If you are curious about learning more on shamanism, two excellent books to look into include Mircea Eliade's *Shamanism: Techniques of Ecstasy* and Michael Harner's *The Way of the Shaman*.

would like nothing better than to roll over and go back to sleep. If you sleep all the way through the night, try to wake up slowly in the morning, pulling yourself out of the dreamstate in stages. As you do this, concentrate on the feel of your dreams, and allow your mind to linger on the dream's imagery. This is the best way to recall as much as possible of your dreams, rather than jumping out of bed and heading straight for the shower. You want to make a gradual switch from one state of consciousness to the other so the content and images of your dreams don't get lost along the way.

Keeping a record of your dreams will help you to determine what, if anything, is visiting you in your sleep. It will also help you to determine whether or not this being has a purpose or a specific message that it wishes to convey to you. Your dream journal will also give you a record for comparison, should anyone else in your house also report similar dreams. If it seems as if an entity is visiting multiple dreamers, have each person keep records of their dreams. Encourage them to compare the details of these dreams only after they have a written record of those details. This keeps everyone honest and it also prevents unintentional skewing of memories. Obviously, when you encounter claims like this during the course of an investigation, you should make all of these suggestions to your client, encouraging them to keep a record of their dreams as well as to assess the possible real-world causes for what they suspect might be tied to their dreams. As an investigator, you should follow up on those causes independently, so you can be absolutely certain of the situation. Most clients do not intentionally lie about their hauntings (though, as every investigator knows, there are always some that do), but sometimes a person's fear will lead them to illogical and erroneous conclusions. Occasionally, perceived spirit attacks are not paranormal at all, but are merely symptoms of the onset of a mental illness. One of your jobs as an investigator is to provide an objective and detached perspective to help your clients get to the bottom of what is really going on. This includes assessing, verifying, or even dispelling the possibility of a paranormal cause.

Terror in the Night

As alarming as the direct invasion of our dreams may seem, dream contact with spirits is not always aggressive or invasive. If a spirit is appearing in your dreams, there's a good chance that it wants to communicate with you rather than intimidate you. The content of the dream itself often reveals the spirit's intentions. Sometimes all it takes is for us to separate ourselves from our initial fear of that very contact in order to clearly perceive the message being conveyed. However, there is no misinterpreting the intent of an entity that hovers threateningly over us in our sleep. Bearing much in common with a phenomena known as a night terror, the nightly predations of some entities skip our dreams entirely and focus instead on our slumbering forms.

Many sleepers have awakened to the sense of a presence in their room. This presence often feels malevolent or, at the very least, threatening. Certain that they are awake and alert, individuals who sense this intimidating presence in their rooms typically try to react—only to learn that they are unable to move, seemingly paralyzed by the unwelcome presence itself. Oftentimes, those who experience this phenomena feel as if they are being pressed down into the bed, or they may experience a sense of violent vibration in their limbs and body. They cannot cry out, so they simply lie there, helpless, as this oppressive entity approaches the bed, looms over them, and sometimes seems to sit or lie on top of them. Those who are able to tear open their eyes and peer blurrily at their attacker often see an indistinct figure, like shadow given form, that occasionally bears a familiar face but most often resembles something from our darkest nightmares.

The experience outlined above is a classic one and while it has many of the hallmarks of a spirit attack, it also perfectly describes a phenomena known as "hag attack." A hag attack, also known as a night terror, is a universal phenomena, closely tied with the physiological process of sleep itself. When we descend into sleep, a portion of our brain shuts down our ability to move so that we cannot physically act

out the content of our dreams. Sometimes, when we wake up, the
process of emerging from sleep is incomplete, and this natural sleep
paralysis has not yet disengaged. Semiconscious and caught in the
hallucinatory hypnopompic state, we realize that we cannot move and
attribute the paralysis to any number of lingering visions that seem to
have crossed back with us from the realm of dreams. Dr. David Hufford, in his landmark work, *The Terror that Comes in the Night*, offers a
full exploration of the myth and folklore surrounding classic hag attacks as well as a knowledgeable summary of the completely natural

processes that lead us to mistake this phenomena for a supernatural experience.

More often than not, the experience described above is really nothing more than a classic hag attack, with its roots in purely ordinary, physiological events. However, nearly all of the symptoms associated with a classic hag attack can also occur in a legitimate spirit attack. This has led to a good deal of dissension between people who believe *only* in the scientific explanation for these experiences versus those who believe in a paranormal explanation. The answer that neither side is usually willing to hear is that both can be correct. Sometimes the experience is just a matter of misfiring nerves and misinterpreted hypnagogic hallucinations. Other times, however, the experience is evidence that a spirit is preying upon someone in their sleep. But how do you tell the difference between two such closely related (and hotly debated) phenomena?

If there are multiple people in the same residence who are all reporting the same experience, it's easy. Although the paralytic function that the brainstem initiates to cause sleep paralysis occasionally results in the sleeper becoming aware of the inability to move, this condition is hardly contagious. The likelihood of two people experiencing identical versions of hag attack in the same place and over the same period of time is extremely slim. To be certain that the phenomena is widespread among residents, take the same steps that you would for dream invasions. Have everyone who is experiencing the phenomena document their experiences. Encourage them to record the date and time of each incident, describing how they woke up, what the room looked like, the position they were lying in, and any other pertinent details of the attack itself. As with dreamwalking incidents, encourage the people who are experiencing the phenomena to compare their notes only after they have each committed their experiences to paper. If, as an investigator, you are coming into the situation after it has occurred, separate the individuals who claim to have experienced the phenomena and interview them separately. Take notes and compare the details of their interviews. If the details match up—especially if the descriptions of the invading entity are significantly similar—then it is highly likely that you are dealing with legitimate spirit attacks.

If you are alone or if you are unaware of anyone else in your residence who is experiencing the same thing, then how can you be certain that the phenomena in question is a spirit attack rather than a simple night terror? There are a few details that are likely to occur in connection with a spirit attack that are highly unlikely to be connected with a hag attack:

- The attack leaves noticeable marks on your body that linger for more than fifteen minutes after waking.

- Continued attacks have a significant impact upon your health beyond what you might expect from a simple lack of sleep.

- You obtain verifiable information about the attacking entity during the course of an attack (a name, a physical description, perhaps a cause of death).

- Another individual witnesses the attack in the waking world.

- You discover that other individuals who have stayed in that location have reported a history of similar attacks.

- During the attack you can clearly read the numbers on your alarm clock and you can verify that this was the correct time once the attack concludes (because a different part of our brain is in control when we dream, letters and numbers in our dreams will shift or appear indistinct. If the numbers on your clock remain clear and consistent, this is a strong sign that you are awake and not dreaming).

As we have already seen, it is unsettling—but not entirely unheard of—for a purely psychic attack to leave distinctly physical marks. Scratches, welts, patches of broken capillaries, and mysterious bruising have all been reported in one incident or another in connection with psychic or spirit attack. As was covered in the previous section, if you suspect that marks have been made by a spirit attack, your first task is to document the phenomena, then to fully explore and rule out all ordinary explanations for the marks. Only when you have ruled out the ordinary should you take the leap to the extraordinary.

If you are experiencing a series of nightly attacks coupled with a noticeable decline in your health, the two may very well be connected. If you find that you are getting sick all of the time or that you are exhausted above and beyond the fact that you have not been getting restful sleep, you should consider the very real possibility that your nightly visitor is feeding off of your energy. As with other physical manifestations of a suspected spirit attack, of course, you should rule out the ordinary before fully embracing the extraordinary. If necessary, seek out a medical professional to be certain there is no underlying physical cause that explains your weakened immune system and other complaints. Keep in mind that, given the way in which our subconscious mind sometimes seeks to communicate with us, it is entirely possible that the night terrors are an expression of an instinctive awareness of a physiological illness, and they are manifesting as a warning for you to get yourself checked out. Cover all of your bases and do not overlook physical explanations based on suspected supernatural phenomena.

Verifiable information connected with the haunting is another good clue that the nightly experiences are attacks rather than night terrors. Many people who report both classic hag attacks and spirit attacks will claim to see the attacker as a shadowy form looming over the bed. Write down a description of the being perceived during the attack. If you are the one experiencing the attacks, make every effort to observe the attacker accurately and record as many details of the entity's appearance as possible once the attack is over. While ghosts very rarely announce themselves by giving their full name, date of birth, and date of death, sometimes it's possible to obtain clear details that will lead to an actual deceased person. When doing your research based on clues obtained from a nighttime attack, do not limit yourself to checking the history of the residence itself. Although it is certainly helpful to know whether or not any previous residents of a domicile died while they lived there, ghosts are not as firmly anchored to the place of their demise as many folk beliefs might suggest. Human spirits have a tendency to linger near the places that were important to them in life, but they are not tied irrevocably to these places. Further, if an old house once stood near a new property, it is entirely possible for any spirits connected with the demolished home to take up residence in that nearby building. Sometimes spirits will cling closely to a friend or family member, following this person to a new location far removed from the place of their death. Some spirits may even take a liking to someone with no discernible connection to who they were in life. Ghosts have whims and desires that are as changeable and inscrutable as those of any living people, and some simply fixate on the first person lucky (or unlucky) enough to notice that they are there.

When research into the identity of the spirit is not possible, there is another investigative technique that can help to distinguish between a night terror and a spirit attack. If the nightly attacks repeat frequently, consider having another person present to observe the sleeper as he or she rests in the location where those attacks typically occur. If another person witnesses the attack and is able to perceive the presence of an entity, this is solid proof that the attack is not simply a dream or night terror. Preferably, the person chosen to sit sentry will possess some ability to perceive and interact with spirits. If you happen to be of a more technological bent in your investigations, consider setting infrared cameras and other sensing devices throughout the room where the phenomena occurs. Personally, I feel that we have yet to construct an instrument as refined as our own natural senses when it comes to perceiving otherworldly phenomena, but sometimes technology is up to the task. Analyze your data carefully, however. Cameras very rarely capture images of spirits in exactly the same way that psychics are able to perceive them—the methods of perception are vastly different, yielding different results. Be open to anomalies and always double-check your results. Consider that equipment failure may also be an indication of spirit activity, especially if that failure is not limited to one piece of equipment and if the failure consistently coincides with a living person's report of the phenomena.

FIELDS OF DREAMS

Due to garden variety nightmares, classic night terrors, and issues concerning sleep paralysis and hypnagogic hallucinations, it is important to proceed carefully where reports of nighttime spirit attacks are concerned. Verify the legitimacy of the claims to the best of your ability and rule out any mundane explanations for the phenomena before committing to the belief that a spirit or spirits are preying on people as they sleep. Once you have verified that a spirit is attacking people at night, either directly interacting with their unconscious bodies or invading the fabric of their dreams, then what do you do? If a spirit can use the pathways of dream to insert itself into someone's mind, how can ordinary people keep it out? One way is to fight fire with fire.

If the problem involves a spirit that invades peoples' dreams, the first place to start is those dreams themselves. A good technique to encourage people to develop is lucid dreaming. Lucid dreaming is the ability to become conscious in dreams. In its most basic form, when someone achieves lucid dreaming, they become aware of the fact that they are in a dream and that nothing occurring in that space is technically "real." This is a wonderful technique to develop if you are prone to having nightmares of the very ordinary variety, because the lucidity you achieve in the dream allows you to conquer your fear of whatever horrible monsters your subconscious conjures up. Are you nightly chased by zombies that hunger for human brains? If you learn how to lucid dream, you can learn to scoff at the nightmare even while you are in the grips of it. Furthermore, if you excel at this technique, you can even learn how to harness the elements of the dream and control them—reshaping the nightmare until the zombies become harmless bunny rabbits, for example.

Lucid dreaming works wonders for ordinary nightmares, but it is also helpful in cases where an outside force has inserted itself into the dreamspace and is seeking to control elements of a person's dreams. First, lucid dreaming allows the sleeper to become aware that the dream is just that—a dream. Fear is a powerful emotion, and it is an emotion that can often be used to control us, making us feel victimized, helpless, and weak. When a person achieves lucidity in a dream or a nightmare, the images encountered in that space lose a great deal of their power to terrify. In the case of spirit attacks, that means the invading entity loses a great deal of the power that it previously held over the victim in the dream. Second, a practiced lucid dreamer can also control elements of their dream simply by exerting a little willpower. An invading entity is using the same tool to insert itself into a dream and control elements within that space. By matching that entity willpower for willpower, a lucid dreamer can do battle in the dreamspace, ultimately driving the attacker out of their dreams.

Some people learn lucid dreaming very quickly, while it can prove to be a very elusive technique for others. The first step to lucid dreaming is of course the ability to remember your dreams. Cultivating lucid dreaming is often a time-consuming process, but if you follow these steps, you should be well on your way to learning the technique:

1. Start keeping a record of your dreams. The more you pay attention to your dreams, the more likely you are to remember them.

2. When you lay down to sleep, think about becoming conscious in your dreams. Do this for several minutes each night.

3. As you fall asleep, say or think the affirmation, "When I dream, I will be aware of the dream. When I dream, I will be in control of the dream."

4. Whenever you step through a door, even in the waking world, train yourself to stop and ask, "Am I dreaming?" Make this a habit so that you will remember to do it even in dreams. Eventually, you will ask this question in a dream and the realization that you are dreaming will make the dream become lucid.

5. When you first wake up from a dream, take time to vividly recapture the dream in memory. Consciously relive the dream. Sometimes, when you do this, you will slip back into the dream, only this time, you will be lucid as you dream.

Researcher Stephen LaBerge is probably the world's foremost living authority on lucid dreaming. He has produced a number of resources to help teach lucid dreaming, including a book and CD, *Lucid Dreaming*. In order to truly master this technique, I strongly suggest that you look into his body of work. I also cover more extensive techniques for learning lucid dreaming in my own book, *Psychic Dreamwalking*, which offers insight into the nature of the dreamspace and how that internal space can be harnessed to interact with both the living and the dead.

Sometimes learning lucid dreaming is not an option. Perhaps the nightly attacks are too pressing and require a quicker fix. When the victim cannot learn how to go toe-to-toe with an invading entity directly in the dreamspace, there are still tricks to shore up the boundaries of that space so the attacker cannot get in. Just like shielding and everything else you have learned thus far, these techniques make use of the fact that our subconscious speaks the language of symbol and ultimately has more control over our energy than we consciously perceive.

Dreams are very prone to suggestion. This is one of the things that makes it so very tricky to ensure that an attack remembered from a dream is actually evidence of a spirit attack—if a person is afraid that a spirit *might* attack them in their dreams, focusing on this fear can lead to some very intense dreams where the subconscious happily provides vivid details on how this attack might be carried out. No actual attack occurs, but the dream remains convincing. This can be frustrating to investigators trying to determine the truth, but it's how our minds work. However, the suggestibility of dreams can be made to work in our favor as well. Nightly affirmations and even mild self-hypnosis can help harness the suggestibility of dreams so that we empower ourselves in our sleep to shore up our personal boundaries and fight off any potential invaders of our personal dreamspace.

The way our subconscious minds work, if you fixate on something before you go to sleep, it is likely to show up that night in your dreams. While this sometimes leads to nightmares permeated with the anxieties that plagued us just before sleep, we can also intentionally fixate on something in order to guide and shape our dreams. If you feel that your dreams are being invaded by spirits, you should attempt to "program" your subconscious to keep you safe as you sleep. For clients who are being preyed upon in dreams, teach this same technique:

1. Get ready for bed as you normally would.

2. Lie down. Ground and center.

3. Concentrate on your breathing, and allow this to help you turn your focus inward.

4. Picture your entire body surrounded by protective light.

5. Tell yourself, silently or out loud, "My dreams are mine and mine alone. Nothing may harm me as I sleep. I am protected. My belief is my shield."

6. Repeat this affirmation several times. Focus on the words and their intent as you drift off to sleep. After several iterations, you may want to shorten it to, "My belief is my shield."

If you are a religious person, you can frame your affirmation as a prayer, asking your higher power to watch over you as you sleep. The traditional child's prayer, "Now I lay me down to sleep" gets a little morbid toward the end, and I don't recommend focusing on the possibility of dying in your sleep, even if you're framing that possibility in terms of getting to heaven. Especially if you are having troubled dreams, you should not fixate on anything that frightens or unsettles you as you go to sleep. Keep in mind that anything you focus on as you fall asleep has a strong likelihood of coloring your dreams. If you feel vulnerable or afraid, you should focus instead on being protected and safe. Be firm but not desperate in these affirmations. As you focus on these things, you are programming your subconscious with your desire to be safe and protected. It will oblige you by maintaining stronger personal boundaries as you sleep.

Another method for protecting your dreams goes one step beyond affirmations to consciously build a protective barrier around your dreamspace. If you (or your client) have responded to the various techniques of visualization describe throughout this book, consider trying this to ward off unwelcome nightly visitors:

1. Get ready for bed as you normally would.

2. Lie down. Ground and center.

3. Concentrate on your breathing for a few moments to help intensify your focus.

4. Once you are focused and relaxed, imagine a typical dream landscape. This can be something you make up right then, or it may be remembered from a past dream.

5. Picture yourself standing in this dream landscape. The dream stretches all around you, but at the farthest edges, it fades to something misty and indistinct.

6. Focus on these outside boundaries of your dreamspace. Acknowledge that this is where your dreamworld ends and where other things might cross over into your dreams.

7. Picture yourself erecting a boundary. It can be a huge, high wall or it can be a ring of charged energy. Whatever you choose, imagine this impenetrable boundary surrounding your dreamspace, keeping it safe.

8. Affirm to yourself silently or out loud: "This is my dreamspace. It is meant only for me. Nothing unwelcome may enter."

9. Focus on the boundary surrounding your dreamspace as you fall asleep. Focus on the words and intent of the affirmation as well. Allow these things to be carried with you as you descend into dreams.

SNUG AS A BUG

In several Native American traditions, including those of the Cherokee and Choctaw tribes, Grandmother Spider is an important figure. A protective goddess, she is credited with bringing fire to mankind in one popular myth. Grandmother Spider is also associated with an item that is believed to protect people's dreams: the dreamcatcher. In the traditions tied to the dreamcatcher, Grandmother Spider is supposed to weave a web that will trap nightmares while allowing good dreams to pass through. Traditional dreamcatchers are woven of sinew or string and are made to resemble a spider web. Over the past few decades, dreamcatchers have been popularized among non–Native Americans, and one can find dreamcatchers big and small in a variety of stores. Some are very traditional in their construction, featuring a small stone or bead in the web to represent Grandmother Spider herself. Some are little more than cheap plastic toys, sold as keychains or items to dangle from one's rearview mirror. The real place for a dreamcatcher is over a person's bed where, if the lore surrounding Grandmother Spider is true, it will catch bad dreams and allow for peaceful slumber.

Faith in Symbols

Do dreamcatchers work and, if so, how? For those who have faith in the protection of Grandmother Spider, that faith alone can help to ensure that the dreamcatcher keeps nightmares at bay. The dreamcatcher itself is merely a symbol of a greater mystery, but its presence invokes that mystery for those who fully understand its significance. In this respect, the dreamcatcher works much the same way as any other protective holy symbol, such as a crucifix or a Star of David. The symbol is more than a mere item because of the meaning it holds for those who believe. The real power of protective objects like dreamcatchers comes from what we ourselves invest in them through our focus, intent, and faith.

Following in the tradition of the dreamcatcher, it is possible to use a physical object to help protect someone as they sleep. Much like the physical cues that can be paired with techniques of shielding, the object in this case serves as an anchor for focus and intent. The object can be an actual dreamcatcher, or it can be any item or symbol that evokes a sense of protection. Keep in mind that meaning is in the eye of the beholder, and you want to select an item that is meaningful and relevant to the person it is meant to protect. For some people this may be a dreamcatcher; for others, it may be a crucifix. If you are setting up a protective barrier for clients, you should sit down and talk to them about their religious affiliation. If the clients are not religious, then consider making use of a symbol that holds meaning for them. I recently worked a case where two young boys were being visited by unwanted spirits. The youngsters were huge fans of *Star Wars,* and so I taught them shielding and other protective techniques using the language of George Lucas. If it takes Jedi mind tricks to make a concept or technique relevant to a client (especially when that client is a child!), don't be afraid to adapt your language to their worldview. The important thing always to keep in mind is that the object itself is a symbol, and the power of that symbol lies in its meaning for the person it is meant to protect.

To use a dreamcatcher or any other symbol to create a protective barrier around someone's bed, perform the following steps. If you are creating the protective barrier for someone else, have them participate in the process as well. Guide them through these steps so they will know how to protect themselves in the future. Protecting your clients is helpful, but teaching them how to protect themselves is the best way to ensure that they will no longer be victimized by a haunting.

1. Hold the protective object in your hands while you ground and center.

2. As your attention turns inward, focus on your energy or connect to the energy of your higher power. Think of protective energy that will keep away nightmares and other things that may invade dreams.

3. Direct this energy to your hands. As you cup the object in your hands, imagine this energy surrounding the object, then filling it up so it shines.

4. As you imbue the object with protective energy, state your intent silently or out loud: "May this [object] shield my dreams so nothing harmful disturbs my sleep." Alternately, you can frame this affirmation as a prayer.

5. Place the object over the bed. As you do so, imagine the energy you have invested in the object shining down and surrounding the bed in a protective net.

6. Before you go to bed each night, touch the object to remind yourself of the protection it represents.

The real work here, of course, is your belief, focus, and intent. Each time you look at the physical item that represents your desire to be protected, you will be reminded of the intent, belief, and focus that you invested in that item during the initial energy work. Touching the item has a similar effect of reassuring you of the item's purpose. Notably, many people unconsciously place protective items around their beds. I can't count how many times I've walked into the bedrooms of a Catholic household and found rosaries hanging from the bedpost. Christians of many denominations place crosses over their beds, and even secularly minded people tend to place pictures of people they look up to near where they sleep. The steps outlined above allow us to take this unconscious behavior and make it intentional and therefore powerful.

If you feel funny about using an item like a dreamcatcher to help anchor your protective intentions, try using the bed itself as your focus. This method is ideal for a four-poster bed, but it can be used anywhere someone lays their head.

1. Ground and center.

2. Gather energy or ask your higher power to work through you.

3. Approach the bed, holding pure, healing energy in your hands.

4. Touch each of the four corners of the bed, starting at the upper right corner and moving clockwise.

5. As you touch each corner, vividly imagine that the pure, healing energy flows from you to the bed. It pours out until it fills the bed and the area surrounding the bed.

6. As you touch each corner, affirm your intent: "At this corner, I erect a barrier so no harm may pass to those who slumber here."

7. When you have touched all four corners in succession, place your hand in the center of the bed.

8. Let all the remaining energy flow down your arm into the bed. Visualize it spilling out and around the bed until the bed is completely surrounded by a softly glowing, protective sphere.

9. Affirm your intent again, saying, "From all directions, I erect a barrier so no harm may pass to those who slumber here."

10. Each time you lay down to sleep, touch the center of the bed once more, vividly imagining the softly glowing sphere that surrounds the whole bed.

Remember that you can phrase your affirmations as prayers, seeking help from your higher power whenever it feels appropriate. If you are doing this protection for a client, walk them through the visualization, then teach them to reaffirm the protection each time they go to bed.

The Least You Should Know

We can be very vulnerable to spirit attack when we sleep, and it is even possible for spirits to invade our dreams. Not every nightmare is a spirit attack, however, and reports of nighttime visitations should be approached with caution. There are a number of physiological explanations for experiences, such as hag attack, and responsible investigators will seek to rule out ordinary causes before committing to the possibility of the extraordinary. The realm of dreams is an ever-shifting territory, and the very uncertainty about how dreams function can lead many people to fear dream contact even when it is not malevolent or harmful. If a paranormal component of a client's nightly experiences has been confirmed, investigators should work with that client to better understand the nature of the contact. Frequently, spirits seek contact in dreams simply to communicate, and there is no reason to fear this contact in and of itself.

Not all spirits are benevolent, however, and some pose a legitimate threat to the client. Some spirits will hover over a client as they sleep, siphoning off vital energy. Others will invade the client's dreams with the intent of frightening or intimidating them. These attacks must be brought to an end.

When attacks involve direct invasion of a person's dreams, there are several techniques that can help create boundaries to keep out the invading entities. Learning how to lucid dream will give a client greater control over their dreams, ultimately allowing them to confront the invading entity within the dreamspace. Lucid dreaming can be difficult to master, however, and so other protective measures can be taken prior to falling asleep. These include visualizations that create an intentional boundary around the dreamspace so that unwanted entities may not enter. In addition to techniques that seek to protect the realm of dreams directly, protective measures can be put in place around the physical body of the sleeper as well. Dreamcatchers or other protective objects can be used as physical representations of these protections, so the client is reminded of the protection in a tangible way before going to sleep. The symbols are less important than their meaning and relevance to the client, and the client should be involved in the process of imbuing these symbols with their intent.

When a spirit is attacking an individual while they sleep, either hovering over their physical form or directly invading their dreams, you should:

1. Teach the person how to ground, center, and shield.

2. Encourage the person to keep a record of their dreams and attempt to cultivate lucid dreams to gain control of the dreamspace.

3. Help the person develop techniques that establish firm boundaries in their dreamspace, so that nothing unwanted can enter their dreams.

4. Help the person shield the place where they sleep, anchoring the protective barriers to a physical object or objects to help reinforce the presence of the protection.

5. If the person has faith in a higher power, they should always be encouraged to seek support from this higher power to protect them in any situations where they feel vulnerable or helpless. Otherwise, they should be encouraged to have faith in themselves.

six

ESTABLISHING BOUNDARIES

Julie came back from her smoke break in time to see me and Irving leaning over his bed, repeating our affirmations about protection. She regarded us quizzically, but withheld comment. When we were finished, Irving sat down on the edge of his bed to think about everything he had just learned.

"Okay," he said, glancing only once over his shoulder at the closet that still gaped on the other side of his bed. "So let me see if I get this straight. The thing we just did with my bed here, it's a whole lot like the shields Julie was teaching me how to do earlier."

"That's right," I said with a nod. "It's all founded on more or less the same concepts."

"So with all this psychic energy stuff, I pretty much decide that there's going to be a wall somewhere, and then it's there. Poof. Is it really that simple?" he asked.

Julie adjusted her glasses as she considered this. "You focus on what you want, and you picture it very clearly in your head," she offered. "Just like I showed you outside. Your intent shapes the energy."

"It's all about willpower," I elaborated. "Mind over matter. If you believe in what you are doing and the images you choose to picture it in have meaning for you, then your energy will follow. But the intent has to be there. You have to believe, and you have to have faith, at least in yourself. Also, it takes some mental work to maintain barriers like that. They're made up of energy—your energy, and you'll feel a certain amount of exertion if you're doing it right."

Irving continued to contemplate these concepts for a little while. Then his face lit up with some internal revelation.

"Why stop at just putting boundaries around my bed?" he asked excitedly. "If I can put a shield around me and I can put a shield around my bed, then why can't I put a shield around the whole house?"

Julie smiled and clapped him on the shoulder. "And you were worried before that you'd never understand this stuff," she said.

"That's really the next step," I told him. "Learning how to maintain boundaries on a small scale is important, but it also helps you learn how to establish boundaries on a larger scale as well. It's all a matter of focus and belief—and how much energy you're willing to put into the work."

"So I could seal up my whole house so these things can never get in again?" he asked.

"That's the idea," I said. "And the thing we were doing with the dreamcatcher, using it as a kind of anchor for your intent, that will help. But before we jump to that step, let me and Julie clear all the stagnant energy out of the rest of the house."

Julie made a face at the mere mention of the work we had been putting off. I can't say that I blamed her. I wasn't really looking forward to it myself.

"That's going to take some time," she observed.

"Well, we don't want to put up boundaries and close all of the crud out there inside of them, do we?" I asked. Then I turned to Irving. "While we do that, why don't you practice with those boundaries? Sit down on your bed and go through the steps to shield like Julie taught you. Only instead of expanding the bubble so it only surrounds you on all sides, see if you can expand it farther, until it surrounds you and your bed."

"Okay," Irving said. "I'm pretty sure I can do that."

"Great," I replied. "And once you've been able to expand it all the way around you and your bed, see if you can't push the boundaries even farther. Try to expand the bubble so it fills up your entire room."

Irving pressed his hands together and closed his eyes, bowing his head as he concentrated. I could already feel a shift in his energy as he gathered power in his center.

"Just be careful that you don't wear yourself out," Julie warned. "You might think that it's all your imagination doing the work, but you're putting energy into those shields. All that energy adds up after a while."

I was gathering up my tools—the tingsha, dorje, and drilbu—for the task that waited for us on the other side of Irving's door.

"Good point," I admitted. "If you start to feel funny, Irving, you should stop. Working with energy is a lot like working your physical muscles. If you're used to doing a lot of exercise, you build up both strength and endurance. But if you haven't done a whole lot of work, you'll need to do a little at a time, at least at first. And if you push yourself too hard, you can strain something." I chuckled, remembering my own learning experiences. Tapping the side of my head, I said, "Of course, with psychic energy, you don't end up with stiff muscles and sore joints the next day. Usually, you know you've done too much when your head starts to ache."

Irving nodded again, and for the first time since we arrived at the house, he seemed genuinely happy and hopeful. He went to work practicing his boundaries and Julie and I headed out to our unenviable task of clearing all the blocked and stagnant energy from the cluttered home.

Making Good Neighbors

In his poem "Mending Wall," Robert Frost famously observed, "Good fences make good neighbors." In the poem, two men are rebuilding the wall that separates their properties. The idea behind the poem's observation is that our interactions with others are improved when there are firmly established boundaries to separate and define those interactions. It's psychologically healthy to be able to enforce your sense of personal space, especially around people who may seek to manipulate, intimidate, or otherwise dominate you. But even surrounded by people you love, personal boundaries are healthy to maintain. With spirits, these personal boundaries become even more important. The concept of shielding relies on our sense of personal space and our ability to reinforce the boundaries of that space through an effort of will.

With shielding, we create a private sanctuary for one, a protective barrier that we can carry with us wherever we go. But our sense of personal space does not extend only to the area immediately surrounding our physical bodies. Consider that, when a home is invaded by a vandal or burglar, the family that resides there feels violated on a deeply personal level. In Jungian psychology, the house is often a symbol that represents the self, and this becomes abundantly apparent in the case of break-ins. When we connect with a residence or even a work area and we truly feel at home there, we extend our sense of personal space to that location as well. This means that when something invades that space—be it a burglar or a ghost—we respond to that invasion on a personal level. Our personal connection to certain spaces is not purely a liability, however. We can use the connection we have to homes and other living spaces to protect those spaces from unwelcome spirits.

There are three main methods for reinforcing the boundaries of homes and living spaces. The first is based on the notion that inanimate objects, such as houses, can nevertheless be imbued with energy to give them form and substance in the realm of spirits. The next is a variation on shielding that extends a person's psychic boundaries to

The Body Electric

Did you know that the human body runs on electricity? Obviously, it's not precisely the same type of electricity that lights the lamps in your home, but a small electrical charge is what carries impulses along your nerves, translating messages from your body to your brain and back again. The electricity that keeps your heart beating can be measured by a doctor using an electrocardiogram (EKG or ECG), and the electrical impulses that course through your brain can similarly be measured with an electroencephalogram (EEG). Galvanic skin response, a technique that measures the electrical charge of our skin, is used in lie detectors and can also help in biofeedback. In systems like Barbara Brennan's *Hands of Light*, the natural electricity that occurs in the human body is equated with the subtle energy of the aura as well as the energy harnessed by energy workers to heal.

include an entire room. The final variation, called warding, sets up specific points of protection throughout a home in order to safeguard it from invasion. The three methods take many of the techniques you learned in the chapter on shielding and apply them to a physical location, rather than one's personal space alone. When we live in a space, we naturally establish some personal boundaries there, just as we naturally have some boundaries to our bubble of personal space. These unconsciously forged boundaries help to make that space more substantial on the Otherside.

Consider the difference between sleeping in a hotel room and sleeping in your own bedroom. There are obvious physical and psychological differences between your experiences in these two places. Your bedroom is a known quantity. It is familiar, private space. You know the layout of the furniture. You know the sounds the space makes at night. Your very familiarity with the space makes it more comfortable. A hotel room, on the other hand, is never as comfortable as your own room. The heating unit makes strange noises. There are noises that come from the hallway or the surrounding rooms that can easily interrupt your sleep not only because of their volume but because they are intrusively unfamiliar. The bed doesn't feel the same. The arrangement of the furniture in the room feels foreign and, if you get up in the night, it's much harder to navigate in the dark because you are not acquainted with the layout. Hotel rooms have been responsible for many a stubbed toe.

But are the physical differences and the level of familiarity the only things that separate your bedroom from a hotel room? What about the *feel* of the room—that ineffable quality that you can't exactly put into words? Is there something *psychically* different between these two spaces?

In feng shui, energy is believed to flow through our environment in gentle currents. These currents are stirred up and strengthened by the passage of human beings. Like walking around and around in a circular pool, we can eventually get the currents to follow our actions if those actions are repeated often enough. This is why, in the case of a home, the front door is seen as the main causeway through which energy follows both to enter and leave the home. The energy follows the repetitive motion of the people who move in and out of that space, as if the energy were water and those repetitive motions built up currents. Notably, several systems in addition to feng shui regard the front door as the main entryway of energy: consider the importance of sweeping unwanted energy out the front door in the hoodoo practices covered in chapter three.

Doors and, to some extent, windows are entry points into a home. Walls, however, create barriers that can block energy out or trap energy in. Why can physical walls pose obstacles to a substance that is not strictly physical itself? According to the principles of feng shui, it all comes down to human beliefs and actions. We perceive walls to be barriers. Physically, of course, they protect a home from the elements. But our very perception, our belief, invests the walls with a certain amount of substance in the spirit world. The longer a building stands and the more people interact with it, investing it with energy even unconsciously, the more those walls become solid and real in the realm of spirits. A hotel room is seen as a temporary space by virtually everyone who spends the night there. By this line of thinking, that means that the psychic barriers inherent in a hotel room are always going to be weaker than the barriers that surround a well-loved and lived-in home. Energy is shaped by belief and intent, and even unconsciously, the living have a constant impact upon it.

If pondering the theories of feng shui seems a little too esoteric for you, let's consider a classic haunting. Years ago, I read about a haunting where a family, upon moving into a new home, regularly heard the sound of footsteps at night. The heavy footfalls would make their way up a set of stairs and stop for a moment, as if the owner of the feet were pausing at the top of a landing. Then the steps would turn and walk across the creaking floorboards of an upper portion of the home. It was apparent to the family experiencing this that they had a ghost, but the presence of this spirit was not the primary thing that puzzled them. The baffling aspect of the haunting involved the location of the sound of these steps: there was no staircase in the house where the ghost walked. Furthermore, when it sounded as if the ghost paused to turn and go through a door to an upstairs room, the spirit actually passed through a blank wall to walk over an area that opened onto empty space. Research eventually revealed that the house had been significantly rebuilt over the years. The spirit with the plodding footfalls was walking up a staircase that had stood for many years, but had since been torn down. A door had stood at the top of those stairs that opened onto another room, but that whole section of the house had since been removed.

This is not a rare phenomena. The folks at *Paranormal State* called me in to assist with the investigation of a home on Chesapeake Bay.

There, a ghost I nicknamed "Old Grumpy" seemed to pace along a specific route that led him through a young boy's room. The ghost habitually walked straight into the closet, and then seemed to continue through the outside wall, as if utterly unaware of the existing architecture. Whenever I attempted to communicate with Old Grumpy, I got an image of him in something like a pea coat, with a cap on his head and his hands thrust in his pockets. The house in question had been built very recently, and Old Grumpy was probably following the ghostly echoes of another home—one that had a porch or widow's walk that he often paced, looking out across the bay.

Sometimes, when a spirit takes a path that no longer exists, that spirit is merely a residual haunting—something like a hologram recorded into the very fabric of a place that repeats the same set of actions, over and over. It makes sense that a residual haunting would follow the floorplan of whatever building stood upon a location when the haunting was essentially "recorded." But Old Grumpy was a sentient spirit, able to communicate intelligently and interact with people. He was no residue. So why did he continue to follow a path that did not physically exist in that home? It's quite simple: buildings have ghosts, too. This answer may seem strange, but it helps to illuminate some of the protective techniques we will be learning in this chapter.

Consider how much care, focus, and attention people put into their homes. They decorate the home to appeal perfectly to their tastes. Sometimes, they even build the house themselves, from the ground up. Even if a family is not so thoroughly invested in the construction of their home, they nevertheless imbue that home with a wealth of emotions. Every wonderful moment, every terrible moment lived within its walls seeps into the fabric of a home, forming layers of energy over the years. Some of this can be swept away like so much psychic dust, but some of it becomes a part of the structure of the home itself, lending form and substance in the world of spirit. The constant, unconscious certainty that a home is a safe haven, a place of warmth, security, and protection adds strength and depth to the walls that the living may never perceive. But, given enough focus and enough time, the building itself becomes real not just in a physical sense, but on a level of spirit as well. We feel this when we walk into certain historic buildings. There is a weight of years that emanates from the very walls, giving the place a sense of *gravitas* that newer buildings often lack. If enough energy has seeped into a structure, even when that building falls, a sense of it remains. It does not have a sentient spirit, but it's as if the bones of the building linger like an echo on the Otherside.

From Casper to *Ghostbusters,* spirits are portrayed as having the ability to walk through walls. This is certainly true of walls that have no more substance than that which is purely physical. But when walls have been invested with enough belief and energy, they stand firm to spirits and to the living alike. The process by which a building gains this kind of substance largely occurs unconsciously. When no direct intention is involved, it tends to take a great deal of time for walls to stand on both sides of reality. However, this process can be greatly speeded up when energy is directed with conscious intent. The first step to helping a family protect their home is to teach them how to turn their living space into something that stands firm in both a physical sense and a spiritual sense.

MY HOME, MY CASTLE

This exercise is something you should do with at least one representative of the family. It's also a good exercise to get in the habit of doing in your own home in order to shore up the natural boundaries of your space. The exercise is founded on the notion that our perception of our homes as safe spaces can help to manifest that safety in the realm of spirit. Try to make this exercise a habit, going over the whole house at least once a month to reaffirm its solidity in body and spirit. This is a good exercise to pair with a house cleansing. Once the stagnant, unwanted energy has been swept out of the home, reinforcing the walls can help prevent further unwanted energy from entering:

1. Ground and center.

2. Start at the top of the house, moving to the front from the back.

3. In each room, touch each of the outside walls in turn. You only need to focus on outside walls.

4. As you touch each wall, take a few moments to reflect upon the solidity of the wall. Vividly imagine the wall standing as a barrier that keeps anything unwanted from entering the house.

5. Allow a sense of energy or power to flow through your hand into the wall. You may wish to connect to your higher power and ask it to flow through you to help reinforce this barrier.

6. As you touch the wall, say to yourself or out loud, "This wall stands against wind and rain, cold and storm. May it stand against the seen and the unseen, holding firm against all intruders."

7. Touch each outside wall in turn and repeat steps 4, 5, and 6.

8. Go through the entire house, moving down toward the front door. When you have covered all of the exterior walls, stand before the front door.

9. As you stand near the front door, close your eyes and focus on the whole house, vividly imaging all of the exterior walls glowing with protective energy that strengthens them against any invasion from the spirit world. Picture the roof and the foundation of the house as well, and imagine that these glow with that same protective light, sealing up the entire home.

10. As you picture the roof and foundation, say to yourself or out loud: "A ceiling above, a floor below, this house stands strong and whole."

11. Step to the front door. Touch this and reflect upon the role the door plays in the home, allowing the people who belong there to come and go as they please.

12. As you touch the front door, say, "My home is my fortress. Nothing unwelcome may enter."

When you are performing this exercise for clients, be certain to explain to them that the exercise involves more than just walking around the house, touching walls, and mumbling a few words. There needs to be focus and intent behind both the actions and the words, and to this end, you should encourage the family to change the wording if it does not appeal to them. Integrate any statements, affirmations, or prayers that seem appropriate. As with every exercise of this nature, the affirmations can easily be changed into prayers and a higher power can be called upon to help reinforce the intent. It never hurts to have friends in high places.

BUILDING A BETTER BUBBLE

It can be fairly time-consuming to go through an entire house, touching each outside wall and affirming its strength on both sides of reality. Because of the concentration and energy involved, some people may also find it exhausting, especially in larger houses. While the repetitive physical actions and affirmations of the previous exercise can be very valuable tools for people who need a little help focusing their desire to be protected, there are quicker techniques you can employ. If you have an aptitude for shielding, it's possible to adapt that technique to form a protective barrier, not just around yourself but around an entire room. It's best to start with a single room, although once you have practiced extensively with this technique, you may find that you can focus enough to extend the shield around an entire building. This offers a quick and easy method for building boundaries around a home. You should practice in your own space first, getting a handle on the process before you attempt to shield a house for one of your clients. This method is deceptively easy once you get the hang of it, although the barriers you erect in this fashion are never permanent. Energy degrades over time unless it is reinforced through unconscious habit or conscious intent. This is why it's a good idea to teach clients how to perform these techniques themselves so, once you are gone, they can reinforce the barriers and take control of their space themselves.

Here's how you set up a protective bubble around a room, using the same basic method as personal shielding:

1. Sit (or stand) roughly in the middle of the room you want to protect.

2. Ground and center, then gather your energy.

3. Reach down and connect to the energy of the earth beneath you. Then reach up and connect to the energy of the heavens as well. Ask your higher power to lend strength to your work.

4. As this energy fills you, turn your attention inward and visualize a glowing ball of light, just as you would when erecting a shield.

5. Vividly picture this glowing sphere expanding outward from the center of your being. Focus on your intent of establishing boundaries and protecting your space.

6. Put more energy and intent into the sphere, and vividly imagine it growing larger and larger. Push the edges out beyond the limits of your physical body, then push them even farther, until the sphere encompasses the whole room.

7. Silently or out loud, affirm your intentions: "May this barrier stand against all that would do harm. May nothing unwelcome be allowed to enter."

8. Touch the floor in front of you and imagine the anchor of this massive sphere passing from you to the earth. Imagine power flowing down into the sphere from the heavens as well.

9. Repeat this visualization approximately once a month, or more frequently if it seems necessary.

There is one very important thing to keep in mind with all of these protective techniques: you won't be able to make solid boundaries in an area if you have weak boundaries yourself. If you are easily frightened, easily intimidated, or easily victimized by others—living or dead—you need to work on your personal boundaries before attempting to extend those boundaries to your living space. This goes above and beyond shielding which, incidentally, will not work very well no matter how much "oomph" you put into it if your emotional and psychological boundaries are poorly developed.

Fortunately, as you work to shore up your personal boundaries, these newfound barriers will naturally begin to extend into your personal space. The more empowered you become, the more ownership you will achieve over your body and your space. This ownership will allow you to create more and more powerful methods of protection for yourself as well as your living spaces.

Symbols of Protection

Since ancient times, people have believed that certain items, words, or symbols have the power to protect individuals and even homes from harm. In the previous chapter, we encountered this idea through the dreamcatcher, a handwoven net in the form of a spider web that certain Native American tribes believed was able to trap bad dreams. We even made use of the dreamcatcher as one method of protecting an

Saint Benedict's Medal

Saint Benedict of Nursia, an Italian born in the fifth century, is best known as the founder of Christian monastic communities. He created the Holy Rule, a set of guidelines adopted by the majority of Christian monastic orders. Benedict is also associated with a holy medal often used by Catholics to ward off evil. The origin of the medal is unclear, although some of its imagery ties back to a fifteenth-century manuscript with an image of Saint Benedict clasping the scroll of the Holy Rule in one hand and a staff ending in a cross in the other. Pope Benedict XIV sanctioned this medal in the mid-1740s. The versions struck during this time bore on one side an image clearly inspired by the fifteenth-century manuscript. On the reverse was a cross with a number of significant phrases, represented by initials. These phrases are likely the reason the Saint Benedict medal is used to protect against evil. They include initials from the Latin phrases for: "May the Holy Cross Be My Light," "Let Not the Dragon Be My Guide," and "Be Gone Satan, Do Not Suggest to Me Thy Vanities."

individual's dreams from invasion by hostile entities. Along these lines, manuals exist from Sumeria, Egypt, ancient Greece, and Rome (as well as many other places) that detail the making of protective charms and talismans. Many of these use a combination of short phrases, symbols, prayers, and the names of various deities to keep evil at bay.

The practice of using items for protection is in no way limited only to Pagan cultures. When a home is in need of protection, the Catholic Church proscribes the use of a medal that is dedicated to Saint Benedict. This medal, bearing an image of the saint on one side and holy symbols on the other, is believed to safeguard a home from pestilence, storms, and every variety of evil. It is considered especially useful in warding off legions of demons. These medals can be placed in the home, typically above windows and doors, or they can be buried around the property to surround the house with blessed protection. The medals, as well as other sacramental items such as scapulars and holy water, are not technically supposed to be approached as amulets or talismans, yet the distinction is a thin one. Holy medals and other items of protection have been used by the Church since the early Middle Ages, and they are the direct descendents of items used throughout the ancient Pagan world.

In the eleventh and twelfth centuries, English monasteries, like the priory at Durham Cathedral, were known to use textual amulets to help heal the sick. These amulets typically took the form of pieces of parchment worn around the neck of the afflicted. The parchment was scribed with special words and prayers and was prepared by one of the monks. These prayers often included Christian blessings and passages taken from the Bible, although foreign words and symbols were sometimes incorporated alongside traditional Christian symbols. The Sign of the Cross was popular, as were the *Arma Christi*—the so-called "Armaments of Christ"—which included a variety of symbols associated with the Passion and Crucifixion, from nails to spears to dice. Because each of these items played a role in his death, these were all seen as weapons that Christ had used to save the world from sin. By extension, they could also be used by the faithful as protection from harm.

The Church had mixed feelings about the use of these amulets and talismans. On one hand, the vast majority of textual amulets were produced by the clergy, for they were often the only people adequately trained to read and write. On the other hand, there was a fear that some of the lay people approached these items with an attitude that verged on idolatry. It is noteworthy to mention that Inquisitors were instructed to craft a talisman containing the Seven Last Words of Christ and wear this to protect themselves from evil when they were interviewing witches and heretics. However, those selfsame Inquisitors actively searched suspected witches for their own talismans, because one of the hallmarks of witchcraft was the use of protective amulets. Many of the protective amulets used in medieval folk magick contained holy symbols and prayers taken from the Bible that made them almost completely indistinguishable from the acceptable talismans produced by the clergy.

Understandably, this led to some confusion as to what constituted a pious Christian use of talismans, as opposed to heretical witchcraft (often punishable by death at the time). Various theologians, including Saint Thomas Aquinas, wrote statements of disambiguation, stressing the fact that the words and symbols themselves were not the reason for the effectiveness of these protective amulets. The real power at work was faith, and the symbols, saints, and prayers, although important, functioned merely as inspirations for that faith. If a person wore a talisman with the expectation that the words and symbols themselves would protect them (rather than their own belief), by Church standards, they were doing it wrong.

I happen to agree with Saint Thomas Aquinas. Holy medals and other objects can be very useful when it comes to protection from unwanted entities. They present one more method that can be harnessed by paranormal investigators to protect a house from intrusion. Warding a home involves setting up specific points of protection either inside or immediately surrounding the home. Oftentimes, these points of protection are represented by physical objects, such as holy medals. Following Aquinas' reasoning, however, if items like this are used, it is important for those using them to understand that the items themselves are not the real source of power. Just as we saw with the dreamcatcher, the item itself is a focus for intent and belief. Furthermore, that belief does not always have to be religious in nature. There are secular and psychological forms of faith—the faith that a person's willpower can influence reality, or the faith that a person's convictions can have a psychological impact on their attitudes and reactions. Whether you approach things from a religious, secular, or psychological perspective is irrelevant, as long as you get results. And, when it comes to protecting a home, it can be very helpful to have a concrete representation of that protection placed visibly to remind the residents that they are safe.

Warding a Home

It is possible to craft your own protective items to place in or around a home. Of course, these items are not worth the materials they are crafted from if they do not directly speak to and inspire the residents' faith. The items are symbols of faith and intent. Sometimes that faith may be faith in another person's ability to craft such an item and imbue it with protective power. For example, much of the protective power invested in Catholic holy medals comes about because those medals were formally blessed by a priest.

Before you select an item or items to use around a house for protection, you should sit down and talk about the family's beliefs. Find out whether or not they follow a specific religion and, if they do not, find out what symbols of protection might have meaning for them independent of religion. Whenever you are cleansing and protecting a family's home, you should always accommodate their personal religious convictions, but this becomes especially important when symbols and items are involved. The items as well as the symbols that appear on the items help to focus intent and belief. Additionally, the very action of placing the items helps to reinforce the sense of boundaries. If there is no mental or emotional connection to the items, however, then they are nothing more than empty symbols—as useless as they are meaningless.

If you use prefabricated items, such as holy medals, to set up wards in a home, you will use a technique that is strongly reminiscent of the exercise with the dreamcatcher, only on a much larger scale. Like the dreamcatcher, the medals become the focal point of your work, but instead of simply protecting a single bed, you will need enough items to place in several strategic areas throughout the house. Before you commit to this, examine the house itself and consider the key areas that need to be warded so that outside influences cannot enter. The main points of entry you should pay attention to include doors and windows. Obviously you will want an item to place over the front door, but you should also consider warding large windows and other doors that allow access into the home. Depending on the layout of the house as well as the general feel of the place, you may not have to ward each and every individual window. But you should have at least one item placed in every room to help shore up the boundaries. The following exercise presumes that you are warding a house with holy medals, but keep in mind that you can use any meaningful item or symbol as your focus. Follow these steps for a basic warding:

1. Ground and center. You only need to do this once, at the very beginning of the work.

2. Have the total number of medals you need for every room in the house collected together in a basket or bowl.

3. Gather the medals into your hands. If there are too many to hold, thrust your hands into the bowl and cup as many of the medals as possible in your palms.

4. Close your eyes and gather energy. You may also wish to connect to your higher power. Allow energy to flow down into your hands, passing from you to the medals.

5. As you allow power to flow into the medals, vividly imagine your purpose. Picture the entire house in your mind, and picture each location in the house where you have decided to place a medal. Focus on protecting the home and shoring up the boundaries so nothing unwelcome may enter.

6. Continue the visualization. Picture a medal placed at each significant point, and picture that medal glowing with a radiant, protective light. Picture lines of this light connecting all of the medals together, to form a web of light that encircles the entire home.

7. Affirm your purpose by saying to yourself or out loud: "May each of these objects be a shield, protecting this home from invasion."

8. Go through the house, starting at the top and moving from the back to the front. Place a medal at each key point.

9. As you place each individual medal, focus again on your intention. Vividly imagine the medal as a point of concentrated light. When you place the medal, it becomes an anchor for that light, and the radiant, protective light spreads beyond the medal, forming a barrier at all nearby windows and walls.

10. For each individual medal, affirm your intention once again: "I place this ward as an anchor of light. May it shield this home from invasion."

11. Finish your circuit of the house at the front door. Place the final medal over this door, once again speaking the affirmation.

12. Once you have placed the final medal, close your eyes and vividly imagine lines of light radiating out from the medal over the front door. Picture the light connecting to each and every medal throughout the house. Each medal glows brightly, and they are all connected by a web of radiant light, protecting the home.

13. Once a month, touch the medal over the front door and repeat this final visualization, or instruct the family to do so.

The objects used for this exercise can be anything from holy medals to tiny crosses to little pieces of paper with a hand-drawn shield. It is perfectly acceptable to make your own items to serve as the focal points when warding a house against spirit invasion. If you make your own items, it's a good idea to use a combination of words and symbols. Words appeal to one part of the brain, and symbols appeal to another. By incorporating both, you are engaging the whole brain, therefore ensuring that the item has meaning on several levels.

Handcrafting the items used in warding can also be very empowering. Let's consider an example. You are asked to ward the house of a family with no particular belief system. They are not atheists, but they don't identify as Christian or any other major religion either. Because the items used in warding are visualized as shields that protect the home at significant points, you decide to draw an image of a tiny shield on a one-by-one-inch piece of paper for your item. The shield is certainly symbolic enough, but to help solidify your sense of purpose, you decide to write an affirmation on the back of the slip of paper as well. You settle on, "Shield this home from invasion." Since you are doing this for a family, you may want to encourage the family members themselves to craft the items. Alternately, you could have a representative of the family, such as the head of the household, draw a shield on all the necessary slips of paper, along with scribing the affirmation on the opposite side.

How does this work help the family? For one, actively crafting the items of protection allows the residents to take control of the protection of their home. Instead of being passive observers as you ward the home, they become active participants who are engaged, body and mind, in the process. The sense of empowerment that arises from this participation will help the clients to feel less like victims. A lot of the sense of a family's vulnerability in a haunting comes from a lack of control. They don't know the rules by which spirits work, and thus they cannot even accurately assess what constitutes threatening behavior from a spirit. Without knowing the rules, they feel helpless, and this sense of helplessness makes them easier targets for attack. By handing them a measure of power and a method by which they can take back their home, you enable them to feel protected once again. Their very confidence in the fact that they are protected will help add strength to the boundaries erected by the wards. All of this is simple psychology. When someone believes they are a victim, they tend to unconsciously telegraph messages to predators that they are weak and vulnerable. Give a person a reason to be confident, and they telegraph a very different set of messages that help to keep predators away. Most predators—living or dead—prefer easy targets and will back away from someone who looks like they could put up a fight.

Variation: Buried Treasure

As previously observed, some Catholics use Saint Benedict medals to protect their homes. Sometimes, these medals are buried on the property around the house. Very frequently, when the medals are buried, one is placed in each of the four corners. The medals themselves are of course symbolic of the protection offered by the saint. But in this case, there is another symbol at work: the act of placing the medals themselves. By walking around the house, the person placing the medals is tracing a barrier that extends beyond the physical walls and encompasses the entire home. By placing medals at each of the four corners, this protective barrier is anchored to the physical world. However, burying the medals has an additional function as well, a function connected with the symbolism of placing things in the ground.

Since the time of the Neanderthals, people have buried their dead. Once the dead are buried, they are believed to make passage to the Otherside. Because we have observed this practice for thousands of years, deep in our collective unconscious, there is an unspoken belief that burying something conveys it to the spirit realm. This connection between the underground and the realm of spirits is something that can be observed again and again throughout the myths of cultures around the world, especially those cultures that influenced our current society. In ancient Greece and Rome, for example, it was not uncommon for individuals to bury little lead tablets in the graves of the dead. These tablets contained requests to be carried out by spirits, everything from prayers for good health to curses upon one's enemies. The tablets could be dropped down wells so their messages could be conveyed to the Otherside, but by placing them directly in a grave, it was believed that the specific spirit of that grave could then serve as a messenger, conveying the intent of the tablet even more speedily to its final destination.

These *defixiones,* or "curse tablets," were a principal part of Greek and Roman magick. Although the Church spoke out against magick, the tradition from which these curse tablets hailed had a direct influence on the talismanic magick of the Middle Ages—and this included the textual amulets produced by the clergy. Burying holy medals in the yard hearkens back to these ancient beliefs and practices. This is not to say that it is mere superstition, but that it builds upon the same powerful symbols that have inspired people for centuries.

To adapt this method of warding a home for your own use, follow these simple steps. Remember to bring along a small shovel or trowel to dig the holes!

1. Ground and center.

2. Collect four items symbolic of protection. As with the warding of the inside of the house, holy medals are assumed, but the items can be anything with significance to the residents of the home.

3. Step out of the house, along with the head of the household or another adult resident invested in the protection of the home.

4. Standing just outside the front door, cup the four medals in your hands. Have the resident of the home place their hands over yours.

5. Close your eyes and focus your energy, moving it from your heart to your hands. Instruct the resident to do so as well.

6. Vividly imagine power flowing into the medals. Picture them shining as brilliant points of light, then picture that light expanding so each medal is the focal point of a powerful pillar of light. Picture these pillars of light standing at each of the four corners of the home, supporting a barrier that nothing harmful may pass through.

7. Affirm the intent of your visualization by saying: "May these medals serve as seeds. May the seeds become pillars of light, standing firm to protect this home." Alternately, you can frame this affirmation as a prayer, allowing your higher power to work through you to empower the medals.

8. Stand at least five feet and no more than ten feet beyond the edge of the house, as space allows. Starting from the front door, walk to the first corner of the house. Move in a clockwise direction and try to proceed in a circular pattern. Take each step with intent, imagining light flowing down and around you, so you leave a ring of light in your wake, surrounding and protecting the home.

9. At the first corner, stop and dig a small hole, three to six inches in depth. Do as little damage to the surrounding grass as possible. Place one of the holy medals into the hole. As you cover the hole, replacing the sod on top, you and the resident should both place your hands on the little mound of dirt that now covers the holy medal.

10. With your hands on the earth covering the medal, take a moment to once again visualize the medal glowing with brilliant light, and that light expanding into a shining pillar.

11. Affirm your intent by saying: "This medal is a seed, and the seed becomes a pillar of light, standing firm around this home." Alternately, you can recite a prayer appropriate to the medal and your intent that it help protect the home.

12. Stand and walk to the next corner of the house. Continue to walk in a rough circle. As you walk, imagine that you trail light behind you. Each step imprints this energy into the ground, forming a ring of light around the home.

13. Place a medal at each of the remaining three corners. Repeat the visualizations and affirmations in steps 10 and 11.

14. When you have traveled all the way around the house, make your way once more to the front door.

15. Stand and face the front door. Take a moment to reflect upon the work. Vividly imagine the medals, flaring like pillars, and the ring of light connecting each of these four points of protection. Picture all of this light growing and connecting until the entire house is surrounded by a protective barrier that stretches high to the heavens and down into the earth.

16. Affirm this protection with a final prayer, or say: "Protection to the north. Protection to the south. Protection to the east. Protection to the west. Protection above, protection below.

In every direction, this house is protected from anything that seeks to do harm."

17. Walk back into the house using the front door. Although you do not need to bury new medals each month, you or the resident should walk the circle around the house and repeat the visualizations and affirmations at least once a month. Consider replacing the medals themselves once a year, removing the old ones (assuming they can be found) and disposing of them in a respectful manner.

The Least You Should Know

Homes can be protected by applying concepts similar to those for shielding, as covered in chapter two. An individual who has practiced shielding their personal space will naturally extend some of this protection to living spaces, but this process can be harnessed intentionally as well. The easiest application of this technique involves shielding a single room. To shield a room, an individual should go through the exact same steps used to shield themselves from unwanted entities and energies. However, once the shield encompasses their personal bubble of space, it should be expanded until it covers the entire room. Rather than having the shield anchored to the individual, which can be exhausting, the shield should be anchored to the space itself. The most helpful visualizations for this involve connecting to the heavens above and the earth below. This way, the shield is rooted to the physical location and is also connected to a higher power.

Individuals who have weak personal boundaries typically cannot shield effectively, and they should not attempt to shield a physical space until such time as they have developed a better sense of their own boundaries. Healthy boundaries include a strong sense of one's personal space, not just physically but emotionally as well. Additionally, a person with weak boundaries is often easily intimidated, manipulated, or dominated by others. In learning how to say no and to establish healthy limits in one's relations with the living, one learns how to maintain similar limits with spirits.

When people feel safe and secure in a space, that sense of security can build up in the very walls, just like any other emotional residue. The longer people live in a particular space, the more energy builds up in the physical structure of that location. This concept is acknowledged in the practice of feng shui, where it is believed that currents of energy often follow the movement of people, and that walls and other physical barriers, because they are recognized as such by people, also serve as barriers to these flows of energy. This essentially allows a house to stand not just in the physical world but in the spirit world as well. This process, although it occurs unconsciously, can be harnessed consciously in order to establish stronger boundaries in a home. By recognizing the strength and stability of a home with purpose and intent, residents can reinforce the walls of that home against spirits.

Warding is another method that can be used to protect a home. Warding focuses on specific points of protection within a house or around it. These points of protection are often represented by physical objects, such as holy medals. The objects used to represent wards must be relevant to the residents' faith. If the family is not religious, the objects should be personally meaningful. Most items used to ward a home combine words and symbols in order to have the greatest appeal, and, like the objects themselves, these words and symbols serve as a way of focusing intent and belief. Perception plays a significant role in all methods of protection, and it is especially important with warding. The placement of physical objects to represent the wards works to remind the residents in a tangible way that they are protected on many levels. When the objects themselves are not visible, as in the case of holy medals buried around a yard, then the act of placing them becomes a most potent symbol that reaffirms this perception of being protected.

Although mental exercises, such as visualizations and affirmations, can play a vital role in helping people to erect boundaries against spirits, faith and prayer are also powerful tools. The faith does not have to be in a particular religion, but in the effectiveness of the protecting act itself. When assessing the needs of a particular family, investigators should learn as much as possible about that family's beliefs and adapt the methods of protection accordingly. Whether protective barriers are erected around a home using energy work, affirmations, or prayer, the end results should always be the same:

- A firm boundary has been established around the home to protect it from intrusion by unwelcome entities and energies.
- This boundary and its method of establishment appeal directly to beliefs and symbols that hold meaning for the family.
- The family has a firm sense of this boundary and is prepared to reinforce the boundary when necessary.
- The residents of the home are working toward developing healthier personal boundaries and no longer feel like helpless victims.

seven

REMOVING
UNWANTED GUESTS

Clearing the stagnant energy from Irving's home was exhausting. All of the physical clutter that choked the space made it hard to concentrate on the spiritual aspect of things. Not only was the physical mess a distraction, but I also knew that it made everything that I was trying to do harder. No matter how much "oomph" I put into my energy work, unless Irving and his mom made a concerted effort to clean up the place, all of my work was merely temporary. If the physical aspect of the house didn't change in a major way, the stagnant energy would build right back up in a matter of weeks. And that's to say nothing of Irving's grandmother, whose slow decline through dementia and into death was creating an unpleasant energy all its own. I understood that the family didn't want to put her into a nursing home, and yet there was an air of neglect about her that told me she would probably have been better off with professional care. But I had been hired to clear out the energy and solve the haunting. Although that allowed me some leeway in suggesting how to clean and maintain the home, I felt my opinions about the grandmother overstepped those bounds. So I just tried to work around her. Compared to her, the clutter was easy to ignore.

Slowly but surely, we cleared the cast-off energy and emotional residues that clogged the space. Each time we finished with a room, we left it feeling lighter and more open, even though none of the physical clutter had been cleared away. Julie and I teamed up to clear one long box-filled hallway, she taking one end and I the other. Eventually we met in the middle and pronounced it clear. Finally, there was one room left: the front sunroom where Irving's grandmother spent most of her day. We could hear the endless muttering of the television through the door.

"I don't really feel comfortable going in there," Julie said.

"Neither do I," I replied. "For a number of reasons."

Julie and I contemplated the door.

"We really need to clean that room out though, don't we?" she asked.

"We do," I said. "And it probably needs it more than most of the rooms. But let me show you a trick. You know how most of the cleansing involves visualization, right?"

Julie nodded.

"Our physical gestures are just symbols. They help us focus. The real work is with the energy. And the energy follows our intent."

"All right," Julie said. "You've only said that about a billion times. So how does that help with the old lady's room?"

I placed my hand against the closed door and smiled. "You don't have to physically stand in a room and make sweeping motions with your hands to clear the energy out," I explained. "If you are really good at focusing, you can clear the energy in the entire house just standing in one place."

Julie glared at me. "Are you telling me that we just cleared this place from top to bottom when we could have just stood in the living room and thought about it real hard?"

"Technically, yes," I said. "But it helps to be present in the space that you're clearing, interacting with it directly. It takes a whole lot of concentration to clear a space from a distance, and you really have to be good at using visualization to guide your energy. When a house is this bad, I prefer to do everything hands-on, because the physical actions greatly reinforce the psychic actions. But in the case of the grandmother's room here, I think we can make an exception."

Julie stared at the closed door and nodded. Adjusting her glasses briefly, she asked, "So what do we do?"

"Stand here. Focus inward. Picture the room on the other side of this door."

"We haven't been in the room yet," Julie pointed out.

"But we have seen the grandmother, and we know what her energy feels like," I reminded.

Julie suppressed a shudder. "You want me to focus on that, don't you?"

"That's right," I said.

"Have I mentioned how much I hate you right now?" Julie teased.

Shrugging, I said, "At least her energy is hard to miss."

Julie sighed.

"All right," I said. "Focus on her energy and use that as an anchor. Reach out into the room. Imagine that you're standing in the middle of the room going through the exact same motions that we've used to clear every other room in this house. Picture it vividly and feel it, as if you are really standing in there, clearing the energy."

Julie and I concentrated in silence for a few moments while, on the other side of the door, the television continued to babble inanely.

"So how do I know it's not just my imagination?" Julie asked.

"Did it feel like you were really doing something?"

"I think so," she said. Then, shrugging herself, she admitted, "I'm not sure."

"Honestly, the best test is to see if other people notice the work. That's how I confirm it. I know what it feels like to reach out and clear the energy, but I wait to hear from people like you or Irving to see if you can tell the difference."

Julie nodded to herself as she considered this. Stepping away from the door, she wiped her hands on her slacks. She had been doing that through most of the cleansing, as if she were trying to wipe the dirt off of her palms. Of course, all of our cleansing had been nonphysical, so neither Julie nor myself had ever touched anything that could get us dirty in a flesh-and-blood sense of the word.

"That's a good indication, too," I said.

"What is?"

"You just wiped your hands on your pants. I bet you didn't even think about it, but on some level, you felt like you'd gotten your hands dirty," I pointed out.

Julie looked down at her fingers and chuckled a bit. "Yeah, I guess you're right. All this clutter is making me crazy."

"Pay attention to your unconscious reactions," I suggested. "I've seen you do that now every single time you've actively worked to clear a room. On some level, I bet you feel all the stagnant stuff still clinging to you. The fact that you did it again just now suggests that you did more than just paint pretty pictures in your head while you visualized the room."

Looking a little haggard, Julie said, "They weren't very pretty pictures."

"The point is, I think we're done with the grandmother's room," I said. I put an arm companionably around Julie's shoulders and guided her back down the hall. As we walked, we passed the room where Julie had first seen one of the shadowy entities in the closet.

"Do you still sense them?" I asked. I already knew my answer, but I wanted to hear hers. It never hurt to get a second opinion, especially where spirits were concerned.

Julie closed her eyes and tipped her head in the direction of the closet, as if listening. She frowned a little as she did so, her pale brows knitted together in concentration. "Hrm," she said, mostly to herself.

"Hrm?" I asked. "What's 'hrm' mean?"

She continued to hold that listening pose for a few moments more. When next she opened her eyes, they seemed brighter somehow, the shades of lavender more pronounced among the blue. "It's like an echo," she said. "Like they're there, but they're not. I don't sense anything in the closet directly, but there's still a sense of a . . . *presence*. Somewhere. Not here, but close to here. Like they took a few steps back and are watching. Does that make any sense to you?"

"I get about the same feeling," I told her. "I'm not going to pretend to understand the geography of the spirit realm, but I think they moved away from the house once we started clearing the energy. It's possible that we pushed them out when we cleared the energy—spirits being energy themselves, that's one of the simplest way to kick certain things out of a house. But you're right. There's a sense that they didn't go far and that they're waiting and watching."

"Waiting for us to leave?" Julie asked.

I nodded. "Probably. They're used to Irving being a victim. We're a new quantity in the home, but if they're intelligent and observant, they'll be able to tell that we won't be around forever. They just have to wait for us to go."

Julie frowned.

"Of course," I added wryly, "They'll be heartily disappointed to discover that we've taught Irving most of what we know, so he won't be much of a victim anymore."

Julie closed her eyes again, trying to pinpoint her sense of the spirits. Her head quested back and forth, and she clenched her fists with effort, probably without even realizing it. After a moment, she sighed again, sounding a little frustrated. "So the energy work pushed them out," she said. "But they could come back? That doesn't seem fair. I mean, Irving had us come all the way out here to get rid of these things, and you're telling me that once we leave, they might just move right back in. Isn't there something more permanent we could do?"

"Don't underestimate the importance of boundaries," I cautioned. "Clearing the energy is only one step. We're going to work with Irving to set up wards and shields around the house to prevent them from coming back in. Of course, nothing we do with energy is as permanent as, say, building a physical wall. The energy work we do degrades over time, and Irving will have to keep up on the boundaries, reinforcing them every month or so. But it should be enough."

"What if it isn't?" Julie persisted. "Can't you just send them into the light or something?"

"Don't believe everything you see on television," I grumbled, and continued heading down the hall.

As it turned out, Irving had the same concerns and questions. Throughout the entire laborious process of clearing the energy in the house, he had waited patiently in his room. When Julie and I entered, he practically jumped up out of his computer chair.

"Are they gone?" he asked. "Did you send them into the light?"

I shot a look at Julie. To Irving, I said, "That's not as easy as they make it seem in the movies. But they're gone, for now."

Irving made that nervous gesture with his hair, and his eyes darted to the closet behind his bed. "For now?" he asked. I could tell that he wanted to ask more, but he wasn't certain where to begin.

"Here's the deal," I said. "The shadows you've been seeing in the closets and elsewhere are actual spirits. They're not just residual hauntings or anything like that." I held up a hand before he could object. "I know you already knew this, but it's best to be sure. Residual hauntings can seem like real spirits, especially when you're talking the kind that repeat a specific series of actions or seem to relive a certain event. But there's no intelligence behind those types of hauntings, so the way you go about getting rid of them is different from hauntings that involve sentient beings. Intelligent hauntings can be either much easier or much harder to deal with than a residue."

Irving looked from me to Julie and back again. Hesitantly, he asked, "So which is it?"

"Sentient spirits," I repeated. "I already said they're not residues."

"That's not what I meant," he responded. "Is it the easy way or the hard way?"

I leaned my back against the door, considering my next few words carefully. One of the most difficult issues in a haunting is the fear people experience when something paranormal intersects with their daily routines. For most people, it's bad enough to know that spirits are out there and that they can sometimes influence our physical world. In those rare hauntings that involve malevolent or at least mischievous entities, it is even more frightening for residents to realize that their otherworldly visitors have taken a specific interest in them and have been behaving with both intelligence and intent.

"I want to try the easy way first," I said. "We've cleared the stagnant energy and, in sweeping all of that out, we pushed the entities out as well. In a few minutes, you're going to come with me and we are going to put up wards and boundaries around the house. That should keep them out."

Irving considered this, and then he asked the same question that Julie had asked. "What if it doesn't?"

"There are a couple of options after that," I offered. "While it's technically possible to send things into the light, I find the very concept presumptuous. I mean, think about it. Here are these spirits lingering on the earthly plane. If they're human ghosts, the general belief is that they're stuck due to unfinished business. Basically, they've got issues, and they can't move on to the next stage of being until they've resolved those issues. And then along comes some well-intentioned medium who just opens up a door to heaven and kicks them through, whether they're ready for it or not? I can't do that. I don't think I have the right to judge whether or not they're ready to move on."

"You know, I hadn't thought about it like that," Julie observed.

"Well, I've thought about it. A lot. And I won't do it," I said. "However, I don't have a problem talking to spirits and helping them make that decision for themselves. Most of the human ghosts I've run into over the years just needed a good therapist to help them sort out whatever issues were keeping them here. The problem is, most therapists don't talk to the dead. So helping them resolve their attachments and leading them to move on that way, I'm cool with. The problem is, Irving, I don't think you're dealing with human ghosts."

"And you're sure they're not demons?" Irving asked.

Julie shook her head. "They're not demons," she reassured.

"There are a lot of things out there, Irving," I explained. "And there's no way any living person could catalogue them all. The most significant differences are between residual hauntings, human ghosts, and non-human entities. The thing with nonhuman entities is they were never people to begin with, so they don't think or act like people. They're native to the spirit realm, and talking to them about their attachments is going to do jack squat to get them to move on."

"All right," he said. "So what can you do?"

"I know two ways to get rid of nonhuman entities more permanently than just shoving them out of the house and figuratively locking all the doors. One involves attacking them—basically going toe to toe on a psychic level and beating them so badly that they don't want to come back. The other involves binding them. I use it as an absolute last resort."

"What's binding?" Irving asked.

Julie perked up, because this was an area she had a lot of interest in. She had spent a great deal of time in high school and college studying the concept of summoning and binding spirits, poring through reprints of old books. I was familiar with many of the historical texts that she had studied, but I was quite certain that Irving was not. A lot of those books were tied in with medieval necromancy and ceremonial magick. Given Irving's Christian background, I didn't want to alarm him with an overly detailed explanation of their contents. Before Julie could continue, I gestured for her to be quiet.

"Basically, you construct a prison and you give the spirit a time-out," I said.

"Well, that's an oversimplification if ever I've heard one," Julie muttered grumpily.

"But it's true," I said.

Irving looked back and forth between the two of us, his gaze a little skeptical. "How do you make a prison that can hold a spirit?" he asked.

"Well, if you have its sigil or its name—" Julie started, but again, I cut her off.

Sighing, I said, "There is a lot of historical thought written on this subject, but essentially, you make a barrier just like you do with shields and wards. Think about taking a jar and putting enough energy and intent in it to make that jar real on the Otherside—as solid there as it is here. Then you put the spirit in it and seal it up tight."

From the look that Julie shot me, she still did not approve of my oversimplification, but she held her tongue. Irving pondered my description, finally asking, "But how does it fit?"

"It's complicated," I said, almost wishing I hadn't raised the topic.

"That part's not complicated at all," Julie insisted. "It's easy. Spirits are energy. The size and shape of the vessel doesn't matter. Those are only physical things. If you compel the spirit into the vessel, it will fit."

"Like a genie in a bottle?" Irving asked.

"Exactly like a genie in a bottle!" Julie replied excitedly. "In fact, the stories about genies or djinn trapped in bottles tie right back to the Solomonic tradition. If you managed to make something like Solomon's brazen vessel, you could trap any type of spirit in it."

Irving's brows knitted together as he tried to keep up. "Solomon's whatsit?" he asked.

"In Jewish lore, the biblical King Solomon is given a ring or a seal that allows him to control spirits," I explained. "And there's a whole tradition based on a few passages in the Bible that talks about Solomon's art—the art of controlling spirits. But all of this is really moot. Binding is not something you try right off the bat. Why cut butter with a broadsword?"

"What?" Irving asked.

"What I mean is you should always take the easiest route first," I explained. "Where human spirits are concerned, try talking to them and setting ground rules. When you're dealing with entities that clearly aren't human, pushing them out and setting up firm boundaries is the simplest step. Though you could technically try talking to them, too. They're not all jerks," I laughed. "Let me go over all the options and see if you don't agree once we're done."

Assessing a Haunting

There are a number of different techniques for removing spirits from a home. However, before applying any of these techniques, it's best to have a firm understanding of what you are dealing with. Different types of hauntings require different approaches. For example, you can try to convince the force behind a haunting to make its peace and move on, but if that force is a residual haunting, all you're doing is wasting your breath. A residual haunting is nothing more than an echo, like a recording imprinted upon the energy of a place. There is no intelligent spirit behind such a haunting, and, as such, there is nothing you can appeal to or ask to leave. Nonhuman entities also present a problem if your main approach to haunting resolution is to try to bring peace to a spirit so it can move on. Entities that were never human to begin with are often native to the Otherside. Not only do they have no interest in resolving their attachments and moving on, in all likelihood, there is nowhere for them to move on to. Because hauntings can be caused by more things than simply human ghosts, it is very important to understand the nature of a haunting before trying to resolve it.

Hauntings fall very broadly into three main categories: residual hauntings, human ghosts, and nonhuman entities. Each of these responds differently to different methods of resolution.

Residual Hauntings

Residual hauntings, what I sometimes term "echoes" or "residues," are not hauntings in the sense that there is a sentient spirit lingering in a specific location. Instead, the residual haunting is a type of echo trapped in the fabric of space or time. The exact specifics of how residual hauntings come about are poorly understood, but the phenomena has been repeatedly documented. Some of the most famous residual hauntings can be found at Gettysburg, where tourists will sometimes encounter whole fields of phantom soldiers reliving the war. In the ancient Greek world, the battlefield at Marathon was known for a similar phenomena. Although many men died at both of these locations, the battalions of ghostly soldiers that replay the fevered pitch of battle over and over are not self-aware. If anything, they are like a recording imprinted on the field of battle itself, possibly due to the intensity of the fighting and the extremity of emotion experienced by those who participated in it.

Residual hauntings are not always as spectacular as ghostly soldiers apparently reliving the last hours of their lives. Any haunting that ceaselessly repeats a specific set of actions is likely to be residual rather than intelligent. The sound of footsteps that wander up the stairs and across the hall every night at exactly three o'clock, the spectral figure of a lady in white who flits through the garden and momentarily stands by the well where she drowned, the doomed queen Ann Boleyn proceeding through the Tower of London to make her appointment with the headsman's axe—all of these are classic residual hauntings. You are dealing with a residual haunting if you observe the following:

- The "spirit" engages in a specific and repetitive set of actions.
- The "spirit" fails to respond intelligently to any attempt at communication.
- The "spirit" displays a fundamental lack of awareness of changes in its surroundings.

- The behavior of the "spirit" fails to change over time.
- The "spirit" only manifests in specific locations or at specific times.

As an investigator seeking to resolve a haunting, it is important to determine whether or not that haunting is residual or intelligent. Intelligent spirits respond to attempts to communicate, even though sometimes that response involves a pointed refusal to communicate. But residual hauntings do not respond to attempts at communication because there is nothing to communicate with—it's just an echo. This means that any attempt to politely ask the ghost to move on will fall upon deaf ears. You cannot resolve a residual haunting by "sending it into the light." Nor can you resolve a residual haunting by exorcising the spirit or even intimidating it into leaving the family alone. All of these methods require there to be an intelligent consciousness at the heart of the phenomena. This may seem as if a residual haunting severely limits the methods you have at your disposal for resolving the phenomena, but never fear. In many ways, residual hauntings are easier to remove than intelligent hauntings because, when it comes down to it, they are nothing more than energetic imprints impressed upon a space. As such, most methods of cleansing built-up and stagnant energy will work to remove a residual haunting. Think of hauntings of this type as a kind of stain upon the house that can be removed with a sufficient application of elbow grease and the methods outlined in chapter three.

The Restless Dead

Intelligent hauntings pose their own issues. The most common tend to be human spirits that linger due to unfinished business. A Buddhist would probably call this "unfinished business" by a different name: attachment. Basically, people who die with unresolved issues or who have powerful attachments to the physical world tend to linger as ghosts. These unresolved issues can be as simple as wanting to see a particular child or grandchild grow into adulthood, or they can be as messy and complex as the issues carried over into death by a young girl who was brutally raped and murdered. Sometimes, the unfinished business only seems important to the ghost itself. One ghost I encountered during the course of an investigation was a man who had built the house the family resided in. He had lived there his entire life and, although he had not specifically died on the property, he lingered because he wanted to see how future residents enjoyed his work. He had no other real attachment beyond the pride he had taken in the construction of the house and a sort of gentle curiosity in watching new generations live and grow there.

When the intelligent spirit is a human spirit, the first thing to keep in mind is the spirit's very humanity. There's an old belief that dates back at least to the Middle Ages wherein spirits are thought to suddenly become privy to the secrets of the universe once they die. This belief is what prompted necromancers in the Elizabethan era and beyond to try to call up ghosts so they could lead the way to buried treasure. This is a rather ridiculous use for a ghost, in my opinion, because the human dead have no better sense of where random bits of gold may be buried in the ground than the living do (unless they buried the gold themselves). In fact, the living probably have a leg up on the dead these days, thanks to the invention of metal detectors.

The vagaries of medieval necromancy aside, the important thing to think about with human spirits is the fact that they think, act, and emote just like the living. The one difference I have noticed in my own interactions is that, if anything, human spirits are even more intensely human than the living. Everything seems ratcheted up a notch for the human dead. Their emotions are more extreme, as are their psychological issues, their hates, their loves, their obsessions—they have had the distractions of the physical world taken away, and all that's left are thoughts and feelings. That complex internal landscape is largely responsible for keeping them attached to the material plane.

It looms large without the minutia of daily life to intervene. Consider, for a moment, those times when you wake up at four in the morning and lie in bed, brooding about every little issue, problem, and anxiety in your life. You are all alone in the dark, and there is nothing to turn your mind away from this internal catalogue of angst, so it repeats and repeats until you are practically paralyzed with the enormity of your life. Imagine that, and now imagine that you are dead and four in the morning is eternal. There is no rolling over and dropping off to sleep, there is no waiting for dawn to come so you can thrust yourself into the bustle of a new day, there is nothing in your world that is louder or more persistent than your thoughts. They cannot be drowned out. From my experience, this is the case with a lot of the human spirits that some psychics call "earthbound."

In many ways, they need a good therapist so they can talk about their hopes and fears, get it all out in the open and off their chests, and then move on to better things. But, of course, the number of living humans who can actually perceive and converse with the dead is few and far between. Is it any wonder then, that when a human spirit finds someone who can perceive it—even just a little bit—that spirit then fixates on that person, seeking to make its presence known in no uncertain terms?

Keep in mind, however, that not all human spirits linger against their will. Some have made a choice to stay, and these are cut from a different cloth than those whose attachments weigh them down to the physical plane. Human spirits that intentionally linger often take the role of guardian or guide. They can still be seen as having attachments—consider the mother who dies in childbirth but stays around long enough to see her child grow into an adult. Sometimes, a mother in this situation lingers unwillingly, bound by her grief and disappointment. But when there is a conscious choice to stay and help from the Otherside, the experience of the spirit is very different. That level of angst and unresolved emotion is absent. The intensity of emotion remains, but most often that emotion involves peace, contentment, or love.

A haunting involving a human ghost has a number of identifiable qualities. You can tell that you are dealing with a human spirit if the spirit

- responds intelligently to attempts at communication
- exhibits intense and very human emotions
- behaves in a recognizably human fashion
- has a consistent and recognizably human "feel" or "appearance" to those individuals capable of perceiving it; and
- presents a definite sense of gender.

Human spirits can be reasoned with and, more often than not, they have no intention of harming or even scaring the people they are haunting. Most human spirits are eager to communicate. They want to be recognized and acknowledged by the living people who occupy the same space that they do. Even some of the more alarming phenomena connected with human spirits are nothing more than fumbled attempts at communication. A human spirit may appear at the bedside of the youngest child in the house, but not to menace him. It may seem as if the spirit has an undue fixation on the children in a household, but in all likelihood, the spirit has also tried to make contact with the adult residents as well. Children are more open and responsive to paranormal experiences than most adults for a variety of reasons. The simplest reason is that adults have often developed a powerful ability to discount or rationalize their experiences. Young children don't often have such a clearly defined sense of what is real or unreal, what is possible or impossible. Therefore, when children wake in the night to the sense of a presence hovering over their beds, they respond viscerally to the experience. Adults are far more likely to simply chalk it up to a bad dream, roll over, and go back to sleep. Of course, this makes it seem as if the ghost in the house is unfairly targeting the children, and even if parents do not believe directly in ghosts, they will become extremely protective at the very thought of *something* scaring their kids.

It seems even creepier that the spirit in question insists on appearing to people at night, while they're sleeping, but as we saw in chapter five, even adults become more open to paranormal experiences at night and in dreams. Certainly, some entities take advantage of this fact to prey upon people, but it is just as likely that a human spirit is simply attempting to communicate in the most efficient manner possible, and those communications are being grossly misinterpreted.

To deal with a human haunting, it is necessary first to determine whether or not the spirit is lingering willingly or unwillingly. If a human spirit has intentionally remained behind in order to watch over or communicate with members of a family, that spirit probably has a very good reason for doing so. In cases like this, removing the spirit should not be your goal. Instead, you should seek to explain to the family what is going on and, if possible, help them to learn who the spirit is and what it wants. Human spirits that linger in this fashion are almost always benevolent, and so they will respond to the family's desires. Thus, if the family is alarmed by the spirit's interactions with a specific child, they should be encouraged to communicate their concerns and to set clear boundaries that the spirit will be expected to follow. Setting ground rules for how the spirit is to behave in the house, around strangers, around children, and around pets will help to resolve the more unsettling parts of the haunting. Some families will still be unsettled by the very fact that a spirit is present in their lives, but if they are taught how to assess real threats and how to govern the spirit's behavior through clear rules and requests, it is not only possible to live with a benevolent spirit, but it can be a positive experience for all involved.

What about human spirits who linger for the wrong reasons, or against their will? Depending on the family, the spirit, and the situation, learning to cohabitate peacefully may still be the best and most efficient solution. Not all human spirits that linger due to unfinished business are bad and not all of them are difficult to be around. Consider the old man in New Jersey, who just wanted to watch people live in his house. The only creepy part of that haunting was the fact that he seemed to fixate on the female resident to the point where she felt he was constantly looking over her shoulder. This was a level of voyeurism that made her uncomfortable, even though she herself knew that his intentions were not bad. In the case of this haunting, as well as others like it, the best solution is to educate the family about their ghostly roommate and encourage them to treat the ghost as such. When people share a home, certain guidelines are established, and there is a division of private and public space. If a ghost prefers to linger in the attic or the basement and, aside from making a few noises now and again, otherwise leaves the family alone, is there really a reason to remove it? Furthermore, if the ghost is that of someone who previously lived in the home, and lived there for many years, doesn't it have a right to feel attached to that space? Working with other people in the paranormal field, at times I've encountered an attitude that only the living have a right to their space and that ghosts have no business being here. And yet, who are we to make that judgment? If a spirit is causing no harm, aside from frightening a family by the pure fact that it *is* a spirit, does it have to be removed? Consider this on a case-by-case basis, but do not overlook the option of just setting ground rules and allowing the fleshly and the ghostly inhabitants of a space to agree to share.

Of course, sometimes a human ghost just has too many issues and it has got to go. I view such spirits as the equivalent of living humans whose psychological problems are so severe that they absolutely must seek professional help and probably would do better in the hands of a facility that can provide full-time care. Even if they are not intentionally malicious or destructive, they can nevertheless be a danger to those around them. When a family is dealing with a human ghost like this, it is probably best to remove it.

Oftentimes, the ghost does not want to cause problems and is honestly seeking help and solace through its attempts at communication. This is good news when it comes to resolution, because it means the spirit will respond positively to communication from investigators and, in all likelihood, once it has been made aware of how detrimental its presence has been to the family, it will reconsider its actions and move on. The best approach to human ghosts of this nature is a ghost hunter's equivalent of talk therapy. Establish contact and try to find out what's troubling the spirit. More than half the time, the problem comes down to recent changes made in the home. I cannot count the number of cases I've been involved with where the family had no trouble with spirits whatsoever until they undertook a series of renovations on the home. Human ghosts are creatures of habit. They are stuck in one phase of their lives, and they often respond very negatively to changes in their environment. They are unable to change, and thus they expect the place of their attachment also to remain unchanged. Of course, in this case, the family has every right to improve upon their space, and this fact needs to be impressed upon the spirit. Change is the nature of the living world, and the ghost needs to be encouraged to accept this change or move on. Every once in a while, you will encounter a spirit that is so resistant to the notion of change that it has even resisted accepting the fact that it is dead. Once again, communication that appeals to the spirit's particular issues and gently leads toward a resolution, or at least an awareness, of these issues is key. Sometimes it is not enough, however, and more extreme measures may be called for. We'll be exploring those later in this chapter.

The Real Boogeyman

While we are on the topic of extreme measures, let's consider the last of the three main categories of spirit: the nonhuman entity. There are a lot of names for things like this, and, in fact, there are a lot of things that fall into this category. Nonhuman entities are a vast and varied bunch, including everything from fairies to shadow people. They were never human, and it is highly unlikely that they have ever been incarnated as living beings. Nonhuman entities seem to be native to the spirit realm. However they began, they began there, and they follow impulses and agendas that are wholly alien to a human mind. Some nonhuman entities are the equivalent of wild animals. While they may have a rudimentary intelligence, they are not native to our plane of existence, nor are they entirely comfortable with that plane. When this sort of entity is encountered in a haunting, it can best be thought of like a raccoon that accidentally wandered into a house and got lost. It's not too happy to be there and it's likely to cause a whole lot of ruckus before it gets out, but in the end, it wants to leave just as much as you want it to be gone.

Other nonhuman entities behave more like vermin that are attracted to our homes by the prospect of food. As we saw in chapter four, most of the time, our energy is that food, and an infestation of this sort of entity can have a drastic and unpleasant impact upon residents' health. Some of these parasitic entities possess only rudimentary intelligence, and they seem to behave more on instinct than anything else. Others are easily as smart, if not smarter, than human beings, and they can be very intimidating when encountered. Their actions and reactions are governed by an intelligence that is clearly not human, and their value systems and motivations are often baffling to us. Some seem drawn to interact with the living purely out of mischief. Others have a definitely malevolent quality to them. When such malevolent entities are encountered, it becomes easy to understand why many cultures have perceived such beings as demons. Cultures that predate Christianity by thousands of years acknowledged that there were some spirits that simply were inimical to the human race. Although rare, they definitively fall into this category of nonhuman entities.

Demonic or not, nonhuman entities probably reside at the heart of a number of myths from a variety of cultures. Poltergeists, tommy-knockers, shadow people, faeries—the terminology seems endless, but it befits a category of beings that is as diverse as it is unfathomable. Poltergeists may or may not fall properly into this category, depending

I am Legion

Some nonhuman entities may be categorized as demons. A traditional religious method for removing demons is exorcism. Although mainly used by the Catholic Church in the modern world, the practice of exorcism actually pre-dates Christianity. In ancient Sumer, for example, demons were believed to cause illness and disease. A specially trained class of priest existed to exorcise these demons and thus cure the disease. One of the ways in which these ancient exorcisms were accomplished involved using a pig as a substitute for the possessed. In a complex ceremony, the demon would be driven out and encouraged to take up residence in the pig. The pig would then be slaughtered, symbolically killing the demon. There is a very intriguing echo of this rite in Mark 5:1–20. In this biblical passage, Jesus is confronted by a Gerasene man who is possessed. The demons inside of the afflicted man proclaim, "I am Legion," meaning that there are many demons harrying this poor fellow. Jesus then drives out all of the demons, sending them into a nearby herd of swine. The swine then go mad and charge to their deaths off a cliff. Witnesses from Jesus' time would recognize an echo of the old Sumerian technique of exorcism. Of course, Jesus one-ups the Sumerian exorcists by removing not one demon, but a whole legion of them—enough to possess an entire herd of pigs!

on the cause of the poltergeist phenomena. Some theories suggest that poltergeist phenomena is actually caused by living human beings— typically girls approaching puberty. The person believed to lie at the heart of poltergeist phenomena is known as a nexus, although whether the volatile psyche of this individual somehow brings about the phenomena through an unconscious application of telekinesis, or if that selfsame volatile psyche provides incentive and fuel for a destructive nonhuman entity is up for debate.

It is not as common to encounter a nonhuman entity in a haunting as it is to encounter a human ghost. This is a good thing, considering the problems presented by dealing with a nonhuman entity. Human spirits are at least predictable due to their very human natures. It is possible to understand why they do what they do (even if it may be hard to forgive them), and there is always a chance that they can be communicated with and appealed to. This is not always the case with nonhuman entities. The very alien nature of these spirits makes it difficult not only to understand their actions and motivations but also to connect with them in any meaningful way. Some of them seem more frightening than they really are because of this alien nature. For others, the alien quality arises from a purity of malevolence that few humans could ever rival.

Nonhuman entities behave with intelligence, but the nature of that intelligence is typically so foreign to us that their behavior can be baffling. Although some of them behave in a manner that is willfully destructive toward the living, it may be misleading to view their actions in terms of good or evil. A tiger is not evil when it slaughters a man. The tiger has neither the ability to premeditate this murder nor the conscience to regret it. Some nonhuman entities function in precisely the same way. This is important to keep in mind when dealing with them. They typically cannot be reasoned with as human spirits can, and it may be impossible to interpret or predict their reactions in terms of human values.

You are dealing with a nonhuman entity if most of the following statements hold true:

- The spirit behaves in an intelligent and/or self-aware manner.
- The spirit exhibits an awareness of attempts to communicate, although it may pointedly ignore these or respond in an unusual fashion.
- The spirit behaves in ways that would be strange or atypical for a human.
- There is a pervasive impression associated with the spirit that seems odd, alien, or somehow wrong.
- The manifestations (sound, appearance, etc.) of the spirit have a distinctly inhuman quality.
- The spirit seems intentionally evasive or misleading, often presenting many mutable personas.
- There is a mocking or manipulative quality to the haunting, as if the spirit views the living as objects, tools, or toys.

Nonhuman entities are often the most difficult to accurately identify, largely because some of them intentionally seek to present themselves as human, and only consistent interaction reveals the façade. Hauntings involving nonhuman entities are also often the most difficult to deal with, because the very alien nature of the entities presents an obstacle to communication. This limits the methods one can use to resolve the haunting. While some of these entities will respond to attempts to communicate, most will not, and so simply asking them to leave the residence ceases to be an option. As observed earlier, communicating with the entity in an attempt to resolve its issues so it can move on also is not an option where nonhuman entities are concerned. Having never been human, these entities don't have issues to resolve, at least not in the sense of issues binding them to the material plane. If the nonhuman entity is causing trouble and refuses to be reasoned wit, you should fall back on some of the more aggressive techniques for spirit removal: forcing the entity out, doing battle with it on its own plane, or binding it. In the next portion of this chapter, we will look at methods for accomplishing each of these. First, however, let us consider one last category of haunting—one that doesn't even involve a ghost.

CURRENTS OF POWER

Residual hauntings, human ghosts, and nonhuman entities are the three main spirits that you may encounter in a haunting. However, there is a fourth category that bears consideration as well, and that's a location-based anomaly. This is not strictly a haunting in the sense that it is caused by a spirit, but it can exhibit qualities that people associate with a haunting. Like the previous categories, this encompasses a variety of things, but all of them are related because they are tied to the physical location of the home. Extremely high EMF, either due to issues with manmade devices located near the home or due to limestone, quartz, or magnetite deposits near or beneath the home, can be considered a location-based anomaly. More esoteric concepts such as ley lines can also be considered location-based anomalies.

Ley lines are associated with the concept that there are lines or currents of power that flow across the landscape. These currents often move in straight lines and are generally thought to be fueled by the energy of the earth itself—either through some geomagnetic force or through an energy that is subtler and more psychic in nature. It should be noted that this is a relatively new interpretation of ley lines. Originally, ley lines were associated with sacred sites, specifically in the British Isles. Alfred Watkins, a businessman from Herefordshire, "discovered" ley lines in the summer of 1921. He observed that many of the sacred sites that dotted the British countryside were connected by straight lines. Sometimes this straight line was represented in the land itself by a wellworn track or path. Although Watkins did not initially develop a theory to explain his observations, fours years later, in his book *The Old Straight Track*, he describes the ley lines in terms of a "fairy chain," connecting ancient places of power.

Ley lines have a number of different cognate beliefs, especially in Asia. Chinese feng shui is partly founded on the belief that there are currents of power that naturally flow through the entire surface of the earth. Called *lung-mei*, or "dragon lines," these currents can have a positive or a negative flow, and it is important to consider these flows before building anything. Ideally, each building project should take into account the surrounding landscape as well as the flows of energy so that harmony could be achieved between earth and sky, wind and water.

Two additional concepts are related to the modern interpretation of ley lines: the vortex and the nexus. A nexus is a point of particular power where a number of ley lines are thought to intersect. Because of the energy thought to flow along ley lines, these points of intersection are believed to contain concentrations of that energy. A vortex is like a whirlpool or storm that spins in the currents of energy flowing through a space. The cause of a vortex is unclear, but, like the nexus, it is a concentrated point of energy. Both of these phenomena are thought to have a profound effect on the energy of a given space. That effect can manifest in a variety of ways, including ghost lights, strange psychic sensations, and physical reactions including headaches and dizziness. Spirits are often drawn to the energy of these environmental phenomena, and so homes that are located on or near them may have legitimate ghosts. However, once the spirits have been removed, you will find that the phenomena continue, or that the home simply attracts more spirits. The real cause of the hauntings, in this case, comes down to the land upon which the home has been built.

Psychics or people who are latent psychics often experience the most profound effects when exposed to the intense energies associated with these anomalies. However, the energy in these locations can

Location, Location, Location!

Ley lines, vortices, and nexuses probably sound like rank pseudoscience, but consider that they may be terms for very ordinary, physical phenomena that we simply do not currently have the capacity to measure. We know that the earth has its own energy, and this energy manifests primarily as geomagnetic force. A whole field of paranormal study, termed "earth mysteries," is devoted to understanding precisely what is going on with location-based anomalies. The fact is that people respond to certain physical locations, often attributing some magical or sacred quality to these sites. The tree where the Virgin of Guadalupe is reputed to have appeared to Juan Diego is the exact same location where people believed that an ancient goddess appeared in pre-Christian times. Many shrines, grottoes, and churches throughout Britain and Europe are built upon the foundations of earlier sacred sites. In some cases, a conscious decision was made to supplant the old religion by usurping these sites, but in other cases, the site itself was simply viewed as special or sacred by everyone who encountered it, regardless of their faith. Consider that there may be some quality to the landscape itself in places like this, either some fluctuation in the native geomagnetic force or unusual sonic resonance that people respond to unconsciously by identifying the site as "sacred."

be potent enough that even ordinary people may be affected. Occasionally, such anomalies attract the presence of spirits, but the anomaly is not a spirit, even though it can be easily confused with a proper haunting.

You are probably dealing with a location-based anomaly if most of these statements are true:

- Nothing related to the haunting responds intelligently to attempts at communication.

- The haunting manifests primarily as strange sensations, odd impressions, or physical symptoms such as headaches or dizziness.

- The haunting is tied to a specific location or locations on the property, and standing in these areas intensifies its effects.

- Nearly everyone exposed to the haunting feels some of its effects, regardless of their level of psychic sensitivity.

High EMF is detectable with proper instruments, and you can show these readings to the family, explaining what they mean. This will not resolve the supposed haunting, of course, but it will explain what is going on. Super-low sound frequencies—found to cause dizziness, nausea, and disorientation in some high-rise buildings—are another purely physical factor that should be tested and ruled out. Other environmental factors, such as carbon monoxide, should also be considered, tested, and ruled out. Low levels of carbon monoxide in a home can produce a range of symptoms including headache, fatigue, dizziness, and confusion—all of which may be mistaken for the effects of a haunting. If the reported haunting includes this range of symptoms, it is critical that you explore the possibility of carbon monoxide poisoning. Carbon monoxide is the leading cause of poisoning deaths in America, and its presence in a home can be deadly. If you have ruled out all of the possible physical causes of the problem and the haunting still adheres to the list outlined above, you are most likely dealing with an energetic anomaly, such as a ley line, nexus, or vortex.

Location-based anomalies are like landmarks. They are a part of the fabric of a place. They cannot be removed like residues or spirits. In all likelihood, the anomaly existed before the house was built, and it was just a matter of bad luck that the house was placed on top of it. If you have been called in to investigate a haunting and you suspect that you are dealing with a location-based anomaly, there is very little you can do to resolve the "haunting" for the family. Although you can certainly educate them about the nature of their problem and teach them how to ground, center, and shield in order to minimize its effects, the anomaly is as permanent as the bedrock beneath the home. If the effects experienced because of the anomaly are extreme enough, the family may even want to consider moving to a new residence. Fortunately, these anomalies are rare, and most of the cases you encounter will involve residues or ghosts. Rather than dwelling on those situations where you cannot offer a great deal of help to your clients, let us consider all the methods you have at your disposal for removing spirits from a home.

First Contact

By far, the simplest method for removing a spirit from a home involves talking to it. When you are dealing with a human ghost (or even multiple human ghosts) in a haunting, this is the first route you should take. It's surprising how many people will endure a haunting without ever attempting to reach out and communicate with the thing that is haunting them. And yet this would solve a great many hauntings. The vast majority of human spirits are simply trying to communicate, and most of their activities are aimed at getting the attention of one or more individuals in residence in order to begin that communication. Human spirits may have a specific motivation for communication. Some have a message they wish to pass on to a living resident. Others have what amounts to a favor to ask of the living. Still others are simply lonely, and they want nothing more than to be recognized and acknowledged by the people living in the home. Ghosts that are lonely and want acknowledgement tend to act out, especially if they feel that there is someone in the house who should be able to hear them, but who is nevertheless ignoring them.

I have seen several cases where human spirits were attracted to a home specifically because they sensed someone there who might be able to respond to them. Hauntings like this are not focused on the home, but on the individual. If individuals like this move, the ghosts are likely to come with them. Even when individuals do not realize they are psychic, the spirits seem to know. It's as if ghosts see the world in black and white, but individuals who are capable of interacting with spirits on their own terms show up in color. Because they stand out, they often act as a beacon for curious, lonely, or mischievous spooks. When someone who (to the spirit) clearly possesses the ability to perceive and respond repeatedly ignores the spirit's attempts at communication, that spirit can become frustrated. A frustrated spirit will often escalate its activities until such time that it gets the attention that it craves. Spirits like this behave much like attention-starved children, pushing every button that they can find until someone responds, even if that response is to yell at them to stop acting out.

If you are not psychic (or if you don't think that you are), how do you talk to a ghost? Most people make the mistake of assuming that only spirit mediums can effectively communicate with spirits, but this is not true. While it often takes a practiced medium to accurately interpret the spirit's side of the conversation, ghosts seem able to hear the living just fine. The simplest way to communicate with a ghost is to speak to it just as you would any living person. If there is a place in the home where the ghost regularly makes its presence known, go to that place and address the spirit. You may feel a little silly at first, since you are essentially talking to empty air, but try to get over any sense of self-consciousness. Speak to the spirit in a genuine and forthright manner. For first contact, follow these steps:

1. Acknowledge the presence of the spirit and let it know that you are open to communication.

2. Don't yell and don't threaten the spirit—at least not yet.

3. Reassure the spirit that it has not been ignored, but explain that there are difficulties in understanding or interpreting its attempts at communication.

4. If clearer communication is desired, let the spirit know that it may have to respond to your questions in a manner that you can perceive, such as knocking, rapping, or affecting the lights.

5. Clearly and gently explain to the spirit the family's response to its activities.

6. Appeal to the spirit as you would a living person to cease any unwanted activities. Clearly state boundaries that the spirit should respect.

7. Extend a desire to help, but explain that the spirit must clearly communicate its needs.

8. Set ground rules for interaction, and explain the consequences of breaking these rules.

9. Do not make idle threats. Be willing to enforce the consequences if the spirit breaks the rules that have been laid out.

The most important part about this first contact is acknowledging the spirit as a real and present being. Sometimes, this acknowledgement is all it takes for the spirit to settle down. It is also important to clarify to the spirit that living people often have a difficult time perceiving or interpreting its attempts to communicate. Nobody likes to be ignored, and if you can explain to the spirit that no one has been intentionally ignoring it, it may become less frustrated and less inclined to act out. You can give the spirit the option of attempting to communicate through means that are not purely psychic in nature. Most often, this involves the spirit manipulating the physical environment through an act of will. When you ask that a spirit produce a physical manifestation in its efforts to communicate, understand that you are asking a lot. Manifestations of this nature take a great deal of energy and concentration on the part of the spirit. Even when a spirit succeeds in making one or two rapping noises in a home, the effort of that response alone may exhaust it to the point where it cannot manage a similar physical manifestation for weeks. Most spirits find it much easier to communicate psychically with the living and oftentimes they are baffled at our inability to respond in kind.

Finally, even if you cannot manage to set up clear lines of communication, you should explain to the spirit that it has been scaring people. Most human ghosts that are simply seeking to connect with the living have no intention of frightening or harming the residents of a home. Appeal to the spirit's humanity. This approach sometimes seems too simple, but if you are dealing with a benign human ghost, laying down a few ground rules about where it can and cannot go in the house and how it should and should not behave can solve most problems. A human spirit that means no harm will respect these boundaries once it has been made aware of the family's desires. This can also work with some benign nonhuman entities. When you know that you are dealing with a human ghost, out of respect for that spirit's lingering humanity, you should always approach it peacefully and politely first. Give it the option to comply. If the spirit continues to act out and the unwanted activities do not cease, then you take the next step.

Talk Therapy for Ghosts

Some human spirits linger in a home for their own reasons. They may seek to communicate with the residents with no ill intent, but the methods of this communication can sometimes be misinterpreted. When a human spirit is benign, often the simplest way of resolving the haunting is to acknowledge the family's awareness of its presence and lay down clear ground rules for its behavior. A well-adjusted spirit will have no trouble complying with these rules and cohabiting peacefully with the living residents of a home. However, not all human ghosts are well-adjusted. For many, the very fact that they still linger close to the physical world is a clear indication of emotional issues. Murder victims, suicides, victims of prolonged abuse, and individuals whose deaths were particularly traumatic often remain until they are able to reconcile themselves with the lingering issues of both their life and their death. Ghosts of this nature are not often pleasant to be around, as they tend to fixate on negative emotions associated with their personal problems. When a spirit of this nature is behind the haunting of a home, the best approach is to try to get that spirit to move on. Rather than presumptuously opening a door to the Great Beyond and kicking the spirit "into the light," a more responsible approach is to give the spirit what it desperately needs: a little therapy.

This method of removing a spirit from a home is founded on gentle, persuasive communication. As with the approach to first contact outlined earlier, you do not need to be a spirit medium to talk to a ghost. Spirits have a clearer sense of us than we do of them, and so all you need to do is address the spirit directly and speak just as you would to any living being. When you're trying to help a spirit deal with its problems, it can be useful to know what those problems are. Do a little research on the house itself, as well as the surrounding area. Check with the local paper and ask permission to view their archives. Speak to any local historians or visit the local library to see whether or not they have a genealogy section. Also learn as much as you can from the family (or previous owners) to see whether or not the spirit is a relative of theirs. The more you know about the spirit involved in the haunting, the better you can tailor your talk therapy to its needs. But even if you do not have solid information about the ghost or its identity, you can still make some general assumptions about its problems if it seems to linger due to unfinished business. Spirits who remain tied to the earthly plane because of emotional issues are often afraid to let go and move past their most recent life. They almost always feel conflicted about some event in their life. They often feel hurt, lonely, or wronged. Some are angry, others are confused. All of them have unresolved issues they feel very strongly about. Address these emotional issues in a general and sympathetic way, all the while encouraging the spirit to let go and move on. Here are some steps to follow if you want to help a spirit move on and leave a residence:

1. Go to a location in the home where the spirit most commonly manifests.

2. Acknowledge the presence of the spirit and let it know that you want to communicate.

3. Establish a sympathetic rapport with the spirit. Let it know that you understand that it is troubled, and that you want to help.

4. Encourage the spirit to be introspective about its problems, reflecting on its hopes and its fears.

5. Acknowledge the importance of the spirit's emotional responses to these problems, but gently and firmly encourage it to let those issues go.

6. Remind the spirit that the life it is obsessing about has come to an end. Be compassionate in your wording and encourage the spirit to approach death as a new beginning rather than an end.

7. Gently and firmly explain to the spirit that the physical world is for the living, and it should not feel tied to its old life.

8. Encourage the spirit to have faith in its own ability to be strong enough and brave enough to move on to the next stage of its existence.

A session like this can get very intense, especially if you are able to connect emotionally with the spirit. Even if you are not strictly psychic and cannot clearly perceive the spirit's words, it is often possible to feel the emotions a human spirit is experiencing, largely because those emotions are so profound. If you are a religious person, you can incorporate some religious wording into your therapy session, but don't overdo it. Unless you are absolutely certain about the identity of the spirit, you have no way of knowing what its own religious convictions were in life. Encouraging a Jewish ghost to trust in Jesus to forgive its sins won't accomplish very much and might even pose a stumbling block in the session. If you choose to employ religious language and symbolism in your session, it is better to be general than specific. Focus on positive things like love, forgiveness, and the possibility that friends and family are waiting somewhere to rejoin the deceased.

Just as with regular therapy, results often do not occur in only one session. You may have to approach a spirit several times before you get results. Allow one or more family members to sit in while you talk with the spirit and attempt to get it to move on. If it seems as if the spirit has not successfully moved on, encourage the residents to speak to the ghost over the course of several weeks, following the same general pattern while stressing sympathy and compassion.

Human spirits often respond to honest and clear attempts at communication. In the case of benign human spirits, setting clear ground rules can resolve most unwanted issues in a haunting. When a human spirit is deeply troubled, communicating with that spirit with the purpose of helping it resolve its problems and move on is another effective method for dealing with the ghost. But, like living humans, some human spirits do not respond well to therapy. Others are either too stubborn or just plain mean. They have no intention of moving on, and when they are actively causing harm, there is little choice but to force them from a home. Nonhuman entities similarly tend to be unresponsive to gentle pleas and compassionate attempts to get them to release their attachments. When you have an uncooperative spirit, whether it is a particularly nasty human ghost or a nonhuman entity, you have to resort to stronger methods. These methods are more challenging, and they should only be attempted by those who are practiced and confident in their use. One of the downsides of taking a more aggressive approach to removing spirits is that the spirits themselves are not likely to be happy about this. They will get angry at you. They will resist your attempts at removal, and some will attempt to retaliate. For this reason, you must be absolutely confident in your ability to protect yourself from these attacks and, if necessary, fight back.

The first option for removing an unwelcome and uncooperative spirit is to sweep the spirit from the home in much the same way you would sweep out stagnant, unwanted energy. This is a variation on techniques covered in chapter three, and it is founded on the notion that spirits themselves are merely energy. This is the least challenging of the more aggressive options, and it is something that anyone can try, so long as they are able to maintain strong boundaries to protect themselves from any attempts the spirit might make to retaliate for getting booted from the house. Here is one variation on the method, outlined in simple steps:

1. Ground, center, and shield.

2. Focus internally on your energy and gather your power. You may also connect to your higher power for assistance.

3. Go to a central location in the home, preferably on the ground floor.

4. Close your eyes and imagine that you are the focal point of a whirling sphere of brilliant force. You may envision this force as light, fire, or even a kind of tidal wave, but be certain to think not only of energy but also of *force*.

5. Focus on this sphere of force and envision it expanding wider and wider. The edges of this sphere are powerful and impenetrable. They push everything out with them, including any spirits left in the home.

6. Vividly imagine the edges of this sphere thundering through the house like a tidal wave of power. Everything is swept before them. Nothing can stand in the way.

7. Envision the sphere of force continuing to expand until it encompasses the whole house, then push it even farther, so the edges expand at least ten feet beyond the house on all sides.

8. Anchor this sphere of force to the ground beneath your feet. You may find it helpful to focus this action with a physical gesture, such as pressing your palm against the floor.

9. Imagine the sphere of force holding everything on the outside. Nothing may re-enter the home. Follow this up immediately by warding the home.

As with shields and wards, you must be confident in your ability to erect boundaries in order for this exercise to be safe and effective. You also need to have a well-developed sense of your personal boundaries, which goes hand in hand with the ability to erect strong psychic barriers. This technique is ideally performed immediately after a full cleansing of the home, although, with practice, you can combine your efforts and use this visualization to clear everything out in one fell swoop.

Keep in mind that this technique makes no distinction between welcome or unwelcome spirits. Instead, like a force of nature, it sweeps everything along in its path. If there are good spirits that are welcome in the home, you may have to invite them back in once you are done. It's also a good idea to give them a little warning before sweeping them out like yesterday's trash.

This technique works best with human ghosts who are not intentionally malevolent, but who are too lost, confused, or emotionally damaged to move on. It is also highly effective in removing those nonhuman entities that behave like animals or vermin. I don't recommend this method for removing nonhuman entities that have behaved with obvious intelligence or malicious intent. An entity that possesses the equivalent of an animal intelligence will move to another location once it's been uprooted from the home. However, intentionally malicious nonhuman entities, or those that have chosen a particular family or location with a specific purpose in mind, will not stay away for long. These require more drastic measures still.

PICKING A FIGHT

As anyone who has investigated a particularly negative haunting knows, spirits can attack the living. Rarely are these attacks physical in nature, although, every once in a while, a spirit attack can be so potent that it leaves marks on a person's flesh. Spirits can, through a concerted force of will, affect things in the physical world. Fortunately for the living, these instances of spirit psychokinesis are rare, and most spooks have to content themselves with psychic attacks. As alarming as it may be to realize that a spirit can have a palpable impact on our health and well-being, most people forget one very pertinent

Spirit Nails

Tibetan Buddhism, as observed elsewhere, has a number of intriguing tools for spirit-work. One of these is a ritual dagger known as a *phurba*. The phurba is essentially a "spirit nail," and it is used in exorcism. From a purely Buddhist perspective, the tool is used in meditation to exorcise a person's inner demons, but the tool grew out of an older tradition wherein the demons were very, very real. The blade is believed to be able to "nail down" spirits, pinning them to the earth so their energy can be harmlessly released into the ground. The blade of the phurba is three-sided, and its handle is a symbolic thunderbolt. When using the phurba for literal exorcism, it can be helpful to think of that handle as an actual bolt of energy slicing down from the heavens to strike the demon or negative spirit. The blade is then thrust into the earth, grounding the energy and driving the spirit down and away. Although the three-sided blade of a phurba is dull and unlikely to cut someone, this spirit dagger is used only on spirits and should never be used actually to strike a living person.

fact: spirits are energy, without a body. But the living are beings of both body and energy. We already have one leg up on the spirits, and even though living individuals tend to overlook their spiritual halves, that aspect is nevertheless a real and integral part of each of us. This comes in handy when we need to meet spirits on their own turf and trade blow for blow.

Before I even address the possibility of attacking a spirit in order to drive it from a home, let me make a few cautionary statements. First of all, I do not recommend this approach for everyone. Some people have a particular knack for these techniques, and that knack often comes with the ability to protect oneself from retaliatory attacks. Individuals who are not confident in their ability to shield and individuals who are not well-versed in energy work would do well to avoid picking a fight with a ghost. Even those individuals who feel confident in their ability to go toe to toe with an entity should choose their battles. Battling spirits is a type of spiritual warfare, and warfare requires strategy. Good strategists know when they are outmatched and should not even attempt a fight. Keep this in mind if you are tempted to consider these techniques. That being said, attacking a spirit is deceptively easy. Like everything else involving energy work, it is all a matter of focus, willpower, and belief. Strong visualization skills are also helpful and will assist with both the focus and the belief.

The first thing to keep in mind is the fact that you are both body and energy. Even though your physical flesh is the most obvious part of your existence, you are still more. Some of us are more consciously aware of this other part of our existence than others, but even those who remain largely unconscious about this spiritual half can still interact on that side of reality. You do not have to be psychic to use these techniques. All you have to do is believe firmly and unshakably that these techniques are possible. There are many different ways to achieve the same goal, but here is a simple approach that will allow you to attack an entity directly and drive it from a home:

1. Ground, center, and shield. Shield aggressively and be prepared to have those shields put to the test.

2. Select a physical item to use as a weapon. This will only be a figurative weapon, as it will serve as a focus for your will. You can choose a cross, a dagger, or any object that has personal meaning for this purpose.

3. Take several moments to prepare yourself, gathering your energy. You can call upon your higher power to strengthen and protect you at this time.

4. Hold the weapon as you focus and vividly imagine power flowing into this object. As energy fills the weapon, envision this energy as something potent and dangerous, like blinding light or fire.

5. When you feel confident in your preparations, seek out the spirit troubling the home.

6. Even if you do not sense the presence of this spirit immediately, close your eyes and envision the spirit. Picture it appearing before you as precisely and clearly as possible. Silently call out to it and will it to appear.

7. Stretch out the arm that holds the weapon and point the weapon at the spirit. In your mind's eye, envision both your arm and the weapon engulfed in brilliant, fiery light.

8. Picture power flowing through you, down your arm, and out of the weapon. It can radiate from the weapon as a wall of force or strike the entity in a single intense beam. The visualization is less important than your intent, and that intent is to do serious harm to the entity.

9. Affirm your intent by stating clearly and forcefully: "I drive you from this house. I cut you. I slash you. I rend you to pieces. Leave this place or be destroyed!" You may also make

this a religious statement, invoking the name of your personal deity.

10. Attack the entity as often as necessary until it flees or appears to be destroyed.

It goes without saying that if you choose an actual weapon as your focus, you should be careful with that weapon. Do not point it at a living person. As you focus on attacking the entity with energy, you may find it helpful to physically strike out with the weapon. In this case, be certain that everyone is out of your way so that no one accidentally gets hurt. Even if the item you have chosen is not a weapon in the strictest sense, be careful not to wave or brandish it toward others. No one appreciates getting whacked in the head with anything solid. If you are using a blade or a dagger, take a few notes from the Tibetans and drive that blade point down toward the floor when you are finished. Obviously, you shouldn't slam the blade into the floorboards, but place the point firmly on the ground in order "nail down" the spirit in the tradition of the phurba.

SOMETIMES THEY COME BACK

Most negative spirits behave like schoolyard bullies. They're all tough around people they don't expect to fight back, but once someone stands up and bloodies them in the nose, they turn tail and run. Spirits that bully the living are used to people who don't know how to fight back, and they are disinclined to target anyone who even looks like they might resist. Oftentimes, simply teaching someone how to shield effectively is enough to get a spirit like this to back off. But, just as with humans, not all bullies are so quick to back down. Although they are rare, there are spirits—mostly nonhuman entities—that will keep coming even after someone has put up a fight. The reasons why they target one person over another may sometimes seem mysterious,

Solomon's Brazen Vessel

The Biblical King Solomon inspired a number of extra-biblical myths. One of the most intriguing of these myths is extrapolated both in Jewish lore and in a document dating to a point between the first and third centuries of the Common Era. This text is presented as having been written by King Solomon himself, although in all likelihood, it is pseudepigraphal, meaning that another author adopted Solomon's name to lend the work more authority and credibility. In the text, King Solomon earns the right to wield power over demons as a result of his great wisdom and piety. God gives him a seal, presumably in the form of a signet ring, that allows him both to summon and bind these spirits. This seal becomes known as the Seal of Solomon. King Solomon binds the first demon in an attempt to save a small boy who has fallen prey to this creature. This demon leads Solomon to the rest, and the text then describes how the Biblical king summoned each of these and put them to work building his temple. To capture one of the demons, Solomon has a bronze vessel prepared. This vessel is scribed with symbols—presumably prayers and names of God, in addition to the Seal of Solomon. When Solomon calls the demon forth, it is compelled to enter the bronze vessel, and then the king shuts the demon up in the vessel, trapping it.

Calling in Professionals

Negative entities—or those entities that can only be labeled demons—are nothing to fool around with. While it is commendable for a team or an individual to want to help a client, it is also necessary to acknowledge when you are in over your head. If a situation becomes too dangerous, frightening, or unpredictable, do not be afraid to seek out a religious authority. Many religions acknowledge the existence of evil or demonic spirits. Exorcism is not exclusive to Catholics but can be found among Hindus, Pagans, Buddhists, and a variety of other faiths. Consequently, priests of many religions are often specially trained in dealing with demonic entities. Even if you cannot convince a priest to come out and specifically perform an exorcism, you may want to consult an ordained member of your client's faith for advice if you are convinced of demonic influence. Many priests, even if they will not specifically perform an exorcism, are willing to come out and bless a home, and this may help everyone involved in a truly negative haunting to feel better.

but they pursue those targets with a singlemindedness that borders on obsession. And that's where binding comes in.

Binding a spirit is a major undertaking, and it is one that should not be considered lightly. The concept is simple: through the use of energy, focused intent, divine assistance, or a combination of all three, a spirit is essentially imprisoned for a lengthy period of time. Typically, some physical object, such as a jar, represents the prison, and seals may be placed upon this jar to further represent the unbreakable nature of the prison. As the Solomonic tradition attests, there is a very ancient belief that a spirit can be bound more effectively by someone who knows its name. A similarly ancient belief suggests that a spirit can be bound by the name of God. In Hellenic magick, the names of a variety of gods are used, perhaps in the hope of covering all the bases should one god prove too weak for the task. Additional systems use the names of angels that are believed to have power over the spirit in question, and still others use sigils—ornate glyphs that depict the names of spirits in symbol. In all of these diverse systems, there is an underlying theme: spirits can be controlled, compelled, and restrained by someone with proper knowledge and skill.

Please don't immediately assume that that someone is you. Picking a fight with a negative entity is a good way to earn that entity's resentment, but attempting to rob a spirit of its freedom will make you an enemy for life—and then some. Nonhuman entities are not mortal in the sense that we understand the term. They have the luxury of time on their side, and it is my belief that they can find us in subsequent incarnations if they bear a strong enough grudge. Many of the traditions that describe the binding of spirits, the Solomonic tradition included, present those bindings as eternal and unbreakable, but it is also my opinion, learned from repeated experience, that nothing is forever, with the exception of the soul itself. What this means in terms of binding is that you might be able to put a spirit away for a very long time, but eventually it will get out. If you happen to still be around at that time, be aware that there is a very strong likelihood that the spirit will hunt you down and attempt to seek revenge. A sentient entity that is truly malevolent and has already proven itself potent and singleminded in one haunting is not likely to have a sudden change of heart just because you gave it an extended time-out. Every once in a while, a binding may be just the thing a spirit needs to reconsider its actions—but don't hold your breath.

I don't want to sound dire here, but I do want to stress the fact that this method should be undertaken only as a last resort. Binding should only be used for truly negative entities and only after they have proven that they are dangerous and not likely to stop causing trouble any time soon. All of those qualifiers should also tell you that, should you decide to bind something of this nature, you should be absolutely confident that you are up to the task. You should be adept at shielding yourself and others and you should be practiced at fighting back should a spirit attack. I should also observe that you do not have to be a magician, a priest, or even a psychic to effectively bind a spirit. As we will see in the next chapter, you need neither fancy training nor fancy tools. All you need is the ability to direct your will and focus your intent, and faith that this action will bring results.

The following steps describe a fairly simple method of binding that does not require the name of the spirit, a sigil, or anything more than focused intent. The physical objects as well as the physical actions involved are meant only to help you focus. All of the power comes from within:

1. Ground, center, and shield. Shield effectively and aggressively.

2. Find a suitable vessel to bind the spirit in. I prefer earthenware jars, but anything will do. In certain areas, they sell little blown-glass orbs called "witch's balls" that are believed to effectively trap spirits. Something like this will also do.

3. Close your eyes, focus inward, and gather power. You may also reach out to your higher power and ask for strength and inspiration.

4. Hold the vessel in your hands as you gather power. As you do, vividly imagine energy flowing down your arms to fill the vessel. The energy infuses the physical walls of the vessel, weaving around and around, until those walls are as real in the realm of spirits as they are in the realm of flesh.

5. Set aside some ribbon and sealing wax. Ordinary wax will do in a pinch. Keep these near at hand when you confront the spirit.

6. Seek out the spirit. You can go to the place where the spirit most typically manifests, or you can clearly envision the spirit coming to you, as described in the fighting exercise. Call the spirit by name if you are fortunate enough to know it.

7. Confront the spirit and be prepared for a fight. Instead of slashing the spirit with a weapon, vividly imagine chains of energy extending from your hands and wrapping around and around the spirit. You may want to seek help from your higher power if you have any doubt about your ability to seize and hold the spirit.

8. Vividly imagine these chains of energy ensnaring the spirit and pulling it into the vessel that you prepared ahead of time.

9. Affirm your intent to bind the spirit by saying clearly and forcefully: "With will and intent, I bind you. With power and faith, I bind you. Into this vessel, I bind you, so you may not go free." You can also invoke your higher power and frame this binding as a prayer. Once again, use its name if you know it.

10. Hold the vessel between your hands and continue to concentrate on the bands of force. Picture these wrapping around and around the vessel, further trapping the spirit within. Place the lid on the vessel.

11. Wrap the ribbon around the vessel, strapping down the lid. Tie the ribbon firmly in place. As you do so, imagine that you are wrapping powerful chains of force around the vessel. If you have enough ribbon, wrap the vessel completely around several times. If not, you may wish to make a wrapping gesture several times anyway, continuing to imagine those chains of force.

12. Once you are satisfied with the integrity of the vessel, place a seal of wax over the lid. If you have actual sealing wax, you may also want to press a symbol of protection, such as a cross, into the wax.

13. You may say a prayer over the vessel, affirming the binding, or you can repeat the affirmation from step 9.

Once you have bound a spirit into the vessel, what do you do? You can either keep the vessel somewhere safe, where you can watch over it and make certain that the binding does not fail, or you can bury the vessel somewhere deep in the earth. The earth is grounding, and it will further trap the entity. The deeper you bury it, the greater a chance you have that the earth itself will trap the entity even if the binding on the vessel gives way. Another option is to weight the vessel down (if it is not already weighty enough) and drop it down a well or in the middle of a deep body of water. Water has different energetic properties than earth, but if the vessel sinks all the way to the bottom, the water, like the earth, will assist in trapping the entity you have bound.

If you are religious, you may consider burying the vessel on consecrated ground, such as a churchyard. Be sure you have permission to do this first. If you choose to keep the vessel around, be certain that it is placed in a location where no one will accidentally open it or break the seal. Keep in mind that even the most potent energy degrades over time, and so you will have to periodically renew the binding in order to be absolutely certain that your unwilling prisoner doesn't break out.

THE LEAST YOU SHOULD KNOW

The first step to resolving a haunting is to accurately identify the cause of that haunting. There are three broad categories of spirits that may be responsible for hauntings. The most familiar of these are human ghosts. The restless dead tend to linger due to unfinished business, which often includes unresolved emotional issues and other attachments that bind them to the memory of their former lives. Some human spirits remain near the living intentionally and should not be considered technically "earthbound." These spirits have decided to stay and serve as helpers or guardians, often for loved ones whom they left too soon. The other two categories involve things that are not human. Residual hauntings are echoes of powerful emotions or traumatic events imprinted upon the energy of a specific location. Although residual hauntings are neither sentient nor human, they are often the products of humans—either living or dead. The final category involves spirits that were never human to begin with. These nonhuman entities can range from spirit beings with the equivalent intelligence of an animal to highly intelligent entities that follow inscrutable agendas of their own. Although not a category of spirit, location-based anomalies should also be considered when assessing a haunting. These phenomena are generally tied to the landscape itself and cannot be resolved using any of the methods outlined for dealing with spirits.

Residual hauntings can be cleared using essentially the same techniques that one would employ to clear any build-up of unwanted energy. When the spirit responsible for a haunting turns out to be human, the best approach is to attempt communication. Although spirit mediums have a more finely tuned ability to perceive and interpret the messages of spirits themselves, anyone can talk to a ghost by simply addressing it like a living being. It is important to keep in mind the essential humanity of a human spirit, and to accord that spirit all the courtesy and respect that one would hold for any stranger encountered on the street. Many human spirits cause disruptive hauntings only because they seek attention, and often these hauntings can be resolved simply by acknowledging the presence of the ghost. Other human spirits have deeper issues that require what amounts to a talk therapy session. Several of these sessions may be necessary to help the spirit to resolve its issues and move on.

Although it has been widely popularized in television and movies, the technique of sending spirits into the light is not recommended. When human spirits linger by their own choice, it is presumptuous to second guess that choice and seek to take away the spirits' free will. When a human spirit lingers due to unresolved issues, attempts to send them into the light may cause them to make the transition to the next state of existence prematurely. It is better and more respectful to help the spirits resolve the issues on their own than to judge them or force them to move on against their will.

Some human spirits are too damaged, stubborn, or malicious to respond to compassionate communication. Although it is still not acceptable to force these to move on, the individuals being haunted by such spirits have rights as well. Living people have the right to a peaceful residence where they can live without fear of harmful or threatening entities. When human spirits cross the line of acceptable behavior in a haunting, they can be removed forcibly from the residence. The first and least aggressive method of removal is to simply push the offending spirits out of the residence along with any unwanted energy. As spirits are comprised wholly of energy themselves, any techniques that clear unwanted energy from a home can also be applied to clear unwanted spirits. This technique is also recommended for removing nonhuman entities that demonstrate an animal level of intelligence or lower. Entities of this nature are highly likely to wander somewhere else once they have been removed from a residence.

More aggressive and malicious nonhuman entities, as well as some exceptionally unsavory human spirits, may have to be dealt with in a more severe fashion. Individuals who are confident in their abilities to shield and work with energy can attempt to lash out and attack spirits in an attempt to drive them from a space. It helps for the individual to have some capacity to sense the location of the spirit, and some method for sensing that the spirit has indeed left the premises. In truly extreme cases, spirits can be bound. This method essentially imprisons the spirit in an object or vessel where it can do no harm. Although simple in theory, this is nevertheless a demanding technique, and it is fraught with a number of potential complications—not the least of which is the bitter enmity of the imprisoned spirit. Binding, when it is used at all, should be reserved only for the most vicious and irredeemable entities and even then, only by individuals confident in their ability to safely complete the task.

Most families call paranormal investigators into a home not only to verify a haunting, but also to resolve the issues caused by that haunting. A haunting can be considered resolved if:

- The residual energy responsible for the haunting has been completely cleared.

- Where the problem is environmental, the family has been educated about its cause and trained in any possible techniques for alleviating their reactions.

- The family has agreed to cohabit peacefully with a spirit that is discovered to be harmless.

- A restless spirit has resolved enough issues that it has either moved on or is no longer acting out in a manner that the family finds alarming.

- A nonhuman entity has been removed from the residence and measures have been taken so it does not return.

In all of these instances, the general energy of the home should be cleared in addition to the removal of any unwanted spirits. The home should be warded and the residents should be instructed in how to maintain healthy boundaries individually and for their home as a whole. These final methods ensure that additional spirits will be dissuaded from invading the home once you have left the scene.

eight

IRVING TAKES CONTROL

Y ou know," Irving said, "I don't think I want you to attack them. I mean, what if that just pisses them off and they decide to take it out on me?"

We were walking around the exterior of Irving's house, and I was talking him through a warding exercise. Julie and I had done a second, more aggressive clearing with Irving in tow just a little while before, pushing the entities that had plagued the poor man even farther away from the home. I had stopped short of attacking the entities, but because there was still a very dim sense of them hovering somewhere in the distance, I had left the option open, letting Irving decide.

"Well," I responded, "The first thing you should keep in mind is that you are no longer a victim. Before, they could take advantage of you because you didn't know how to protect yourself. But now you know how to ground and center, how to shield, and how to set up boundaries around your home. You're no longer easy pickings."

"You still really need to try cleaning the inside of your house," Julie pointed out. "There's a reason these spirits picked you. You're sensitive, just like me, so you can see and respond to them. But the inside of that house just makes things worse. Stuff gets trapped in there. I have to wonder whether or not a couple of the things we kicked out didn't find their way in by accident and then got lost."

"Really?" Irving asked, looking to me.

"The state of the house didn't help, and I think all that stagnant and trapped energy was affecting your health and probably everyone else living there as well," I replied. "But Julie's right about the spirits being attracted mainly to you. Most spirits want attention of one kind or another. The more attention you give them, the more you encourage them to pester you. Think of them like stray cats. You put food out for one, and suddenly every cat for miles is mewling at your door, wanting a handout. Paying attention to the spirits that wander past here is just like feeding stray cats. You need to ignore them, even when you do sense them nearby."

"Ignore them and they'll go away," Irving said, intoning the words like they were his new personal mantra.

"That's part of it, but you also need to stop fixating on them," I cautioned. "Don't worry about whether or not they're out there. Don't obsess over every strange feeling you get. Don't wonder whether or not every little sound you hear in the house is really the spirits creeping back in to attack you. Work on your boundaries and focus on positive things in your life. Focus on your music. Do things that make you feel happy, safe, and secure. Even if something scary does happen, like you have a bad dream where the spirits return, try not to give in to your fear. Be firm in the fact that you are no longer a victim and that you no longer have room in your life for these entities."

"And I should set up these wards about once a month from now on?" he inquired.

"Yes, and keep practicing how to shield. Change the space you live in by cleaning it out. Change your attitudes so you don't feel helpless anymore. All of this will go a long way to keep these entities from coming back and preying upon you."

"Thank you!" Irving declared. Quite unexpectedly, he gave me a hug. Throughout our entire investigation, he had carried himself like someone with an aversion to physical touch, but this was a heartfelt and sincere embrace. To me, it spoke of his growing confidence and his newfound ability to feel comfortable in his own skin. When he was done with me, he threw his arms around Julie as well, practically bowling her over. Laughing, she adjusted her glasses, which had been knocked slightly askew upon her nose. Warmly, she hugged him back.

"Feel free to call me if you need anything," I told him. "Even if you just want to talk."

"I will. Thank you!" he said again.

Julie and I packed up and headed out. Irving stood in the driveway, waving with one hand and clutching my business card like a talisman in the other. Once we had gone a little ways down the road, Julie asked, "That house. I mean, the clutter, the dying grandmother—do you really think we made any difference in the long run?"

"I think we made a difference for Irving," I said. "You saw him when we first showed up. Was that the same guy, standing in the driveway and smiling at us as we drove away?"

Julie considered this. "No, I guess not. He seemed a lot more open and relaxed."

"Well, even if all we did was give him the confidence to fight back, I think we accomplished something of value today," I asserted. "Hand me those directions, will you? I'm not sure about the next few turns to the highway."

Julie shuffled through a stack of papers that I kept wedged under the armrest.

"It should be the one on top," I offered, trying to keep my eyes on the road.

"I don't know how you keep anything straight here," she grumbled. "Have I pointed out recently that your organizational skills could use some work?"

"It's the artistic temperament. Blame my mother. I inherited it from her," I replied. "Did you find them yet?"

Julie sighed, still shuffling. "All I see are the directions that we followed getting out here."

"Yep, those are what I want. I just go backwards through the steps."

I felt more than I saw Julie roll her eyes at me. "You get lost a lot, don't you?" she teased, handing over the hastily scrawled paper.

I laughed. "Sometimes I end up taking the scenic route," I admitted. "But I always get where I'm going in the end!"

After we had successfully gotten onto the highway (my severe lack of direction notwithstanding), Julie returned to the subject of Irving and his haunted house.

"I still don't like the fact that those creepy shadow things didn't seem gone, so much as they just felt distant," she observed, frowning. "Boundaries are all well and good, but it still seemed like they were just waiting for the right opportunity to return."

"I don't know," I responded. "I think Irving will surprise you."

As it turned out, Irving surprised both of us.

Several weeks later, I received a phone call. It was Irving. At first, I couldn't tell if he was excited or terrified, he was talking so fast.

"Slow down," I said. "Are you okay? What's going on?"

On the other end of the phone, I heard him take a deep breath, then slowly release it.

"Irving?"

"I caught it!" he proclaimed. "It came back for me but I caught it. Could you come up here, just to see if I did it right? I don't want it getting out."

Perplexed, I asked, "You caught what, Irving?"

"One of the shadow men. They went away and I practiced my boundaries and my shields just like you said, but the other night, one of them came back. So I found a jar and did that binding thing, and it worked. I caught it. I put it outside by the stump."

"You bound the spirit?" I asked, not really believing it. "Are you sure?"

"That's why I want you to come out here. Please?" he asked. "Take a look at the jar and tell me if I did it right. I know I probably shouldn't have tried it, but I wanted to take care of things on my own."

"Um, sure, Irving. I can be there in a couple of hours."

I hung up, then called Julie.

"Want to go on a little road trip again?" I asked.

"Where to?" she replied. She sounded kind of sleepy, like she was napping, and my call woke her up. Naps in the afternoon. Some days I missed being a college student.

"Back to Irving's place," I said. "He says he thinks he trapped one of the shadow men in a jar."

"He did what?" Julie demanded, achieving wakefulness immediately.

"I'm not sure what to think of it myself," I said. "He wants us to check his work."

"You can't possibly think he managed to bind anything," she responded. "I mean, he was a wonderful guy and everything, but a month ago, he didn't even know what a shield was."

"Well, let's go see. Are you up for it?"

"Let me get ready," she said. "I was taking a nap."

"I could tell," I laughed. "I'll swing by on my way up there. Maybe in an hour or so?"

"Sounds good."

Just in case things had gotten bad again at Irving's place, I collected my tingshas, dorje, and other tools. Then I printed out directions again because, by then, I'd already lost the previous set. On the ride out to the farmhouse, Julie and I bantered back and forth, speculating about what was waiting for us in Irving's jar. Both of us were skeptical about the fact that Irving had actually succeeded in binding anything, although I allowed for the possibility that he'd managed to do *something*. Julie, who had spent years studying the Solomonic art, was less charitable. She simply refused to accept it.

When we got there, Irving was waiting at the top of the driveway. This was a very different person from the worn and haggard man we had helped out only a few weeks before. For one, Irving was smiling, and it was a smile that reached all the way to his eyes. His hair was neatly combed and the dark circles around his eyes had begun to fade. In addition to the obvious physical changes, there was a distinct difference in his energy as well. He seemed more animated, more confident, and more present in the world.

"Wow, you're looking good, Irving," I said, getting out of the car.

Behind him, I could see a pile of boxes and trash bags stacked up near the side of the house. Julie spied it at about the same time I did.

"You've been cleaning?" she asked.

Irving shrugged modestly. "A little at a time," he said.

"Slowly but surely gets the job done," I reminded. "So what about this jar you've got?"

Irving's smile broadened, his eyes sparkling with pride. Making a gesture for us to follow, he turned and headed toward the stump in front of the house. Hunkering down, he pulled a cardboard box from among some weeds next to the stump. Triumphantly, he held the box out for our inspection. I recognized it as one of the many boxes that had once cluttered the inside of the house. The flaps of the box had been taped shut.

"Can I open the box?" I asked.

"I think so," Irving said. "There's a coffee can in there that you can open, too, if you want." Suddenly sheepish, he said, "I bound it in a peanut butter jar. It's the best thing I could find at the time."

Julie and I exchanged glances. Suddenly very unsure of what I might find, I set the box down on the stump and opened it up. Sure enough, there was a coffee can resting on its side at the bottom of the box. There was also a sense of pressure that I could sense almost as soon as I opened the box.

"Do you feel that?" Julie whispered, leaning over my shoulder to peer inside.

"I sure do. Curiouser and curiouser," I muttered, mostly to myself.

Standing there in the high grass that sprouted around the stump, the golden light of the afternoon slanting down around us, Julie and I both reached for the coffee can at once. As soon as our hands closed around it, that sense of something—a weight or a presence—grew stronger. I could tell that Julie felt it as intensely as I did, because her eyes flew up to meet mine at the same time that I stared over at her. Suddenly, the afternoon seemed dimmer, even though no clouds had obscured the sun.

"Whoa," Julie whispered.

"Open the coffee can?" I asked.

For a moment, Julie hesitated, then she nodded.

I peeled back the yellow plastic lid. Inside, the jar rattled hollowly against the sides of the coffee can. I reached in and grabbed the jar. As soon as I did, I heard something like a buzzing in my head. The same phantom buzzing vibrated up my wrist as I grasped the peanut butter jar. It felt for all the world like an angry swarm of invisible insects was trapped inside. I held the jar up to the light. It was hard to see inside, primarily because Irving had wrapped duct tape around the jar so many times that only little slivers of the clear plastic jar itself were visible. Peering in between the duct tape, I could tell that the jar was empty of anything physical, and yet that emptiness looked cloudy somehow, like the air had clotted together on the inside. No matter how many different ways I held the jar up to the light, that cloying shadow remained. It was clumped in the middle of the jar, an amorphous, dark thing that was not physically there and yet was also undeniably present in the jar. From the buzzing, it was clear that it was not happy about being there.

"Um, wow," Julie said as I passed the jar over to her. She went through nearly the exact same set of steps that I had, holding the jar this way and that, lifting it to the sun and peering through to the impossibly cloudy center.

"Did I do it right?" Irving asked. "I can see it there, like a shadow. And it's pissed. I don't want it getting back out again."

Still stunned by what I was sensing, I took the jar from Julie and poked it some more. Belatedly, I noticed that Irving had scribed a cross in what looked like permanent marker on the duct tape that crisscrossed the lid.

"I don't know what to say," I admitted.

Julie was equally taken aback. "Solomon's brazen vessel," she said, almost in awe. "He made Solomon's brazen vessel with duct tape and a peanut butter jar."

"It would appear he did," I responded. Turning to Irving, I said, "I don't think that thing is getting out any time soon."

"What should I do with it?" Irving asked.

Noting the shovel that leaned up against the stump, I said, "You were thinking about burying it?"

He nodded.

I put the peanut butter jar back into the coffee can. I couldn't help but suppress a delighted laugh when, as I sealed the lid of the coffee can, the sound of buzzing insects that I did not hear with my physical ears suddenly became muffled. Irving had written on the plastic lid of the coffee can, probably with the same marker. I didn't read the words. The words didn't really matter. Irving had MacGuyvered a spirit-jar with little more than raw intent. And duct tape. I guess the bumper stickers were right—it really does hold the universe together.

I looked down at the cardboard box as I held the coffee can. "Maybe a shoe box, instead. Something a little more durable," I suggested. "This thing's too big and the cardboard will just fall apart the minute it gets wet. I approve of the set of three vessels to bind it, though. It seems appropriate, somehow."

"I did good, then?" Irving asked.

"I think you did fantastic."

A wise man once said, if you have faith the size of a mustard seed, you can move mountains. He wasn't kidding.

nine

AN END, AND A BEGINNING

When I first started putting this book together, I knew that I wanted to tell Irving's story because that investigation, more than any other before it, really proved to me how the victim can become the victor with just a little guidance and support. Irving not only took everything he learned during our investigation to heart, but he also innovated on it once we were gone. He is the perfect example of what can be accomplished with a little faith, belief, and intent. But now that his story has been told, and a number of lessons have been learned along the way, we find ourselves nearing the end of this volume.

I personally find it hard to end a book. There's always more stories to be told, another exercise I could probably squeeze in. Of course, if I tried to cram every possible bit of information on this subject into one book, it would probably be thousands of pages long. I don't really want to write anything that long, and I'm fairly certain that no one would want to read it. But it's important to note: there is always more. Every exercise outlined here has countless variations. As such, you should approach all of the exercises as guidelines only. I've described the techniques that work best for me, but all of us have different symbols and beliefs that inspire us. Try the techniques as they are written to familiarize yourself with their underlying concepts. Practice them so you can get a solid handle on those concepts. Then experiment and innovate and make them your own. Tailor them to your unique and personal style, because all of these techniques have their power in you, not in the exact wording or symbols.

I've tried to explore a number of different traditions and belief systems throughout this book, especially in the "Beyond Belief" sections, expressly so you can play around with a number of variations. Since the dawn of time, humanity has developed methods for dealing with spirits. From exorcism to shamanism, from Tibetan ritual tools to the folk magick of hoodoo, there is a wide variety of symbols, styles, and approaches that may or may not appeal to you. The real work, after reading this book through once, is to learn more about the traditions that did reach out and grab you. And if nothing here seemed to speak to you on a profoundly personal level, you should embark on the wonderful journey of developing a system all your own.

Before I leave you to explore your newfound skills, there are a few topics I want to address. The first has to do with developing sensitivity to the world of spirits. I suspect that some readers have waded through these chapters with a vague feeling of frustration, worrying all the time that they are not psychic enough to accomplish the techniques as described. I think such readers are simply laboring under a false belief, because everyone is psychic to one degree or another. Sometimes, I think we should do away with the term "psychic" entirely, simply because it conveys a sense that these abilities are special, like some gift bestowed upon only a privileged few. In my experience, there are some people who have a keener sense of the otherworldly, but they're no different from people who happen to have 20/20 vision or exceptionally acute hearing. If I took off my glasses right now, I wouldn't be able to read the text in front of me, but that doesn't make me inferior to someone with better vision. Psychics like myself simply have more intense impressions, which make it harder to deny those impressions or to rationalize them away. It doesn't mean that folks with less intense impressions are inferior. It doesn't even mean that those impressions aren't there. But, when one sense is weaker than another, it is very natural for people to begin to rely on their stronger senses. If your psychic impressions happen to be weak, that doesn't mean they don't exist. Chances are, you respond to them anyway. You simply do so in such an instinctive and automatic fashion that you never even question where that particular bit of information is coming from.

While they don't make corrective lenses for the third eye (at least not yet), there are some things you can do to help hone and develop your own sixth sense. Read on!

BUILDING SENSITIVITY

The first step to honing your psychic perceptions is to start paying attention. As I said in the previous section, you almost certainly have had psychic impressions. However, you have probably also responded to these in such a natural and automatic fashion that you never recognized them as "psychic" in the first place. Once you learn how to recognize these impressions for what they are, you can begin to tune into these senses more consciously, taking control of your psychic side. Here are some tips to help you start to recognize your daily psychic experiences:

- When you first walk into a building, such as a shop or a home, pay attention to all the impressions that you get. How does this place make you feel? Does it remind you of something? Do you experience any physical sensation upon first walking into this space? Perhaps a song suddenly leaps to mind. Maybe you experience a brief flash of emotion, or a similarly brief series of images that play through your mind. Stop and ask yourself what these could be telling you. Then, stop and ask yourself where this information is coming from. If you can't pin down a physical cause for these impressions, it's very likely that you are responding psychically to the energy of the space.

- When you meet someone for the first time, pay attention to any sensations or impressions you experience that do not seem to have a rational physical cause. Analyze these impressions. What do they tell you about the person? After you've parted ways, it may help to write down these initial impressions. As you get to know the person better, how accurate were your impressions? Can you identify any physical sense that telegraphed this information to you? If you can't, try to remember how those impressions manifested. If you can identify how your psychic impressions speak specifically to you, you will have a better chance of recognizing them in the future.

- In your daily interactions with others, pay attention to your shifts in mood. Do you suddenly experience a certain emotion or set of emotions when you interact with a specific person? Is there a logical reason that this person should inspire these emotions in you? If these emotions seem strange or foreign to you, yet you experience shades of them each time you interact with this person, consider that the emotions could be coming from them, not from you. You can test this by making a conscious effort to close yourself off the next time you interact with the person. Shield yourself from them, just as you learned in chapter two. If the foreign emotions fade or go away entirely, there's a strong chance that what you were experiencing is empathy. This is the psychic perception of other peoples' emotions. Once you identify the experience, you can recognize it in future.

All of these are very simple exercises based on self-analysis. The goal is to pay attention to all of your sensory input and try to track down the nuggets of information that come from a source that is other than your five physical senses. If you can isolate these experiences and recognize them for what they are, you will have a better chance of identifying your psychic impressions in the future. The more you tune in to these senses, the more open you will become to their input.

There are many additional methods for honing your psychic impressions. Some of these can even be fun. My mother used to make a game of psychic development with me. We used a deck of cards. In later years, I learned that what we were doing with a plain playing deck was a variation on experiments run by the Rhine Institute with a special deck called Zenner cards. Zenner cards have five very simple figures on them, each in a different color. Although you can buy or even make your own set of Zenner cards, I feel that my mom's method works just as well. Here's how you play:

1. Get a plain deck of playing cards. Shuffle the deck thoroughly.

2. If you have a partner to play with, have them sit across from you and select one card at a time. Your partner should look at the card but hold it in a way that you cannot see the face of the card. If you are playing alone, you should just pick the first card off the top of the deck and hold it up with its back to you.

3. Concentrate on the card and try to determine whether it is a black card or a red card.

4. Write down your impression, then turn the card over to check your results. If you are playing with a partner, you can alternately have them keep score, writing down in a column from one through fifty-two what each card was.

5. Once you have gone through the whole deck, tally your results. By the law of averages, you will probably get at least twenty-five cards right. If your tally is significantly higher or significantly lower than this, it may be an indication of psychic ability.

6. Play the game several times in a row, comparing your results each time. If you are feeling really confident in your abilities, try to determine the suit in addition to the color of each card.

It's ideal to play this with a partner, because it's generally easier to pick up impressions from another person rather than an inanimate object. That's why your partner should look at each card that is drawn and really concentrate on that card. The idea is for the partner to telepathically send you the details of the card. Drawing the cards by yourself involves a very different set of psychic abilities. It is interesting to note that some people do markedly better with a partner to actively send images of the cards. If you are afraid that your partner is somehow sending you unconscious physical cues about the nature of the cards, consider sitting in different rooms, or back to back so you cannot see one another.

You may have raised an eyebrow when you read that getting a significant number of cards wrong indicates psychic ability as much as getting a significant number right. In the Rhine Institute trials, they found that people who did not believe in psychic abilities sometimes nevertheless demonstrated some level of psychic awareness. Typically, this manifested as a marked propensity to guess the cards wrong, well beyond what the law of averages suggested that they should have guessed wrong. The sheer number of wrong guesses seemed to suggest that these anti-psychics had some sense of what was really on the card, but they were so determined to prove that psychic abilities did not exist that they consistently gave wrong answers. This phenomena does not have to be limited to people who disbelieve in psychic phenomena. Performance anxiety can also play a role in encouraging people to doubt or second guess their accurate impressions. If you tally your results and discover that you are skewed in the direction of incorrect answers, try to think back to your impressions of each card. What was your absolute first impression? And why did you give the answer that you did? You may find that you were getting very accurate impressions of the cards, but because these impressions came so easily, you doubted them and gave a difference response. A lot of people expect psychic perceptions to take a huge effort or to manifest with all kinds of Hollywood-style bells and whistles, but that's not the case. Psychic impressions often manifest so quickly and naturally that they can be easy to overlook or second guess. Keep that in mind the next time you get a sudden flash of insight and find yourself thinking, "Nah, that couldn't be . . ."

If you are interested in exploring other exercises for psychic development, the card game outlined above appears in one of my other books, *The Psychic Energy Codex*, along with a wide variety of additional exercises. That book is specifically written as a manual of psychic development, and it also offers tips on how to start a study group so everyone can work on honing and testing their talents together.

YOUR ENERGETIC TYPE

I believe that everyone has psychic ability, and thus everyone can not only sense energy but work with it to one degree or another. However, not all abilities are created equal. Anyone can pick up a pencil and draw a human figure. For some of us, the drawing that results will only be a stick figure. Others have enough artistic talent to produce an image of astounding realism and beauty. We recognize talent when it manifests in connection with our other senses. Some musicians have perfect pitch. Many artists have an eye for shade and color that baffles the rest of us. Senses, and the abilities tied to them, differ in their intensity, degree, and application.

Psychic senses are no different. I believe that most psychic perceptions boil down to an ability to sense energy, and I have observed that there are three basic energetic types that influence not only the nature of peoples' perceptions but also the talents they tend to possess when it comes to working with energy. I feel that these energetic types are based on how a person naturally interacts with energy on a fundamental and instinctive level. The energetic type is not a limitation, as people can learn to grow beyond the boundaries that it sets, but it represents a kind of psychic default that becomes important when someone is first learning how to harness their abilities.

These energetic types are a lot like personality types, because there are other qualities in addition to energetic ability and sensitivity that go along with them. Like personality types, they paint broad and generalized pictures of people, and there are exceptions to every rule. Some people do not fall neatly into one category, although you will find that nearly everyone has a preferential type. Identifying this energetic type can help also to identify a person's natural strengths and weaknesses when working with energy. This is the real reason why these energetic types are important. If you can determine which type fits you best, it can help you better understand how your own energy works—and how best to work with that energy.

The Connecting Type

Connecting types have energy that does just that: it connects to everyone and everything around them. These people like to reach out to others, and touch can be very important to them. They find that just about any day can be improved by a hug, and every activity is improved with the presence of friends. Outgoing and gregarious by nature, their energy is also open, sometimes to the point of vulnerability. They are highly sensitive to the energy in the world around them, especially emotional energy. These people are not only sympathetic to the emotions of others, but they respond psychically to those emotions as well. This can sometimes lead connecting types to be overwhelmed by the emotions of others, even as they are driven to be around other people. One of the first steps connecting types need to take in controlling this is to learn which emotions come from them and which emotions are coming from the world around them. Since it is their nature to connect, they do not always have very firm personal boundaries, so this can be a challenge. Sensations of any sort tend to be very immediate for connecting types, and they often react impulsively to whatever they feel without much reflection about why they feel these things or where certain impressions may be coming from.

In a negative haunting, a connecting type is almost always the first to be overwhelmed. A haunting does not even have to be overtly negative in order to push these people to their limits, for they feel and respond intensely to everything they pick up. The challenge for a connecting type is to learn how to tone down their impressions. Since it is in their nature to connect to everything around them and to feel these connections deeply, they are often indiscriminate in what they allow to affect them. Connecting types are like strings on a musical instrument that are tuned too finely—every sound causes them to vibrate, even if they themselves remain unplucked. Shielding typically makes connecting types feel closed off, disoriented, or claustrophobic since so much of their experience of the world hinges on their sense of connection. However, in order to cope with life, connecting types should at least learn how to filter, and they should try to stay grounded—even though this, also, does not come naturally to them. They can be great assets to a team because of their sensitivity, but when that sensitivity goes uncontrolled, they can also be distracting. They will flit from perception to perception, feeling everything too deeply, and they may not always be able to make sense of all of the information constantly flowing in. Spirits love connecting types because they are so free with their energy—intentionally and otherwise. Connecting types can use this willingly to reach out to spirits and offer up some of their abundant energy to help the spirits manifest. The downside to this is that negative entities, sensing this abundant energy, may seek to take it unwillingly. Connecting types are the most common of the three types to develop parasitic attachments because of their combination of abundant energy and weak personal boundaries.

The Protecting Type

Protecting types are the polar opposites of connecting types. Where connecting types have very few boundaries, always reaching out both physically and energetically, protecting types are all about boundaries. They have plenty of energy, but they tend to keep it to themselves. They do not generally like touching or being touched, unless they are 100 percent comfortable with the people doing the touching. Even then, protecting types sometimes feel as if they have perpetual barriers in place, and they often have a kind of mental "inner sanctum" where they keep their most vulnerable aspects walled away from the world. Protecting types may not always be big and strong in a physical sense, yet they often carry themselves in such a way that most still get this impression. They also tend to be very practical individuals, grounded in a mental sense as well as an energetic sense. They are those rock-solid, dependable people others naturally look to for support.

Many protecting types are so naturally grounded and shielded that they never even realize that they are psychically sensitive. They have so many efficient barriers in place that even the most negative hauntings leave them unfazed. Where a connecting type has long ago collapsed due to overwhelming energy, a protecting type may stand there, puzzled about all the fuss. This leads a lot of protecting types to become skeptics, because they very rarely share the impressions and experiences that others claim to have. Again, this is not because they lack sensitivity, but because they have such naturally powerful shields that it takes an amazing amount of energy for something to get through. Even if a spirit directly attacks a protecting type, the impression of this attack may feel muffled or dim. It's certainly not enough to make the protecting type feel nauseated or dizzy, and it may be subtle enough that the protecting type can simply rationalize the experience away. These powerful barriers can also intimidate spirits, especially entities that prefer to play the bully. Bullies like easy targets, such as connecting types, and protecting types are anything but. Although it can frustrate a protecting type who is honestly seeking a paranormal experience, many spirits will not even bother trying to get through those rock-solid shields.

Protecting types face a set of challenges connected with their natural shields. First of all, they are most comfortable when they are shielded, and it goes against the grain of their nature to open themselves up enough to truly connect. Dropping their barriers and opening up can make protecting types feel exposed and vulnerable. When they can even manage this, they are not at their best: they often feel self-conscious, anxious, and uncertain. Despite this, protecting types should learn how to tone down their potent barriers, and the first step toward this is first to realize that those barriers exist. It is entirely possible for protecting types to sense and work with energy and in fact, they are quite good at it. But they can be hindered by the expectation that their perceptions should be as powerful and obvious as the perceptions of others. For protecting types, this generally is not the case. Instead, they need to learn to listen for very quiet and subtle cues. They almost always have good instincts, and easily half of those instincts are influenced by psychic impressions. If protecting types can learn to relax their barriers, even a little bit, they will become more open to experiences, even though they are highly unlikely ever to have an experience that leaves them feeling completely overwhelmed. This is actually one of the greatest strengths of the protecting type. Even in the face of the most negative haunting, protecting types can hold their ground. In addition to this, they can also learn how to extend some of their rock-solid protection to others, helping them to shore up their personal boundaries, fight off attacking spirits, and ground and center.

The Directing Type

Directing types are not as closed off as protecting types, nor are they as wide open as connecting types. Directing types engage in a certain amount of give and take with the energy in the world around them, but it is give and take on their terms. Directing types are typified by their need for control. They are highly sensitive to energy and in many ways, their systems rely on their interaction with it. But where connecting types approach that interaction in terms of emotion, directing types tend to intellectualize it. They are the individuals most likely driven by a need to study, to analyze, to understand, and to *know*. Although directing types do not always end up in charge of organizations, they almost always end up in some position where they are calling the shots. They are not always natural leaders, but they do tend to be natural organizers. A directing type tends to look at everything—even people—in terms of utility. This can lead them to seem cold and unemotional, but directing types approach emotions in much the same way they approach everything: on their terms and their terms alone.

Control is the driving force behind a directing type's interaction with energy. Even though these people tend to be very sensitive to energy, this need for ironclad control can sometimes lead them to discount their psychic impressions. Directing types intellectualize everything, and few paranormal experiences hold up to their relentless self-analysis. They also need to be absolutely sure that something is paranormal before committing to such a radical interpretation. In many ways, this habit is just one more expression of directing types' need for control, for they hate being wrong about anything. This overwhelming need for control grows out of two main factors that are fundamental to the directing type's basic experience. First, directing types do not shield well, and they tend to be highly sensitive and responsive to energy. Second, they tend to respond to powerful psychic impressions in a very physical fashion. Changes in energy often literally make directing types sick, and this, combined with their natural sensitivity to energy, often inspires their need for both explicit understanding and explicit control.

As is the case with the other two types, the directing type's greatest weakness can be their greatest strength, depending on how it's handled. Connecting types live in the moment and tend to respond to each experience without much thought. Directing types, on the other hand, stop, analyze, double-check, and experiment rigorously. Provided they can relax their need for control on a personal level enough to truly open themselves up to an experience, they can become some of the most insightful psychics out there. Because directing types are good at harnessing energy and imposing their will on it, they are also good at some of the more complicated aspects of energy work, such as lashing out and attacking spirits. All of that obsessive control leads to one powerful force of will, and if this can be honed and directed, the effects are nothing short of astounding. Directing types also need to be careful not to overdo things or to push themselves too far. They often expect more out of both their bodies and their minds than is reasonable. Their all-consuming drive may get results, but it helps to remind them that they can't be efficient if they've worked themselves into the ground.

Know Your Type, Know Your Role

If the descriptions above seemed confusing and left you wondering where you actually fit, there is an easier way to distinguish between the three types. This method comes down to how each of the three types tend to approach the world. Connecting types are emotional. Protecting types are practical. Directing types are intellectual. If you feel that you fit more than one of these, consider which approach you take most often—especially in new situations. This will give you an idea of your default. Go back and re-read the section describing that type, and honestly compare your strengths, weaknesses, and habits to the qualities outlined in that section.

If the first one simply does not resonate at all, re-read the passage for your secondary response. Remember that these categories are broad and sweeping generalizations and that not all of the qualities have to fit word for word. The most important qualities you want to match up have to do with your openness to energy and your initial response to interacting with it. This can help shed some light on problems you may have encountered performing any of the exercises in this book. Connecting types often find it challenging to ground and shield. Protecting types find these to be so easy that they doubt whether or not they've done them at all. Directing types are likely to get hung up on all the possible ways they might misinterpret their results or accidentally confuse actual psychic experiences for the placebo effect. Taking the suggestions at the end of each passage on how to overcome the downsides of each type will likely help you to improve your performance overall.

Knowing your type, as well as the types of others, can also help you to better organize a group and delegate tasks among the members of that group. Given their natural tendencies, you are probably not going to want a protecting type to attempt to channel an entity. Nor should a connecting type be your first choice to do battle with a malevolent spirit. This comes down to pure managements skills. In the workplace, it's very obvious: you pick a person's job based on that person's skills. There is nothing wrong or judgmental in being honest about people's shortcomings. In fact, it's safer for everyone involved if you know that certain members of your team should probably not be given certain tasks. As a team member yourself, you should be brutally honest in your assessment of your own skills, acknowledging where you may stumble and where you shine. This line of thought brings us to the final point I want to address: ethics.

Responsible Ghost Hunting

The field of paranormal investigation, although not new, is still under development. Although there are many theories about what constitutes the paranormal and there are many different methods for studying and documenting paranormal phenomena, there are still no set standards that dictate how one should run an investigation. Given the diversity of the paranormal community, this is both a good and a bad thing. On one hand, it's good that individuals are allowed to pursue their investigations using their own methodology. There are no restrictions on what belief system a person should adhere to when pursuing the paranormal. The field has skeptics, psychics, Christians, witches, and everything else in between, all unified by their interest in the topic of ghosts, even if they are not unified in their ideas of what ghosts are. This diversity is wonderful, and I think it adds a great deal to the field. It allows for a number of different perspectives, and it ensures that no possible approach to understanding and interacting with the paranormal is overlooked.

The bad part about a lack of standardization within the community is the problem of ethics. There are no set guidelines for pursuing an investigation. There are no rules that clarify right and wrong behavior, and, in addition to the lack of rules, there is no manner of oversight to protect individuals who are haunted from unethical investigators who may be interested only in selling their opinions, feeling special, or just bilking people out of money. I do not think that it is wise or even possible at this point to institute standards of investigation. The community is too diverse, and what constitutes a proper investigation for a skeptical team may be radically different than an investigation run by a team made up predominantly of psychics. I personally believe that all of these many different approaches and points of view help to enlarge our collective experience and understanding of the paranormal, and it would be a mistake to institute anything that might limit this diversity. That being said, ghost hunters should make an effort to maintain certain personal standards, and the most important of these standards is a strong sense of ethics, especially where clients are concerned.

One of the first things an ethical ghost hunter should accept is the fact that the field of the paranormal is still a speculative science. Nothing is known for certain. Paranormal investigators deal with theories and suppositions, not facts. Clients do not always understand this. In their search for an explanation that helps their experiences to make sense, clients may even be reluctant to accept that most answers are possibilities rather than absolutes. It is imperative for investigators to present their findings in terms of theories and educated guesses. It is wrong for a group to go into a house and present their opinions and findings as the absolute and only possible interpretation of a haunting. One of the things that keeps all of us coming back to the field of the paranormal again and again is the fact that no one has all of the answers, and even the answers that we think we have can still be debated. Although an observation about a haunting or an explanation for a haunting can be presented as a strong possibility, do not take advantage of a client's need to believe by presenting anything as pure fact. When using technological methods of gathering evidence, you should review the evidence with the client and explain the technology to them, but you should ultimately leave it up to them whether or not to accept that particular piece of evidence. You can certainly offer your opinions, and you can explain why those opinions are educated and *likely* to be right. But, out of respect for your clients as well as for your fellow investigators, acknowledge the uncertainty that still exists as a part of the paranormal field in general.

Uncertainty is a part of even the most scientifically run paranormal investigations, but the issues presented by personal interpretation and human fallibility become magnified tenfold when the investigation is mainly psychic in nature. I speak as an individual who runs primarily psychic investigations, and so this is not a statement that is biased against psychics. However, it is *extremely* important to acknowledge the limitations of psychic perceptions when investigating paranormal phenomena for a client. A psychic should never present his or her impressions as absolute facts. Psychic perceptions should always come with qualifiers such as, "this is what I feel," or "this is my interpretation." Offering qualifiers for your impressions does not negate the value of your psychic abilities. Instead, just as with technological evidence, it allows the clients to decide for themselves what they are willing to accept and believe. In my opinion, one of the greatest wrongs one person can commit against another is to attempt to force a belief upon them. Furthermore, psychics who present each and every one of their perceptions as hard facts have failed to truly understand the nature of their gifts. Psychic perceptions are filtered through the lens of the human mind. That mind, by virtue of its very humanity, is fallible. As with technologically obtained proof, clients should be encouraged to question psychic evidence, to put it to the test, and ultimately to decide for themselves. Like technicians, psychics can certainly explain their credentials, offer references, and give clients access to old case files that indicate their typical level of accuracy. But the decision should always be left with the clients. Once again, in this field, there are no absolutes.

Obviously, I feel very strongly about these things. I think these issues are very important to consider, especially in a field where clients are often asked to pay for the services of ghost hunters. I am not opposed to charging clients for services. Everyone's time is valuable, and paranormal investigators are no different. It is not always convenient to haul equipment and people out to a haunted location, and time spent investigating a haunting is time that investigators cannot spend doing other things. Some remuneration is both polite and appropriate, but the pricing should be fair. It can be all too easy to capitalize on a client's fear and sense of victimization. Some clients are willing to throw money at a ghost problem in the hope that it will just go away, and responsible ghost hunters should make an effort not to take advantage of people who feel that desperate about a situation. If a sense of honor or personal responsibility does not seem to be motivation enough, also consider that if you take advantage of clients, those clients are likely to spread the word and give you—and by extension any other investigators in your area—a bad name.

Rather than ranting endlessly on this topic, let me suggest a set of simple rules that every ghost hunter should consider following. I think of them as a kind of ghost hunter's manifesto:

1. Respect the living and the dead.

2. Follow the laws of the land.

3. Leave a place in as good a state as you found it.

4. Respect the belief systems of others.

5. Present all psychic impressions with the proper qualifiers.

6. Do not take advantage of another's ignorance or fear.

7. Communicate the difference between theory and fact.

8. If you take clients, be honest, sincere, professional, and forthright.

9. Never be afraid to admit when you are out of your depth.

With these nine simple rules in mind—and armed with both common courtesy and common sense—you can be a credit to the field of paranormal investigation. One thing many of us may forget is that we all reflect upon one another. Each time any of us visits a client, speaks at a convention, or even offers our opinion on an Internet message board, we represent the field of paranormal investigation to others. One of the main motivations of that field is to learn more about the paranormal so that we may better understand how we interact with it, and how it interacts with us. A secondary part of that motivation is to help others. We help by gathering and sharing information. We help by explaining the techniques that have worked for us in the hopes that they will work equally well for others. We help by pursuing experiences from a variety of different perspectives so that, collectively, we can create as complete a picture as possible of what is really going on. And, for those people who do not willingly make the paranormal a part of their everyday lives, we help by empowering our clients, teaching them how to protect themselves and encouraging them to reclaim the security of their homes. If we do it properly, with respect and sincerity, it is a noble task.

Clearing Houses, Changing Lives

As observed earlier, this book does not represent the only right way to cleanse negative energy and protect people from hauntings. However, by drawing together concepts and theories from a wide variety of sources and seeking to achieve a balance between skepticism and belief, I feel it is a resource you will be able to turn to again and again. If there is an underlying lesson that can be found at the heart of every exercise here, it is that the real power to cleanse and protect arises from your own focus, intent, and belief. These three things—more than any number of symbols, prayers, or gadgets—are the greatest weapons in your arsenal against the unknown. As we explored both skepticism and belief, I hope it is clear by now that your personal worldview does not change the effectiveness of these techniques. You can be a Catholic, a Jew, a skeptic, or a witch, and these methods will all work equally well, because they harness innate human abilities that exist regardless of how we choose to interpret them.

One of the most rewarding aspects of ghost hunting, at least for me, is helping clients regain control of their lives. Even when a haunting is not overtly negative, it can still be intimidating. The existence of nothing more than a residual haunting can be very upsetting to people who do not ordinarily make a pursuit of the otherworldly a part of their lives. Many ghost hunters are less interested in resolving hauntings for clients than they are in gathering evidence of hauntings, but even this pursuit ultimately helps to put peoples' minds at ease. The more we learn and the more we share, the more we expand our understanding of this field. As you have read, a good portion of haunting resolution is achieved by helping clients to gain confidence in uncertain situations. When people feel like victims, they are far more likely to be victimized. If you can educate people about how hauntings work, what constitutes a negative haunting, and how to identify something that is paranormal but nevertheless harmless, you help them achieve that confidence.

Techniques like grounding, centering, and shielding may seem deceptively simple, and yet they constitute the most essential groundwork for every other method of psychic self-defense. Learning about energy—how it flows through spaces and how to clear it—is a skill that will help you in nearly every haunting you encounter. Furthermore, it is a skill that you can pass along to your clients so they can better assess their own situations and maintain their living spaces so they are less likely to attract ghosts. A great deal of psychological techniques go hand in hand with these methods, but don't think that this means that the techniques are all in your head. When it was first founded, psychology was named for the study of the soul, and there is no coincidence that many of the techniques used for harnessing and directing energy are also techniques used to harness and direct one's willpower. The two go hand in hand, and what one group of people may call magick, another can easily call mind over matter. Just as symbols are less important than their underlying meanings, the names you call the methods are not important. The real importance lies in your results. If you trust nothing else, trust those results, especially because those results are what clients are seeking when they come to you to resolve a haunting.

The realm of the paranormal presents a vast undiscovered country that we are still seeking to map. We will be mapping it for a long time, and by its very nature, we may never be able to map it all. But through our repeated experiences and our willingness to share the lessons of those experiences with others, we can at least set up guideposts to help others navigate the treacherous areas. Just because ghost hunting draws us into exploring the unknown does not mean that we have to venture into the shadows unarmed.

SOURCES AND
SUGGESTED READING

This book covers a wide range of topics and introduces many diverse traditions from around the world. Because I encourage my readers to branch out beyond this work, I've included a chapter-by-chapter list of books that I consulted while writing this book together with other texts and websites you can explore to help enlarge your own understanding of the topics covered here. The books are not in alphabetical order but instead are arranged in the general order of appearance for each topic.

CHAPTER ONE

Jung, Carl G. *Jung on Active Imagination*. Joan Chodorow, ed. Princeton, NJ: Princeton University Press, 1997.

Andreas, Steve, and Charles Faulkner, eds. *NLP: The New Technology of Achievement*. New York: Harper Paperbacks, 1996.

Hall, L. Michael, and Barbara P. Belnap. *Sourcebook of Magic: A Comprehensive Guide to NLP Change Patterns*. 2nd edition. Norwalk, CT: Crown House Publishing, 2004.

Gawain, Shakti. *Creative Visualization*. Revised edition. Navato, CA: New World Library, 2002.

Andrews, Lynn V. *Teachings Around the Sacred Wheel*. New York: Tarcher Books, 2007.

Bonewits, Isaac, and Phaedra Bonewits. *Real Energy*. Franklin Lakes, NJ: New Page Books, 2007.

You may also want to look into my own book on working with energy and developing your psychic abilities: *The Psychic Energy Codex*. San Francisco, CA: Weiser, 2007.

Chapter Two

Brennan, Barbara. *Hands of Light: A Guide to Healing Through the Human Energy Field*. Toronto: Bantam Books, 1988.

Penczak, Christopher. *Ascension Magick: Ritual, Myth, & Healing for the New Aeon*. Woodbury, MN: Llewellyn Publications, 2007.

———. *The Witch's Shield: Protection Magick and Psychic Self-Defense*. St. Paul, MN: Llewellyn Publications, 2004.

Cuhulain, Kerr. *Magickal Self-Defense: A Quantum Approach to Warding*. St. Paul, MN: Llewellyn Publications, 2008.

Fortune, Dion. *Psychic Self-Defense*. York Beach, ME: Weiser Books, 2001.

Chapter Three

Sargent, Denny. *Clean Sweep: Banishing Everything You Don't Need to Make Room for What You Want*. San Francisco, CA: Weiser Books, 2007.

SantoPietro, Nancy. *Feng Shui: Harmony by Design*. New York: Berkeley, 1996.

Barrett, Jayme. *Feng Shui Your Life*. New York: Sterling Publishers, 2003.

Yronwode, Catherine. *Hoodoo Herb and Root Magic*. Self-published, 2002.

———. "How to Use Bath Crystals, Floor Washes, and Spiritual Soaps in the Hoodoo Rootwork Tradition." http://www.lucky mojo.com/baths.html (accessed December 17, 2008).

Borden, Adrienne, and Steve Coyote. "The Smudging Ceremony." http://www.asunam.com/smudge_ceremony.html (accessed November 22, 2008).

Dorje, Ngakpa Rig'Dzin. "Ultimate Gesture: The Ritual Objects of Tibetan Tantra." *Sacred Hoop Magazine,* Issue 7, 1994.

Brennan, J. H. *Occult Tibet: Secret Practices of Himalayan Magic.* St. Paul, MN: Llewellyn Publications, 2002.

Chapter Four

Allen, Sue. *Spirit Release: A Practical Handbook.* Berkeley, CA: O Books, 2007.

Belanger, Jeff. *Communicating with the Dead.* Franklin Lakes, NJ: New Page Books, 2005.

World Health Organization. "Electromagnetic Fields." http://www.who.int/peh-emf/en/ (accessed November 23, 2008).

Filan, Kenaz, and Raven Kaldera. *Drawing Down the Spirits: The Traditions and Techniques of Spirit Possession.* Rochester, VT: Destiny Books, 2009.

Martin, Malachi. *Hostage to the Devil: The Possession and Exorcism of Five Living Americans.* San Francisco, CA: HarperSanFrancisco, 1992.

Fisher, Joe. *The Siren Call of Hungry Ghosts: A Riveting Investigation into Channeling and Spirit Guides.* New York: Paraview Press, 2001.

Ingerman, Sandra. *Soul Retrieval: Mending the Fragmented Self.* San Francisco, CA: HarperSanFrancisco, 2006.

Laycock, Joseph. *Vampires Today: The Truth About Modern Vampirism.* Westport, CT: Praeger, 2009.

You may also want to look into my own book on psychic vampires: *The Psychic Vampire Codex.* Boston: Weiser, 2004.

Chapter Five

Ullman, Montague, and Stanley Krippner. *Dream Telepathy: Experiments in Nocturnal Extrasensory Perception*. Charlottesville, VA: Hampton Roads Publishing, 2003.

Van de Castle, Robert. *Our Dreaming Mind*. New York: Ballantine Books, 1995.

LaBerge, Stephen, and Howard Rheingold. *Exploring the World of Lucid Dreaming*. New York: Ballantine Books, 1990.

Hufford, David J. *The Terror that Comes in the Night*. Philadelphia: University of Pennsylvania Press, 1982.

Eliade, Mircea. *Shamanism: Archaic Techniques of Ecstasy*. Williard Trask, trans. Princeton, NJ: Princeton University Press, 2004.

Harner, Michael. *The Way of the Shaman*. 10th anniversary edition. San Francisco, CA: Harper, 1990.

Kalweit, Holger. *Shamans, Healers, and Medicine Men*. Boston: Shambhala Press, 1992.

Wangyal Rinpoche, Tenzin. *The Tibetan Yogas of Dream and Sleep*. Mark Dahlby, ed. Ithaca, NY: Snow Lion Publications, 1998.

You may also want to read my own book about dreams and psychic experience: *Psychic Dreamwalking*. San Francisco, CA: Weiser, 2006.

Chapter Six

Ewing, Jim PathFinder. *Clearing: A Guide to Liberating Energies Trapped in Buildings and Lands*. Findhorn, Scotland: Findhorn Press, 2006.

Skemer, Don C. *Binding Words: Textual Amulets in the Middle Ages*. University Park, PA: Pennsylvania State University Press, 2006.

Gager, John G., ed. *Curse Tablets and Binding Spells from the Ancient World*. New York: Oxford University Press, 1992.

Ott, Michael. "Medal of Saint Benedict." The Catholic Encyclopedia. Vol. 13. New York: Robert Appleton Company, 1912. http://www .newadvent.org/cathen/13338a.htm (accessed September 5, 2008).

Catholic Online. "Catholic Encyclopedia: Medal of Saint Benedict." http://www.catholic.org/encyclopedia/view.php?id=10309 (accessed September 5, 2008).

Chapter Seven

Wilson, Colin. *Poltergeist: A Classic Study in Destructive Hauntings.* Woodbury, MN: Llewellyn Publications, 2009.

Price, Harry. *Poltergeist: Tales of the Supernatural.* Cheltenham, Glos., UK: Bracken Books, 1993.

Guiley, Rosemary Ellen. *The Encyclopedia of Ghosts and Spirits.* New York: Facts on File, 2009.

Nesbitt, Mark. *Ghosts of Gettysburg: Spirits, Apparitions, and Haunted Places of the Battlefield.* Gettysburg, PA: Thomas Publications, 1991.

Watkins, Alfred. *The Old Straight Track.* London: Sago Press, 1970.

Devereux, Paul. *Haunted Land: Investigations into Ancient Mysteries and Modern Day Phenomena.* London: Piaktus Books, 2001.

Ashe, Steven, ed. *Qabalah: The Testament of Solomon.* Glastonbury, UK: Glastonbury Books, 2008.

Leitch, Aaron. *Secrets of the Magickal Grimoires: The Classical Texts of Magick Deciphered.* St. Paul, MN: Llewellyn Publications, 2005.

Ankarloo, Bengt, and Stuart Clark, eds. *Biblical and Pagan Societies.* Witchcraft and Magic in Europe series. Philadelphia: University of Philadelphia Press, 2001.